SOFTENING the *edges*

Assessment Practices That Honor K–12 Teachers and Learners

KATIE
WHITE

FOREWORD BY
CASSANDRA ERKENS

555 North Morton Street
Bloomington, IN 47404
800.733.6786 (toll free) / 812.336.7700
FAX: 812.336.7790
email: info@SolutionTree.com
SolutionTree.com

Visit **go.SolutionTree.com/assessment** to download the free reproducibles in this book.

Printed in the United States of America

Library of Congress Cataloging-in-Publication Data

Names: White, Katie, 1977- author.

Title: Softening the edges : assessment practices that honor K-12 teachers and learners / author, Katie White.

Description: Bloomington, IN : Solution Tree Press, [2017] | Includes bibliographical references and index.

Identifiers: LCCN 2016051337 | ISBN 9781943874071 (perfect bound)

Subjects: LCSH: Educational tests and measurements--United States. | Educational evaluation--United States. | Individualized instruction--United States. | Competency based education--United States.

Classification: LCC LB3051 .W48845 2017 | DDC 371.27/1--dc23 LC record available at https://lccn.loc.gov/2016051337

Solution Tree
Jeffrey C. Jones, CEO
Edmund M. Ackerman, President

Solution Tree Press
President and Publisher: Douglas M. Rife
Editorial Director: Sarah Payne-Mills
Managing Production Editor: Caroline Weiss
Senior Production Editor: Tara Perkins
Senior Editor: Amy Rubenstein
Copy Editor: Evie Madsen
Proofreader: Miranda Addonizio
Text and Cover Designer: Abigail Bowen
Editorial Assistants: Jessi Finn and Kendra Slayton

Acknowledgments

I have worked for the North East School Division (NESD) in Saskatchewan, Canada, as a teacher, administrator, and system leader. This book is dedicated to my education colleagues, who have willingly (and sometimes unwillingly) listened to me in classrooms, hallways, workshops, and offices as I lived much of the content you will read in this book. It is through powerful conversations, co-planning and co-teaching, facilitating professional learning, and, above all, listening, that I have learned how to be a teacher in the true sense of the word. I will forever be grateful to the NESD.

I also dedicate this book to the students of the NESD. Their faces, their minds, and their hearts are the reason I get up every day and devote my life to this work. Many of them probably don't even know my name, but I hold their future in my mind as a beacon that guides my work.

Lastly, I acknowledge my family, who keeps me propped up in the moments I need it and inspires me to be the best whole person I can be. To my dad, who was my teaching hero; to my mom, who lives the definition of wholeness; to my husband and daughters without whom I am lost, I thank you. You have made sure I live with softened edges.

Solution Tree Press would like to thank the following reviewers:

Alfredo Barrantes
Director, Assessment and Data Management
Cartwright School District 83
Phoenix, Arizona

Stacie Beaman
First-Grade Teacher
L. J. Daly Elementary School
Fayette, Missouri

Jeff Bush
Government and Economics Teacher
Kent Innovation High School
Grand Rapids, Michigan

Sandra Kitts
Kitts Consulting
Moose Jaw, Saskatchewan
Canada

Jim Knight
Fourth-Grade Teacher
Pearl S. Buck Elementary School
Levittown, Pennsylvania

Stacie Nickols
Coordinator of Elementary Social Studies
McKinney Independent School District
McKinney, Texas

Heidi Paterson
Science Teacher
Preeceville School
Preeceville, Saskatchewan
Canada

Will Remmert
Principal
Eagle View Elementary School
New Prague, Minnesota

Jim Smith
Lighthouse Learning Community
Wayzata, Minnesota

Mandy Stalets
Mathematics Teacher
Thomas Metcalf Laboratory School
Normal, Illinois

Jennifer South
Seventh-Grade Math/ELA Teacher
High School PE Teacher
Melfort and Unit Comprehensive Collegiate
Melfort, Saskatchewan
Canada

Visit **go.SolutionTree.com/assessment** to download the free reproducibles in this book.

Table of Contents

Reproducible pages are in italics.

About the Author

Katie White is coordinator of learning for the North East School Division in Saskatchewan, Canada, and an educational consultant. With more than twenty years in education, she has been a district and in-school administrator, a learning coach, and a K–12 classroom teacher.

Katie was an integral part of her school division's multiyear journey through renewed curricula and standards-based assessment and reporting. She helps develop and utilize strong assessment and grading practices that support teaching and learning in classrooms. Her focus is on helping educators develop a personalized understanding of the connections among curriculum, assessment, and instruction. She has developed multiple supports for teachers and administrators as well as facilitators of school-based professional learning. She is a co-moderator of the All Things Assessment (#ATAssess) Twitter chat and a frequent contributor to the *All Things Assessment* blog (http://allthingsassessment.info/blog).

Katie received a bachelor of education and master of education in curriculum studies from the University of Saskatchewan.

To learn more about Katie's work, visit www.kwhiteconsulting.com or follow @KatieWhite426 on Twitter.

To book Katie White for professional development, contact pd@SolutionTree.com.

Foreword

By Cassandra Erkens

As educators, we have often heard about the art and science of teaching, but we have seldom considered the art and science of assessing. If anything, assessment has been a largely clinical task, shrouded in technical discussions, and a predominantly scientific endeavor laced with designing perfect prompts, gathering sufficient evidence, triangulating data, validating inferences, monitoring for controls and variables, and drawing accurate conclusions. But in *Softening the Edges: Assessment Practices That Honor K–12 Teachers and Learners*, author Katie White masterfully reshapes the face of assessment to be as much an art as it is a science.

The Science of Assessment: A Fresh Perspective

Assessment includes technical aspects that we cannot ignore. Much has already been written about the granular details of how to accurately design and effectively use classroom assessments (for example, Ainsworth, 2003; Black & Wiliam, 1998; Stiggins, Arter, Chappuis, & Chappuis, 2004; Vagle, 2015; Wiggins & McTighe, 2005). White contributes to this field and offers a fresh perspective on the extant literature. Specifically, she helps her readers integrate critical concepts with practical examples, meaningful questions, and applicable strategies.

Softening the Edges offers educators a comprehensive yet accessible path for navigating the assessment process from start to finish. White helps teachers integrate important concepts in the field by *showing* her readers the connections. Using stories, charts, reflective questions, and examples, she illuminates the tight relationships between assessment and instruction, precision and flexibility, formative and summative assessment, and, most importantly, student learning and teacher learning throughout the assessment process.

As she navigates the details of assessment development, White provides concrete ways to implement the work. She argues that targets are more than statements of what students will learn, and they are more than indicators for assessment development—targets inform the instructional actions teachers must take to make the learning visible and available to the learners. White illustrates learning continuums that illuminate the connections among targets, learning progressions, proficiency levels, and specifically, the reflective questions teachers must use to guide instructional decisions when moving all learners forward. White's handling of the nuts and bolts of assessment helps teachers delve deeper so they can integrate assessment practices in meaningful ways.

While addressing the technical aspects, White reminds us to challenge our own assessment work. This is a field, she notes, that does require precision but in the context and service of building hope and efficacy for our learners. She writes:

> If we believe an assessment has fallen short, we may consider using that evidence as formative evidence only and seek more information in a different way. If each assessment was strong, we may begin to ask ourselves, "Did the learners struggle with a particular piece the first time, and do we know this learning gap was addressed the second time?" If so, then the most recent evidence is the most reliable. (page 177)

The evidence we ourselves generate through the assessment process must sometimes be further investigated or impeached. In this, and so many other ways, *Softening the Edges* provides clarity to many misunderstandings within the science of assessment.

For far too long, debates regarding formative and summative assessment have raged in the field (Can formative assessments be graded? Are summative assessments the end of learning? If one is better, why is the other even necessary? and so on). With this fresh look at assessment, White renders the debates meaningless. She argues that the issue has little to do with the mechanics of assessment and everything to do with the human dynamics involved in the assessment process.

The Art of Assessment: The Master's Landscape

From the seemingly insignificant comment a teacher might share in passing to the influential test score a teacher will ultimately assign, assessment is deeply personal. Throughout *Softening the Edges*, White reminds us that assessment work is *human* work. She writes, "We bring our own humanity to our learning spaces and there, we meet human learners. . . . Together, students and teachers can co-construct conversations and experiences that impact us well beyond our time together in the classroom" (page 12). With humanity squarely in the center of our work with students and learning, there can be no hard lines in the art of assessment.

Like an artist with a canvas, White uses personal stories, metaphors, and imagery to contextualize important concepts. Her poignant illustrations help readers put empathy back into an assessment routine that can be sterile and sometimes heartless. As early as chapter 1, White reminds us that "Students . . . are complete and changing, just like adults" (page 14). And throughout the book she reminds us that teachers, like students, can also learn and evolve through the assessment experience: "We need to become comfortable with ourselves as professionals. We need to trust our observations. Once we do, we are free to experiment with learning experiences. We can move beyond paper into a three-dimensional world" (page 90). Like art, assessment makes life infinitely richer for everyone involved. It must be functional, yet aesthetically inviting. It must remain responsive and continue to evolve.

Painter Georges Braque (1952) once noted that science is meant to reassure, but art is meant to disturb. The true art behind *Softening the Edges* lies in the author's ability to gently but rightfully disturb the traditional assessment arena in which students and teachers alike have been prematurely and thus wrongfully labeled and judged. Instead, assessment must remain open to discovery and possibility. It is about uncovering insights into the self while discovering truths about the world around us. We must rethink our work with assessment, White contends, softening our hard lines of monitoring, measuring, scoring, evaluating, and moving on. She builds the masterful argument that we must slow down enough to enjoy the journey and relax enough to appreciate the gifts we find in each other along the way. In the end, assessment must support the human endeavor to learn *and love*.

Preface

I once watched a ninth-grade student work through practice questions on a homework assignment. She worked diligently and confidently for forty-five minutes, but every three or four minutes she would sigh as she moved from one question to the next. Eventually, I asked her why she seemed so distressed when she was clearly able to complete the practice without much difficulty. She told me that she hated her homework assignments. When I asked her to explain, she said:

> Here's how it works. Teachers teach and then they give about six hours of practice and it doesn't matter if you "get it" after two. People who get it spend all that time working and those who don't get it don't do it at all. But nothing happens to them except their final may not go that well.

I then asked her why she continued to do practice homework when she clearly didn't need it, and she replied, "I don't know. I guess I don't want to disappoint anyone."

On another occasion, I was working with a learner to prepare for a test. As part of our study session, I asked him to predict what topics and major concepts he thought would appear on the assessment; I asked him to consult his notebook and determine the key aspects of the course. He seemed to resist this approach, muttering that it was useless to try to predict what the teacher might ask on the test. He stated that he had tried this approach in the past and it just hadn't worked. He explained:

> If you ask students to learn something for an assessment and then it doesn't appear on the assessment, you are teaching them that assessments aren't going to be about what we learn. It becomes a bit of a trickery session where kids try to guess what you're going to pick, as opposed to learning what they need to know, and it makes me feel pessimistic about studying because assessment is a game. But that's the reality of high school. It sucks.

Both stories highlight challenges surrounding assessment in our current education context. In both cases, the students felt discouraged and frustrated by how formative and summative assessment occurs in their classrooms. They practice when they don't need to and are denied the opportunity to enrich understanding. Their time is hijacked by inauthentic assignments, and their energy is consumed with frustration at a perceived lack of consistency in the expectations placed on their peers. They complete work as a matter of compliance as opposed to investment. They are uncertain of criteria for success. They are unsure how to spend their valuable time when preparing for assessment, and they lack confidence in their teachers to align student needs with a measured response. They feel ill-equipped to experience success and control over their own learning, and they lack trust in the system. Even more troublesome in both stories is a resignation that things will never change and that their feelings and perceptions will never be heard or acted on.

It is clear that assessment has a bad reputation. Students may see it as verification of self-doubt or confirmation of a belief they hold about themselves and their value as learners. Teachers may see it as a necessary evil that manifests in nights of endless marking, comment making, and calculating. Parents may see it as a reflection of their child's behavior, intelligence, or even their own parenting. The idea of assessment holds a strong connotation for each person based on prior experiences and conditioned responses over time.

There are many reasons why assessment seems at odds with a vision of nurturing students and teachers in our schools. Evaluating, grading, marking, testing, scoring—each word holds tremendous implications for teachers. As educators, we steel ourselves every day to wade into the world of assigning value to student learning. It can be an unpalatable process, and yet we collectively share an understanding that it makes up a large part of what we do in our classrooms. However, when we view assessment as a mandate, and when we view our actions of assessing as diminishing what we are able do in our classes and how much we are able to meet student needs, it is no wonder current assessment leaves much to be desired.

When I work with new teachers, I notice our conversation always seems to circle back to assessment: specifically, summative assessment (evaluation) and reporting. There is a tangible and collective panic to figure out how to engage in this process before discussing anything else. When I ask about this urgency, they share how much they worry about *getting it right.* They understand that assessment can immediately impact their relationship with students. They see reporting as accountability to parents and to the system as a whole.

I understand these beliefs and the anxiety that accompanies them. However, I am concerned for new teachers because of what assessment seems to represent for them and because of how they *feel* about it. There is very little confidence when they speak of designing assessment events that reflect learning. I wonder what has happened over the course of these young teachers' educational experiences to have fostered this degree of anxiety and pressure when it comes to assessment. Perhaps their personal experiences with assessment shaped certain perceptions about what it means for teachers and learners. Maybe the tremendous swell in public debate surrounding accountability, standardized testing, and teacher evaluation has added to their anxiety. Simply searching the Internet elicits a vast selection of headlines with high emotional weight: "Stop the Testing Circus" (Rotherham, 2015), "Teachers' Unions Fight Standardized Testing, and Find Diverse Allies" (Taylor, 2015), "High School Seniors Aren't College-Ready" (Camera, 2016), "Teacher Evaluation System Is Latest Education Battleground" (Bowie, 2014). There is rarely a day that passes when the fight for ownership of education doesn't make itself known in mainstream media. The stakes may seem very high to these new teachers.

Students also may feel conflicted by assessment. I hear their frustration with assessment practices and their assertion that there is no way to advocate for their learning needs. I see their reluctance to explore feedback, and I hear their desire to have their work be valued or assigned a number because this is what they think school is about—that this number is the only thing that matters in the end. I worry about our students, and I wonder how their schooling has shaped them and their beliefs about assessment. I worry about the degree to which a single number impacts their perception of their ability and their options for the future. I have heard students declare a lack of ability in a specific area based on a single assessment result. I have seen students become painfully discouraged after an assessment event and refuse to even discuss the result and options for future learning. I have heard students mutter, "I failed," while handing in an assessment, even though the word *fail* has not been used in their classroom all year. I have retrieved students from bathrooms after they have become ill in anticipation of an assessment event. Assessment is causing stress for these students, and this stress reflects perceptions about assessment and how it works. If these patterns are not addressed, the stress will continue, potentially reducing achievement, optimism, and joy in learning through assessment.

Assessment has taken on a more sinister connotation in the larger landscape of education and politics. Terms like *high stakes*, *standardization*, *tracking*, *academic dishonesty*, *retention*, and *teacher evaluation* have shifted the meaning of assessment for many people, including teachers, students, and families. Sometimes it is hard to imagine that assessment could come to any good inside our schools anymore.

Nevertheless, I assert optimism for the word *assessment* and everything it *could* mean. I believe in assessment because I know that when used correctly, it is one of the most powerful tools available for holistically supporting students on their learning journeys. I believe in assessment because I love learning and the gift it offers human beings. I am optimistic about assessment because I love our schools and the people who live large portions of their days inside them. I see schools as places of joy and curiosity; wonder and practice; challenge and support. I love the relationships that flourish inside our buildings. I have nothing but hope that we can nurture schooling experiences where the focus continues to rest on these relationships among all people in schools as well as the relationships between the students and their own learning stories. I love that assessment can support these learning stories, build relationships, and foster curiosity, joy, efficacy, and healthy challenges for adults and students alike.

Introduction

Shortly after I began working as an educational consultant, I was driving to the airport with a colleague after we had spent three days facilitating a session on assessment with a large group of teachers. It had been challenging work, and I was trying to make sense of the experience by talking it through with my colleague. I was mostly concerned with how challenged the participants seemed to feel about the assessment design processes we were working through. They seemed burdened by so many stresses—multiple sets of standards; state testing as well as district assessments; and learners who were coming to school hungry, tired, and disengaged. Discussing assessment as an essential component of the learning process seemed to really challenge their beliefs about the work they were doing and their roles as educators.

As a Canadian, I was also trying to make sense of the education paradigm in the United States and the implications of this paradigm on my message and my facilitation. My colleague patiently explained the history of U.S. education reform and the resulting assessment reform. It was a long drive to the airport, and we talked through many important aspects of our work. My own experiences in coming to understand assessment had been personally and professionally challenging, and I already had a sense of the difficult nature of this topic, but I began to see that assessment was truly loaded with misunderstanding and harsh realities for teachers and students.

As we drove, we passed through rock formations alongside the highway. The light shifted over the red igneous cliff faces as approaching rain clouds began to alter the shadows along the edges of the stone. It made me think of the lines and edges that our education system has created in relation to assessment; the rules and processes that, to many teachers, seem static and non-negotiable. I started to think about the shifting effects of light on the edges of the rock, depending on the time of day, the weather, or the perspective of the viewer, and I began to wonder if it were possible to shift our view of assessment in the same way—by changing the conditions under which it is viewed and by changing the perspectives of the viewers. Would these kinds of shifts soften the edges of our relationship with assessment? Would they change how we see assessment and how our students experience it?

On that drive with my colleague, I began to recognize that assessment had taken on a solid form in the minds of the teachers with whom we had worked. It was a *thing*, an entity. It seemed vast and unmanageable all at the same time. It seemed like when teachers interacted with it, they felt a small pain, as if cut by the edge of the practice itself. I began to think that the work we were doing with these teachers was to take this hard edge of assessment and round it or smooth it out, so when teachers began to work with it, it would no longer hurt. I knew we needed to shift the perception of assessment as a thing into assessment as a process. We had to take that hard line or edge and turn it into something that was approachable, flexible, and manageable. Like a carpenter sands the edge of a table before inviting people to eat at it, like an artist skillfully blends a hard line into a soft transition between land and sky, or like a chef adds a spoonful of sugar to the vinegar to make the sauce less acidic, we were trying to invite changes or additions to assessment practices that softened the edges by addressing the needs of both teachers and students in the service of learning. By doing so, we were supporting the development of an assessment paradigm that is approachable, gentle, and not at all overwhelming.

The Metaphor

This book is about eliminating hard edges from our assessment practices and inviting soft edges through considered choices. It is about shifting the idea of assessment as an entity separate from learning to assessment as a process, integral to growth and development, and flowing in and out of the learning experience. Just as carpenters, artists, and chefs make the choice to soften the edges between two things in order to neutralize extremes, refine sensations, or create impressions of seamless transition, so too do educators. However, instead of sanding off edges of wood, blending land with sky, or mixing vinegar with sugar, teachers have the opportunity to blend their assessment decisions with the commitment to nurture and support both their own and their learners' needs. When assessment practices align with the intellectual, emotional, physical, and social needs of the people involved in the assessment relationship, soft edges exist. In contrast, hard edges form when some or all of these critical needs go unaddressed throughout the assessment process, and without careful adjustment, those hard edges will derail even the strongest assessment practices.

During assessment processes, when we consider the needs of our students beyond the intellectual realm, we are attending to the *whole student*. Addressing the multiple needs of our learners is not new to teachers—we often provide food and school supplies to students who need it; we ensure consistency and safety within the walls of our classrooms; we provide exercise and rest in balanced proportions. Despite this, considering emotional, physical, and social needs is often not part of a discourse on assessment. However, if we do not attend to all parts of a learner while assessing, we can engage in practices that may be designed to support intellectual development, but instead infringe on a student's emotional or social safety and undermine any gains in intellectual development we may have made.

The terms *hard edges* and *soft edges* are metaphors for the degree of alignment that exists among the beliefs, values, and needs of educators and learners, and the ways assessment is experienced in classroom spaces. The metaphor speaks directly to the relationship between the whole person and assessment. When the edges are softened, assessment practices blend one learning experience into the next and allow students to feel smooth transitions, growing confidence, and recursive content and skill development. Softened edges allow both learners and educators to relax into the learning, adjusting and reflecting as needed and responding within a context of trust and support. Learning to recognize the hard and soft edges of classroom assessment experiences will invite both teachers and students to examine their roles, beliefs, and actions and redesign everyday assessment practices to meet the intellectual, physical, social, and emotional needs of all of those in a classroom.

When we engage in processes we don't fully understand or we implement practices we don't fully accept, we can feel frustrated, resentful, confused, and unheard. These emotions indicate a hard edge, and both teachers and students can feel these hard edges in classroom experiences. When the edges are hard, we have likely infringed on some aspect of the whole self and, without intention, may have caused emotional harm, social challenge, or intellectual difficulty to ourselves or our learners. For example, when we preassess and see students' confidence suffer, we know that in our attempt to support their intellectual growth, we have inadvertently challenged their emotional safety and formed a hard edge. The pain students may feel when encountering a practice they don't understand may be sharp and unexpected.

As a result of encountering many small hard edges over time, students may feel marginalized or voiceless in assessment and instructional practices. They may not have been given time to make sense of what was happening to them in their learning environments. They have become part of a story but have no agency in designing the plot, and this, in turn, impacts their emotional and intellectual well-being. At times, students may feel there is a difference between what they understand about themselves and how their classroom experiences reflect their skills and knowledge. This can result in a lack of growth and engagement and indicate a hard edge.

This lack of student growth and engagement, in turn, creates a hard edge for teachers because learners are not invested in the processes we have designed and our need for efficacy is challenged. When trying to determine whether an assessment has developed a hard edge, we can ask ourselves if some aspects of our design choices are impacting our own emotional, intellectual, physical, or social safety. Are students invested in the learning we have so carefully crafted? Are we spending more time grading papers than our learners spend reading our feedback? Are we discouraged by the lack of progress students are showing?

When we are caught in a cycle of hard edges, something will have to shift to soften things for everyone and ensure our assessment architecture supports all aspects of the whole person. *Assessment architecture* refers to "a layout of the plan teachers will use to monitor learning throughout a unit of study" (All Things Assessment, 2016a). By attending to the diverse needs of our learners and ourselves, we can ensure that our blueprint for assessment is flexible enough to address needs as they arise but thoughtful enough to accomplish the intellectual growth we are intending to develop.

Whether modifying existing assessment tools and approaches or creating them anew, the practices explored in this book are intended to either remove a hard edge or create a soft edge of learning and offer empathic approaches to classroom assessment and reporting that honor the intellectual, physical, emotional, and social needs of both teachers and students. To further clarify these concepts, see table I.1 for select indicators of soft and hard edges.

Table I.1: Indicators of Hard and Soft Edges

Hard Edges	Soft Edges
• Teachers, students, or both feel boxed in by a practice. • Teachers, students, or both suffer emotional pain as a result of a practice. • A teacher's or student's sense of self and intellectual, physical, emotional, or social capacity are diminished by a practice. • Teachers, students, or both feel helpless as a result of a practice. • Teachers, students, or both feel a separation between who they are and what they do.	• Assessment processes invite flexibility, responsiveness, and creativity for teachers and students. • Assessment practices support investment, compassion, and optimism for teachers and students. • Teachers and students experience efficacy and agency in decisions about their own actions. • Teachers' and students' voices are heard, and physical, emotional, intellectual, and social needs are met.

All students have a learning story. These stories are powerful because they represent an accumulation of all the learning experiences a student has had over time. Each day is a page in this story, each year a chapter. The main character in the learning story is the child, and teachers are the supporting characters who ensure the plot is filled with achievement, efficacy, and empowerment. Ultimately, we want to support a story of learning that contains the right balance of success and challenge, wonder and consistency, creativity and competence.

When we establish a strong understanding of what we are trying to accomplish in our school system, we are better able to meet the diverse needs of both teachers and learners and support the creation of a positive learning story. This means we design actions that reflect this understanding and create classrooms that offer students the voice and confidence they deserve. This, in turn, supports the teachers who will walk alongside learners as they develop their learning stories.

The stories of the teacher matter, too. When the edges are softened in our assessment practices, we no longer feel boxed in or helpless, scrambling to defend a grade or explain a reporting decision, because we can take control of our assessment and the instructional decisions that emerge from the information we gather. We feel capable of describing our philosophical beliefs, and we can make sure our everyday practices align with these beliefs. We experience flexibility, responsiveness, and creativity. Furthermore, our practices support investment, opportunity, and hope for learners. We assert ownership of classroom experiences and build the capacity of students to be true designers of their own learning stories. In a classroom where the assessment edges are soft, all voices are heard, and everyone's needs are met.

Softening the edges is not about going easy on students, reducing the rigor of the learning experiences we construct, or offering bonus points or easy tasks. Instead, it is about having enough respect for our learners to ask as much of them as they can give. Make no mistake—our learners can give a great deal. The potential of our students is astounding when they are met with high expectations, engaging purposes, and clarity about the strategies and skills they are working to develop. Edges are softened when the primary focus of our classroom work is to develop the relationships necessary to support risk taking, deep reflection, and passion. These qualities are as important for teachers as they are for students. A truly strong assessment and reporting system supports the development of this vision for every person in a learning space.

We want all learners to leave our school system filled with background information, strong skill sets, resilience, confidence, and the determination to accomplish whatever they decide will occupy their days. We cannot facilitate these goals by going easy on students. We can't develop these attributes by making school a series of meaningless tasks for inauthentic purposes (grades) and a single audience (the teacher). We also cannot hope to nurture confident, independent learners by shutting them out of decision making and rendering them voiceless. We have to believe in our students so deeply that we refuse to accept less than their best. We have to believe in ourselves to accomplish this very complex vision for each learner. To do less and be less is simply not an option.

The Audience

While *Softening the Edges* very specifically explores ways to address these issues, it is not intended as an introduction to assessment. There are many other sources that introduce the fundamentals of assessment thoroughly (for example, Chappuis, Stiggins, Chappuis, & Arter, 2012; Davies, 2011; Guskey, 2015; O'Connor, 2007; and Wiggins & McTighe, 2005). For additional works, please refer to "References and Resources" beginning on page 205. Instead, *Softening the Edges* is for teachers who have been dabbling in unpacking or unwrapping learning goals but may not feel completely comfortable utilizing this work for real-life learning. It is for educators who have tried preassessments and formative assessments and experienced some discomfort or frustration at the way they affected students and the time they seemed to take away from learning. This book is for teachers who have tried many research-based practices but feel some challenge to align them with the reality in their classrooms. It is for teachers with experience in the world of assessment.

Educators know that teaching involves much more than simply spending time with students. To make classrooms run smoothly and productively, teachers must research, plan, instruct, assess, and respond to student needs. At times, even the most careful planning does not anticipate in-the-moment needs of learners or interruptions to the schedule of the day (assemblies, announcements). The skills required to meet the needs of diverse learners within a school environment are astoundingly complex. It is challenging to be a teacher.

A common experience for many educators involves spending most of their time out of the classroom planning units, preparing upcoming lessons, and assessing completed student work. Understandably, it is difficult to also find time to engage in a growing body of literature that attempts to capture and define good teaching. Staying on top of research is challenging, and sorting through a myriad of suggestions, tips, techniques, and studies can be a daunting task for time-pressed teachers. Teachers may explore this research under hurried circumstances, with little time for thinking deeply about the implications of the information or experimenting with the most effective ways to apply the ideas in a classroom setting.

As a result, teachers work through processes that administrative directives require and approaches they have been introduced to in conferences, workshops, or other professional learning sessions, perhaps without fully understanding the reasons for doing so. Classrooms can become a patchwork of techniques and strategies, with little opportunity to reflect, refine, and redo. Understandably, teachers may feel disengaged with initiatives and disenfranchised by mandates. Everything can feel isolated and separate, conveying a sense of things piling up as opposed to fitting together.

Even for experienced educators, the challenge remains that our classrooms are filled with an infinite number of variables. This is the nature of human work. Labeling an approach as *the* approach just doesn't suffice. Each approach may be helpful, depending on the circumstances and needs of the people involved. Perhaps the most important thing to do, for both ourselves and our students, is to sort out what we *believe* about learning and the purpose of school. This book takes the position that any decision we make inside our classrooms has to emerge from our values, beliefs, and needs. It has to honor who our learners are as whole people, and who we are as their teachers.

The Teacher Voice

It is important to acknowledge that throughout this process of exploring our craft within the classroom context, our identities as teachers will shift when we step outside comfortable practices and try new things. This changing perception of who we are within our work impacts the choices we make every day. Like our students, we bring our own previous experiences, prior knowledge, and life circumstances to our role. We have the same need for empathy and compassion. We need opportunity and time for reflection. Our whole person must be nurtured and our voices must be heard. Ken Robinson (2015) explains, "There is no system of education in the world that is reliably better than its teachers" (p. 264). When the education system ignores teacher voice, it becomes increasingly challenging to feel like we have a voice at all. We may begin to question the need for risk taking and research, for reflection and discussion. However, when we minimize our own thoughts and ideas, we minimize our voice, which ultimately deprofessionalizes the work of educators as a whole.

D. Jean Clandinin and F. Michael Connelly (2000) describe a classroom as a *shared space*. It is a place where stories are lived in a shared, but private environment. Alongside that notion is the idea that teachers and students are continually building a classroom culture that is very personal to those within that room. Relationships serve as the foundation, and practices become comfortable and predictable; everyone learns the rules of engagement, including the teachers.

The primary challenge with this model of education is that as teachers, we are not often afforded the chance to reflect on our practices with others. Clandinin and Connelly (1995) explain, "What is missing in the classroom is a place for teachers to tell and retell their stories of teaching" (p. 13). Without this opportunity to reflect and collaborate with others, we are left to manage the effect our work has on our sense of who we are as educators. Making time each day to meet with colleagues and share struggles and celebrations can often be enough to move us into our next round of risk taking and reflection. Documenting, together, the results of new practices and approaches can invite an increasingly sophisticated understanding of our assessment practices.

Teaching is incredibly complex, and educators are relentlessly asked to change practices, to shift beliefs, and often to do it alone. Our voices are not always heard and certainly not considered when many decisions are being made by district, state, or national leaders. Regardless of the intention of their decisions (to improve learning, to increase accountability, to enhance available resources, to reduce spending), these decisions impact us and our students. Carol Ann Tomlinson, Kay Brimijoin, and Lane Narvaez (2008) identify the unexpected degree of emotional response to change:

> We are unaware of or unprepared to deal with the implications of change in classroom practice. We tend to deal with the change on a superficial level, tend to neglect fidelity to the change, and are often unprepared to deal with the fear, tension, loss, and conflict that inevitably accompany change. (p. 11)

The absence of opportunity to reflect on our experiences and tell our stories means our ability to change and still retain a strong teaching identity is challenged. If we are left to manage on our own in the shared spaces we create with our students, we do not have the opportunity to hear the voices of others. In circumstances where isolation is the norm, we could then ask which voices have the most volume. Do we most strongly hear the voices of administrators and the initiatives they deliver? Is it the voice of the students and their needs we attend to most, or is it the voice of our own experiences and identity heard most clearly? In the midst of change and shifting practices, being given the opportunity to listen to multiple voices gives us much-needed support for exploring who we are.

Softening the edges requires finding the time to reflect on our own processes within our school context and refine them in alignment with our personal philosophies about teaching and learning. Advocating for the need to do this may be difficult, but it is an essential aspect of change and growth. Richard DuFour (2015) says, "We have yet to establish a cultural norm in which working and learning are interwoven, ensuring educators are continuing to grow and learn as part of their routine work practice" (p. 79). Supporting ourselves and each other on our own learning journeys is vital for equipping us to do the same for the learners in our classrooms. We have to make time to slow things down and explore classroom moments a little—clean off the dirt of stories, egos, and daily stimuli, and see what is underneath. We need time to contemplate the significance of our classroom experiences to better understand ourselves as teachers.

Giving educators the opportunity to develop assessment practices that serve our need to learn who our students are and respond with confidence, accuracy, and integrity is another way of softening the edges. It honors the important relationship between teachers and students and respects the teachers' responsibility to apply professional judgment to learning contexts—in essence, *reprofessionalizing* teaching. This requires trust in students' learning potential and our own ability to capture that potential. If we are going to change the story of assessment in our schools, we are going to have to shift our processes. A new story cannot replace an old story without time to reflect and alter things bit by bit.

To work toward softening the edges, teachers must be invited to work together to come to collective understanding and shared purpose. Creating common collaborative assessments and working together to analyze student work and determine the next steps on the learning journey is a highly empowering practice that also has the benefit of greater student learning. Over time, collaborating and reflecting allows our practices to be more efficient and effective. Slowing down for a while means speeding up overall. Creating a collective clarity in our practice empowers us, as individuals, to invite change, creativity, and wonder in our shared classrooms. Teachers need the chance to experiment together and determine the effects on learning, learners, and their own well-being. Collaboration and reflection practices are essential to softening the edges for teachers while at the same time giving teachers a voice in the midst of change.

The Structure of the Book

Softening the Edges explores assessment, focusing on aspects of the whole person and leaving room for future discussion and questions. We will consider *whole* as being *integrated*, not complete or comprehensive. This invites us to take our assessment practices, dust them off, and reimagine how they could better serve the needs of those they are intended to serve. There are many ways we can adjust our practices to support student learning while at the same time supporting our need to ensure we are making a difference.

Chapter 1 explores critical understanding about assessment, and chapter 2 introduces the learning continuum that teachers must use to ensure effective assessments that honor the whole person. Without this foundational understanding, softened edges become very difficult to establish and maintain.

The remaining chapters each explore a different aspect of assessment: preassessment (chapter 3), formative assessment and feedback (chapter 4), self-assessment and goal setting (chapter 5), summative assessment (chapter 6), and reporting (chapter 7). These chapters establish a conceptual understanding of each assessment focus and answer the question, How do I put this into action? These chapters address both background information and steps for engaging in strong assessment practices. Each of these chapters includes extensive reflection questions to consider as we embark on softening the edges of our assessment practices. The prompts can be used to reflect on assessment architecture, student responses to assessment, and personal feelings about how assessment is working in the classroom. Each of these chapters also includes two reproducibles—one to help identify practices and circumstances that can create hard edges, and another providing specific and practical recommendations for ways to ensure soft edges. Both teachers' and students' voices are explored, and consideration is given to the best ways to support everyone's needs while nurturing an empowering and engaging learning environment. Readers can use these tools as quick references, to refresh their memories, or to discuss the contents during collaborative work and professional development.

Softening the Edges is about bringing out the best in our students and in ourselves by assessing well and nurturing the whole person's needs. Let's get started!

CHAPTER

1

Assessment and the Whole Person

In my first year as principal in a brand-new community, I spent the summer before school trying to figure out how to be an administrator. I thought about all the practicalities: the school discipline process; how I would communicate with staff; what kind of school-home relationships I would engage in; and how I would manage playground supervision and assemblies. The list was endless. I interviewed teachers and surveyed the students to determine where they felt they needed support. I did all the homework I could think of until I felt like I was drowning in details and plans. In spite of all this preplanning, I still felt I was missing a focus on the most important things—students and learning. In short, I was preparing myself to be a great manager but I was missing the leadership part. It took an event in my personal life involving my daughter to clarify what I was missing—a mission and a vision. I needed to step back from the details and look at the bigger picture.

Around this time, my young daughter developed what seemed to be a small infection in her finger. We thought we were responding appropriately by putting a bandage on it, keeping it clean, and hoping it would clear up. We went away for a family holiday and while we were away, her infection worsened, and we decided to visit a clinic. The waiting room was empty, and our daughter was quickly ushered into a treatment room. As soon as the doctor entered, it became clear he was not a pediatrician, nor did he have much patience for young children. In the course of our fifteen-minute visit, he yelled at both me and my daughter, accused me of ignoring my child's needs, and treated her injury in a very painful and abrupt manner. We left the clinic completely shaken by the experience.

This doctor treated my daughter's injury, the infection cleared, and the pain disappeared. However, the damage to our mental health lasted for quite some time. It was through this experience that I came to understand some very important things about my role inside schools—the methods I may consider using as an administrator may work, and I may get the results I am hoping for in my school, but the end does not justify the means when dealing with human beings. It was important for me to ensure that the processes I chose to shift practices in my new role would also respect the people involved in the process. I needed that doctor to treat my child's injury *and* honor her whole being. I needed empathy and kindness as her parent. It was not enough to manage the problem; the problem was a human problem, and the response needed to equally respect the humans involved.

This event led me to realize that the students in my school had similar needs when it came to their learning and assessment experiences. A single assessment event is a moment in time, but it is wrapped up in context, tone, choice, emotions, and beliefs about what assessment is and its role in the complete learning cycle (which includes goals, experiences, assessment, reflection, and response). How learners experience assessment will shape attitudes and determine how they receive it in the future. Assessment, depending on the context surrounding it, can either support continued learning or stop it dead in its tracks.

Following the event at the clinic and my discovering this connection between an experience and the humans engaged in it, I chose three words to guide my work every day, and those three words still hang on my wall nine years later: *safety*, *love*, and *learning*. The order is intentional, and the direction these words have provided me cannot be overstated. The work we do as educators is human work. We bring our own humanity to our learning spaces and there, we meet human learners. When we engage in assessment after considering how each choice we make will impact learners in multiple realms, we are softening the edges of assessment. Together, students and teachers can co-construct conversations and experiences that impact us well beyond our time together in the classroom. If we are going to teach humans and assess human learning, we need to honor the needs of the whole person.

Understanding the Concept of the Whole Person

The term *whole person* expands on the more familiar term *whole child*. Carol A. Kochhar-Bryant (2010) explains, "As school professionals become increasingly concerned with the academic performance of students, they are more aware of the need for educating the *whole child*—attending to cognitive, social-emotional, physical, and ethical development" (p. ix). The expansion to *whole person* is a recognition that educators, like students, have complex needs, and attending to the needs of both groups is critical. When we feel we have failed because a student unexpectedly performs poorly and withdraws from engagement or resists formative instructional discussions, often due to their engrained negative perceptions of assessment, not only are student needs not being met but our own need to impact learning in a positive way is challenged. It is important in these moments to pause and reflect on the experiences we are having holistically. We may need to explore our own responses to situations as well as those of our students. We may need to move beyond intellectual needs and explore social contexts, physical demands, or emotional safety. Multiple factors can impact any experience and anticipating needs can be challenging. It is also helpful to remember that, "being a learner, the holistic teacher has to discover new knowledge, and the primary mode of discovering knowledge is to undertake research" (Patel, 2003, p. 273). Giving ourselves the time and space to be reflective and responsive is one way of ensuring the edges can become soft once again.

When we explore aligning our assessment choices with the needs of the whole person, it is critical to remember that the edges must remain soft (and the needs of the whole person must be met) for both learners and their teachers to create and nurture holistic education experiences. The notion of whole adults educating whole students opens up discussions about how the story of learning is experienced in schools. What does it mean to educate and nurture? Are we responsible for educating all parts of a person? While there are many important questions about holistic learning to consider, this text will focus more narrowly on assessment practices that honor the whole person. This is not an attempt to ignore or simplify the complexity of education. Holistic education is complex in and of itself, and one book can't cover the concept's entirety. However, considering the importance of the whole person impacts our assessment decisions and is crucial to softening the edges.

Assessing the Whole Person

Introducing the concept of the whole person into an examination of assessment invites a conversation about how our instructional and assessment decisions impact the development of a human in multiple realms—socially, emotionally, intellectually, and physically. When we invite students into an assessment experience, are they intellectually active or passively compliant? Are we inviting questions and self-exploration, or are we telling our learners how to think and feel? Are we exploring our next steps with curiosity and critical thinking, or are we defining each move and narrowing the focus in a manner that removes a strong purpose? Are learners part of the assessment and learning conversation, or are they standing outside it? Is the story theirs to create, or are they simply consuming our story? Winifred Wing Han Lamb (2001) reminds us, "We should view children as partners in learning, as adequate people rather than as inadequate adults" (p. 210). When assessing, there are a number of foundational philosophies we must keep in mind.

The following list articulates the philosophical beliefs that underlie the connections between assessment and the whole person. Each of these beliefs provides a lens through which to develop and support practices to soften the edges of assessment.

- Students are not incomplete. They are complete and changing, just like adults.
- All students can learn, and all adults can learn.
- We show students and adults respect by believing in them and challenging them.
- We show respect for students when we help them build independence and believe they can be independent.
- Clarity builds confidence, and confidence in learners can be nurtured through choices adults make.
- Students are different from each other, and this difference is a gift, not a complication.
- Learning occurs within tension, risk taking, and mistake making, but in a safe environment.
- Assessment can support hope, efficacy, optimism, and joy.

Through our assessment practices, we want to promote integrated approaches, not fragmented focuses. Our exploration of assessment and the whole person is about breadth and balance (McLaughlin, 1996). Softening the edges involves increasing our belief in students by allowing our assessment practices to reflect the best-of-the-best knowledge, rich understanding, and strong connection making.

Identifying the Benefits of Assessing the Whole Person

When we make the choice to soften the edges of assessment for our students and attend to their wholeness, we produce learners who are intellectually active while also developing their inclination to be empathic, kind, caring, and fair. We instill a desire to be creative and curious while also ensuring the ability to be disciplined, self-directed, and goal oriented. We support the development of critical thinkers who are confident and free to express their needs and hopes. We nurture students who clearly feel cared for and valued for precisely who they are (Commission on the Whole Child, 2007).

Creating environments and experiences that foster these learner characteristics is part of the broader purpose of our work in schools. When we use these outcomes as a filter for the choices we make in our assessment practices, we can begin to see how our choices may nurture or contradict these characteristics in students. The soft edge of assessment attends to and supports the development of the whole student.

Learning is a complex dance between environments, experiences, and the social, intellectual, and emotional needs and conditions of human beings. Reflecting on how our instructional decisions impact all parts of a person increases the likelihood of environments that support growth, risk taking, safety, love, and belonging, all of which indicate a softened edge.

Understanding Assessment

If we are going to soften the edges of our assessment practices to honor the whole person, we must ensure we clearly understand the fundamentals of what assessment is, as well as why, when, who, and what we are assessing, and how best to capture all that it entails accurately, reliably, and in a way that is accessible for everyone. Knowledge leads to efficacy for both teachers and learners, and efficacy indicates a soft edge. Spending time deepening our assessment knowledge is vital to supporting learning and bringing out the best in everyone.

What Is Assessment?

An *assessment* refers to a specific tool used to measure and document learning within a specific context in relation to a goal. Goals can include *learning goals* (I use this term throughout the book to generally represent terms such as *standards* or *outcomes*) or behavioral goals. The broader practice of *engaging in assessment* refers to the continual intention and act of capturing learning in the moment and making inferences about the degree of a learner's understanding in relation to a goal over time.

A strong argument can be made that humans are constantly engaging in assessment. For example, we may think: *I have to make it to work by 8:00 a.m. and it is now 7:30 a.m. I had better leave now or I won't make it on time.* And then later: *Well, I was wrong. I needed forty-five minutes to get to work.* Perhaps we engage in this mental conversation: *Oh, here comes a puddle. I had better jump now or I will hit the water. Oops! Not enough distance on that jump!* In fact, any time we clarify a goal, take action, and measure our efforts in relation to our goal, we are assessing. It is an incredibly natural process and a vital part of our decision making every day.

For assessment to be primarily embedded in the learning cycle, it must remain *formative*. Paul Black and Dylan Wiliam (1998) clarify the meaning: "[Formative assessment is] all those activities undertaken by teachers, and/or by students, which provide information to be used as feedback to modify the teaching and learning activities in which they are engaged" (pp. 7–8). Through daily learning experiences, we ask students to practice the individual skills and knowledge that build toward the learning goal so that, over time, students can synthesize those skills into deeper understanding.

Ideally, the impact of daily formative assessment is to increase the chances that decisions and actions meet goals. The consequences for not achieving goals on our first attempt are simply to learn, adjust, and try again. This cycle of goal setting, action, and reflection is naturally organic and part of the learning development that humans experience. Black and Wiliam (1998) assert the impact of formative assessment: "The research . . . shows conclusively that formative assessment does improve learning. The gains in achievement appear to be quite considerable . . . amongst the largest ever reported for educational interventions" (p. 61). It is this kind of assessment that we recreate in our classrooms to promote student learning. As Cassandra Erkens (2009a) explains, "If we understand what we are trying to accomplish instructionally with *each learner* . . . we can use the assessment process to leverage the outcome" (p. 16). When we co-construct goals alongside students, invite them to take risks, and engage in actions that will serve as a springboard for reflection, we are fostering an assessment practice that supports hope and growth. This kind of learning environment meets the needs of both ourselves and our learners and softens the edges of classroom experiences.

When we feel students are ready, we engage in *summative assessment*—moments when we measure progress, consistency, and independent proficiency in relation to goals. These moments are akin to the learning "performance" or "game" and require synthesis and connection making inherent in the larger learning goals. According to Richard J. Stiggins and colleagues (2004), summative assessments are designed to measure student learning and "are used to make statements of student learning status at a point in time to those outside the classroom" (p. 31). When these summative moments become a celebration of hard work, practice, feedback, and engagement, the edges remain soft for teachers and students. When they do not reflect these things, summative assessment and reporting become unclear, unfair, and convoluted. In these instances, we may find ourselves falling back on *magic math* to tell us how students are doing. We look to our gradebooks filled with numbers, and we depend on the calculation of a single score after averaging, weighting, and converting to tell us whether learners are proficient or not. The number of variables involved in this type of process makes the resulting score have an unclear meaning. This approach can create stress and lack of confidence for all involved, ultimately producing a hard edge. Instead, we can engage in summative practices that truly validate growth and invite us to report progress with confidence and clarity to concerned stakeholders (parents and the school community).

Why and When Are We Assessing?

Assessment doesn't have to be a bad word. In fact, assessment should be part of the learning cycle. If assessment just equates to a report card, we need to reconsider our practices. Assessment is something we are always doing—from preassessment to formative assessment, through feedback and relearning, to observation and demonstrations of learning—and essential in supporting the human need to grow. When assessment is solely used to rank and sort students, we are risking our learners' emotional safety and potentially stagnating opportunities for their continual development, thereby creating a hard edge. Instead, with constant engagement in assessment, we can continue to make decisions about our instruction and how to invite even more learning from all students, regardless of their ranking. Assessment should be optimistic and hold the promise of success. We have to believe all students can and will learn and that this process is never-ending. This is the nature of a student-focused, learning-driven education system. DuFour (2015) explains, "In the end, creating a learning-focused culture requires an organization to answer this question: Are we here to ensure students are *taught*, or are we here to ensure that our students *learn*?" (p. 103). We may also ask ourselves whether we are here to measure past learning or to support future learning. Is our work about building walls and documenting who climbs over them, or making sure all our learners have the tools and supports to get over any wall life places in front of them?

Being clear about our reason for assessing ensures an assessment system that is multidimensional, inclusive, proactive, reliable, accessible, and future focused. If we need to know whether a student is ready for the learning goals we are about to introduce, we can design a preassessment, which occurs before learning. If we want to ascertain the effectiveness of our daily instruction, we craft smaller formative assessments, which occur during the practice and acquisition of learning. To plan for differentiation in our instruction that is responsive to student needs, we can create a common formative assessment, which we may deliver at a key point during the learning process in order to inform the next chunk of instruction. We can engage students in self-reflection and goal setting through self-assessment several times throughout the learning journey. If we want to capture learning after much practice and movement toward proficiency, we can engage students in a summative assessment. We can use reporting to communicate student progress toward learning goals at various key points during the year. Developing a clear understanding of why we are assessing, when it best makes sense to do so, and then sharing this understanding with our learners fosters emotional safety and is vital to ensuring soft edges for everyone.

Who Are We Assessing?

One could argue that assessment in a classroom measures students' learning *and* the teacher's instruction. When teachers use assessment to augment the relationship between the learning experiences they design and the impact of those experiences on the learner, it serves the needs of both parties. Understanding ourselves as teachers is as important as understanding our learners. If we are going to respond to student needs as a result of what our assessments tell us, we also have to know our own strengths and preferences. Engaging in personal reflection is key to developing instructional practices that meet the needs of students. We must reflect every day in preparation for receiving the assessment information we gather about our students so we respond in ways that nurture the needs of both ourselves and our learners.

Knowing our learners is important in signaling when and how we should assess their learning. We must find time to know our students in all their complexity. Making time to observe them while they learn, listen to them as they interact with their peers, and support them as they take risks is all part of figuring out who they are. Knowing their strengths and challenges helps ensure our assessment practices capture their understanding fully and avoid the unnecessary hard edge of bias or privileging. It is critical that we ensure we do not inadvertently ask students to demonstrate their understanding in ways that are contrary to cultural norms (for example, self-assessment is difficult for learners from cultures where talking about oneself is considered bragging). We also have to be careful we are not framing our prompts around contexts with which they may not be familiar (for example, asking students to calculate the area of a swimming pool when they have never gone swimming in anything besides a lake). Without an awareness of our learners and their personal contexts, we could privilege certain students who have had specific experiences over those who have not. We could also require assessment processes that offer an advantage to students who have access to materials, technology, or time that others may not be able to access.

To ensure we know our students, we must also find time to talk to them about their lives outside school. It is important to find out who has supports and who doesn't. We must ask students how much homework they have, whether they have job or childcare responsibilities, who they spend time with, what their cultural beliefs and traditions are, what technology they have access to, and how they see the world. This allows us to avoid asking more of them than their circumstances outside of school can accommodate. This way, we are also in a better position to set up our students for success.

Robinson (2015) asserts, "All students are unique individuals with their own hopes, talents, anxieties, fears, passions, and aspirations. Engaging them as individuals is the heart of raising achievement" (p. 77). Knowing our students enables us to understand when and how to encourage risk taking and provides insights into their beliefs about themselves and their abilities. When we know our students, we understand the roadblocks preventing their success and can identify the best supports to help them create new stories about their potential.

What Are We Assessing?

We assess a myriad of things inside our schools. We assess students' academic growth and behaviors. We assess their ability to apply strategies to new learning experiences and to comply with our requests. We assess their willingness to take risks and their ability to work well with others. This range of assessment on a wide variety of goals is important in ensuring responsive classrooms.

However, when we blend academic assessment with behavioral assessment and practice data with summative data and report it as a single code or number, we are unable to offer feedback specific enough to be helpful, which creates a world empty of true formative assessment and neglects our learners' intellectual needs. We may also prevent students from understanding where they are going and how close they are to getting there, and eliminate their ability to self-assess. Mixing academic, behavioral, process, and product goals together into one measure makes instructional agility—an intentional instructional adjustment a teacher makes in response to assessment evidence—next to impossible, and it muddies our reporting practices. As Carol Ann Tomlinson and Jay McTighe (2006) point out, "A grade should give as clear a measure as possible of the best a student can do. Too often, grades reflect an unknown mixture of multiple factors. . . . How effective is such a communication system?" (p. 133).

The solution is to start by being crystal clear about what we are assessing and to assess it using concise criteria so teachers, students, and families know what is being explored and what proficiency will look like when it happens. Ken O'Connor (2007) asserts, "Students and parents need to understand that achieving in school is not about only 'doing the work' or accumulating points. . . . We want students to understand that school is about learning" (p. 6). *Unpacking* or *unwrapping* learning goals is important so we can first clarify for ourselves what we want students to know and then preassess our learners to gauge their foundational readiness and possession of the needed building blocks for the academic learning journey. This process also allows us to be crystal clear about the targets we set along the way that will support our learners to meet them. Throughout this book, I will use the terms *targets*, *"I can" statements*, and *stepping stones* to refer to the distinct skills and knowledge students will need to learn and develop as they work toward the larger learning goals. We identify these skills and knowledge when we unpack the learning goals. Being clear about these items by unpacking them from the learning goal allows us to recognize when a student is proficient and ready to engage in enriched learning opportunities. After unpacking or unwrapping our learning goals, we can be sure that when we measure a student's progress toward the goals, we know we have captured exactly that and nothing else.

At the same time, we can also evaluate students' growth of skills such as collaboration, communication, critical thinking, and creativity. These behaviors and competencies should be assessed and reported separately from academic goals, but teachers must similarly clarify the criteria for proficiency. Being clear about what we are assessing is essential to assessing it accurately and reliably and reporting it clearly, transparently, and accessibly.

How Are We Assessing?

Tom Schimmer (2014) reminds us, "The reality is that all assessment methods have their place in a balanced assessment process, but the learning target needs to be matched with the assessment method that will most accurately allow students to show what they know" (p. 42). There is no single way to assess learning, and this allows us to meet multiple student needs with a softened edge. However, to avoid assessment methods that are disconnected from our learning goals, we must first clarify what we are assessing before we determine how best to do so. At the heart of assessment is clarity, and we can only achieve this clarity by choosing assessment methods that invite students to demonstrate the skills and knowledge articulated in the learning goals. Furthermore, we also need to ensure our assessment results are reliable, so measuring our goals on more than one occasion to confirm the accuracy of our assessments is optimal.

Once we know why and what we are assessing and we engage in it when it makes sense and in a way that honors our learners, the options for how we assess open up. Selected-answer questions, open-ended questions, performance tasks, demonstrations, and discussions are just some options. If we are formatively assessing the smaller building blocks of a learning goal, for example, we may decide that selected-answer questions, such as multiple choice, matching, and true or false, are the quickest way to capture this in-the-moment learning and may be the most effective way to efficiently capture recall or conceptual understanding. However, if we are inviting the summative demonstration of a complex learning goal, we may design a performance task to measure this degree of learning. Attending to the kinds of learning indicated within a learning goal (and within the smaller building blocks that the goal comprises) is an important step in determining how we will assess students. In chapter 2, we will clarify the learning continuum, which can help us with this process.

Clarity affords us the opportunity to have fun, experiment, and engage our learners in authentic processes and products. Our professional understanding allows us to watch and listen to our students and determine where they are on their journeys so we can invite them to explore further, take risks, and celebrate growth.

Changing the Assessment Paradigm

Many educators have come to associate assessment and the standards-based movement with rigid rules and boundaries that can impede learning. As a response, many new education trends have emerged, including Genius Hour, problem-based learning, and flipped learning. These approaches are often positioned in contrast to the traditional paradigm. They are engaging and student focused, and it is no wonder they get much attention. With the current tension in the world of education around standardized assessment, teachers may be left believing they have to choose between a focus on standards or exploratory learning. Teachers may design lessons around learning goals most of the time but try to sneak in inquiry and creativity when they can find the time. This can result in a fractured approach to teaching and learning, where students long to move away from test preparation and learning goals and move into the fun days when they can engage in topics of their own choosing. As teachers, we may feel some choices we face when planning and assessing are stark, and we long to nurture engagement for our learners. Engaging in this type of either-or paradigm can be troubling. Often, however, these paradigms are *false dichotomies*.

Our beliefs about these false dichotomies can not only impact the decisions we make around assessment and instruction but can also impact the language we use when we speak about learning. In our rush to get things done, prepare for high-stakes tests, and fit in the learning goals we are required to teach, we may be communicating a message about assessment that ultimately affects how students are positioned in relation to learning. Bringing an awareness to the false dichotomies we may perceive and the language choices we may be inadvertently using could help us to make assessment everything it could be and learning everything we hope for.

False Dichotomies Between Achievement and Creativity

The task of making classroom decisions is not without doubt and conflict. We can sometimes feel conflicted between defining a goal ahead of time to ensure we are supporting all students and not being overly prescriptive in classrooms. We want a solid place for creativity and innovation for both ourselves and our students. We want to bring ourselves to the learning space and meet students there so we can co-construct meaningful experiences, discussions, and explorations of interest. However, we also know that learning goals are the reality in our education systems and it would be unrealistic to deny or ignore them—and tragic to fail to invite students to explore the things society has determined are important for them to learn.

However, the reality is we don't have to choose! Goals in specific areas do not necessarily marginalize creativity (Reeves & Reeves, 2016). Formulaic learning doesn't have to be the cost of achievement in school. We can honor students' skills and interests within our explorations of what our system has decided students should learn. Mary Catherine Bateson (1994) states, "When you are able to attend to something new or to see the familiar in a new way, this is a creative act" (p. 10). With creativity and freedom to explore ideas in a multitude of ways and with a willingness to work alongside children, we can actually do both. We can develop our learning goals while engaging in creative acts.

We need to be receptive to the related combinations of playfulness and discipline or responsibility and creativity. Creativity is developed and enhanced through a combination of creative acts and the assessments that capture these acts. Robinson (2015) says:

> Being creative is not about having off-the-wall ideas and letting your imagination run free. It may involve all of that, but it also involves refining, testing, and focusing what you are doing. It's about original thinking on the part of the individual, and it's also about judging critically whether the work in process is taking the right shape and is worthwhile, at least for the person producing it. (p. 147)

Edges are soft when we explore ways to assess *and* meet the creative and intellectual needs of our learners.

How We Speak About Assessment

Even when we approach education with the intention to empower and the desire to nurture the whole student, our language can often contradict these aims. Although unintentional, the language we use about assessment and its connection to learning can be at odds with what we are trying to communicate and accomplish. We may tell students that practice is important for developing learning but then ask them to rush through an assignment because time is short. We may explain that self-assessment is about developing independence and determining how they perceive their own progress toward goals but then use phrases like "Tell me what you liked" or "Justify to me why you made the choice you did," implying that the audience for a self-assessment is still just the teacher and not themselves. Our language reflects our beliefs, and our beliefs impact our decisions. As Anne Burns (1992) notes, "The teacher's verbalisations reflect something of the interplay between belief and decision-making constantly operating beneath the surface of more observable classroom language and behavior" (p. 63). When we hear students talk about *point grabbing* (demanding additional marks for effort or compliance alone) and how to *get out of work*, we need to examine the paradigm our language is establishing and the effect it is having on the beliefs of our students in our shared spaces. Furthermore, the language around assessment we use as adults both reflects and forms our own beliefs.

The messages in our language around assessment practices and learning can be subtle, but over time can establish a wider belief about what assessment is for, what it means, and who it serves. When our language aligns with our assessment practices, and both communicate responsibility and authentic purpose, we can avoid the dreaded question, "Is this for points?" Table 1.1 provides some examples of language considerations.

Table 1.1: Language Considerations

<table>
<tr><th>Instead of . . .</th><th>Try . . .</th></tr>
<tr><td>We need to help students make connections in their answers.</td><td>Students will make connections in their answers.</td></tr>
<tr><td colspan="2">This is a subtle difference, but anytime our language implies who is responsible for the learning, and that person is someone other than the learner, we have set ourselves up for an ownership problem. Our language must always communicate a belief that students are responsible for their own learning and that we believe they can handle that responsibility. We cannot let ourselves believe that we will make anyone learn; the finesse of teaching is creating circumstances in which students are able to learn and then gradually releasing that responsibility to them.</td></tr>
<tr><td>This counts; this doesn't count.</td><td>Every bit of learning matters, and every bit of learning counts.</td></tr>
<tr><td colspan="2">In reality, everything counts if it is part of constructing new understanding. As long as we continue to delineate, we inadvertently create a paradigm where formative assessment, practice, and daily learning do not count and will not be taken seriously. When we use these terms, we reinforce point grabbing and undermining intrinsic motivation. However, clarifying the difference between learning and assessment to improve versus reporting is important when talking about formative and self-assessment. Our work as educators is to know where our students are going, to support them in reaching those goals, and to verify learning once it happens. At the core of these responsibilities is professional judgment, and when we are making reasoned and well-informed judgments, everything counts. Learning counts.</td></tr>
</table>

continued →

<table>
<tr><th>Instead of . . .</th><th>Try . . .</th></tr>
<tr><td>We will be covering . . .</td><td>You will be learning . . .</td></tr>
<tr><td colspan="2">Covering is a verb that relates solely to the teacher. When teachers refer to covering content, they are often referencing the work they need to do with the course topics and resources. Again, this implies that the teacher—and not the student—owns the content. The student is passive in this equation. True learning happens when the learner is an active participant. We have to move from discussing what we are teaching to discussing what students are learning.</td></tr>
<tr><td>Prove your understanding; justify your thinking.</td><td>Support your understanding; clarify and expand on your thinking.</td></tr>
<tr><td colspan="2">While we certainly want our students to be persuasive and comprehensive when they communicate understanding and share opinions, these terms again can imply that the sole reason for doing so is to give the teacher what he or she wants to hear; the teacher becomes the only audience and purpose. Asking students to prove or justify their thinking to us can establish a singular purpose dependent on another person's opinion. This isn't all bad, but we want to shift the purpose away from the teacher and toward the students' personal messages and encourage their commitment to ensuring they are clearly represented. We can achieve this by searching for audiences and purposes that invite true student investment, supporting their students' desire to be heard and understood. In those cases where the teacher truly is the sole audience, changing our language to reflect a purpose that rests with the student is important. Prompts like "How can you ensure your message is clear and convincing to others?" is a slight shift in language but reminds students that their message is what is most important.</td></tr>
<tr><td>This is worth ten points.</td><td>This will show your understanding and hard work.</td></tr>
<tr><td colspan="2">When we state that an assignment is worth a grade or a certain number of points, we can inadvertently communicate that the only reason to do the assignment is because it has a quantifiable value. We engage our learners in a game, where they weigh their effort against the value of an assignment. Students who are accustomed to experiencing failure will often see this reward as insurmountable, while high-achieving students ready themselves for playing the game of finding the best way to please the teacher. We want the learning experience to be intrinsically motivated as much as possible. Assessment responses show learning, and this is worth more than any grade.</td></tr>
</table>

<table>
<tr><td>Great response. I am impressed.</td><td>Thank you.</td></tr>
<tr><td colspan="2">When we offer students feedback like this, we can create a cycle of compliance and a desire to please the teacher as opposed to thinking deeply. This can greatly reduce creative and critical thinking as well as risk taking. Before we know it, students are looking to us to confirm learning, and the opportunity for self-regulation is lost. Furthermore, students will also acquiesce to those in the room who everyone accepts as being the knowers. Praise like this can support this paradigm and diminish participation when it is handed out to some. Simply thanking students for thinking without offering general praise can better support students in developing independence and authentic engagement.</td></tr>
<tr><td>I am going to . . .</td><td>Your job is to . . .</td></tr>
<tr><td colspan="2">It is important to consistently place the responsibility for learning where it belongs—in the hands of the learners. We can offer support, but it is far more valuable when that support follows self-reflection and goal setting by the student. Too often, we step in too early, believing this is what good teachers do. We have to empower students in their quest for knowledge.</td></tr>
<tr><td>Once we finish this unit . . .</td><td>This learning leads us into . . .</td></tr>
<tr><td colspan="2">One of the biggest misconceptions our education system perpetuates is that learning has a beginning and an end. Our day is divided into timetabled segments, and our teaching is divided into subjects and units of study. This can promote the idea that the skills and knowledge students gain in a unit only matter for a short time. Students will cram for assessment events and leave learning behind as soon as the marks have been given. To shift this story, we have to continually strive to connect learning for students. Learning is continual and so, too, is assessment. New learning replaces old; clarity takes the place of misconceptions. The skills and knowledge we gain in one unit will serve us in future learning. These connections need to be explicit.</td></tr>
</table>

Our language around assessment and learning reflects the positions both teachers and learners hold in relation to what happens in classrooms. The reflection can, in turn, create a self-fulfilling prophecy (Merton, 1948). Lee Jussim and Jacquelynne Eccles (1992) explain the power of beliefs to create reality. Our beliefs about assessment impact our language, which, in turn, can affect our students' beliefs, creating a cycle. Therefore, it is critical to examine both our beliefs and our language around those beliefs. Do we acknowledge that assessment is a relationship between people; between content and context; and between the tool and the people using the tool? Or is assessment an event to be done by students, for teachers, for the purpose of generating a number value? When we make a statement, does it honor the intrinsic value of learning, or does it imply motives for assessment that do not relate to learning?

When learning is tied to *extrinsic valuing*, it removes any intrinsic value it may hold. Our language choices are indicators of our beliefs about assessment, and they can influence what our students come to understand about themselves, their learning, and their reasons for being in our classrooms every day.

Final Thoughts

It is time to reimagine assessment and write a new story that honors both teachers and students. Assessment can support rich learning experiences that attend to all parts of the people who engage in them. Students can explore assessment alongside teachers, and together they can create a new narrative for what the process means and what it becomes in the classroom (Clandinin & Connelly, 1995). Assessment can make learning more creative, more expressive, more diverse, and more responsive when it is viewed in a new way. It is time to soften the edges of assessment and align our practices with our beliefs about learning and students' needs.

Questions for Reflection

The following questions for reflection have been divided into three sections: (1) architecture, (2) student response, and (3) personal response. The architecture questions invite consideration of how we design our assessment processes to ensure our assessment choices reflect learning accurately and reliably. The student response questions prompt us to consider assessment choices from the perspective of the learner. The personal response section asks us to reflect on our own beliefs about assessment and consider these beliefs in relation to decisions we may make. Each question is intended to act as a catalyst for deeper thinking and may lead to new questions. Taking time to reflect on one or two at a time, through journaling, conversation, or as part of a group discussion, can help determine aspects of assessment that may have a hard edge and those that we have successfully softened.

Architecture

- Do you have a personal philosophical belief about assessment? How does it connect to the purpose of education?
- How often do you explicitly engage students in discussions about their lives? What are some of the ways you do this? How will this help you meet their needs?
- To what degree are you able to build a relationship with each student you teach?

- What are your reasons for assessing students? How often do you assess them?
- How often do you have the opportunity to reflect on your assessment practices, choices, and results? Is it enough time?
- How often are the audience and purpose for student products someone other than you and for a reason beyond grading?
- How prepared are your students for the next grade level at the end of the term or school year? If they aren't prepared, why not? Could you change this? Why or why not?

Student Response

- How do your students act when receiving assessment information? What are the conversations that accompany assessment?
- How often do your students ask questions about assessment?
- How often do your students volunteer information about themselves? Why?
- How confident are your students in making mistakes? How confident are they in responding to mistakes?
- How comfortable are your students in taking risks and trying new things?
- What language do your students use when talking about assessment? Record some of their words and phrases. What do these word and phrases indicate?
- How engaged are students in your classes? When is engagement highest? When is it lowest? What does this tell you?
- How often are students invited to be creative? To be curious? To be critical?
- To what degree does each of your students feel cared for and valued? Do you need to address this for any students?
- To what degree are your learners' intellectual, physical, emotional, and social needs being met by your assessment choices?

Personal Response

- How often do assessment results surprise you?
- How often do you discuss assessment with students?
- How often do you invite students to co-construct learning and assessment experiences?

- How much say do you have in how students are assessed? To what degree does this frustrate you? How could you address your own efficacy?
- To what degree do you have strong professional knowledge about assessment?
- To what degree are your intellectual, physical, emotional, and social needs being met by your assessment choices?

CHAPTER

2

Instruction and Assessment Planning Using a Learning Continuum

Travel has been a family priority for my daughters' entire lives. We have journeyed overseas and camped close to home. Each time we head somewhere new, I vow to wander without a clear agenda and let the day unfold completely on its own. This never happens, though, because every day my daughters wake up and ask what we are doing that day. For years, they have resisted my attempts to play things by ear. They insist on learning our destination each day. I have come to understand that knowing where we are going provides them with a great sense of comfort and control—in having a sense of where we might end up despite not being exactly sure how our journey will unfold. As Schimmer (2014) says, "Maybe it's just human nature—we crave some element of predictability and find comfort in knowing a little about the future" (p. 70). Blending the desire for adventure with the need for clarity supports a softened edge.

This is the same reason why knowing our learning goals empowers and reassures us at the same time. If we know where we will end up, it gives us so much more freedom to meander and explore the landscape on the way. When our destination is clear, we feel more able to experience missteps, take risks, and imagine possibilities because there is reassurance that we will get to where we want to go in the end. The alternative is much less palatable. Starting with a wide open space and then trying to measure a discreet aspect in that landscape of possibility is very challenging for both the teacher and the learner. Instead, we can start with a target and then open up the learning space as wide as desired and necessary. In the end, we return to the target and measure progress against it by using a *learning continuum* (in some literature referred to as a *learning progression*). In this chapter, we will explore the concept of the learning continuum, examine the stages of creating learning continuums, and note challenges we may encounter when working with learning continuums.

Understanding the Learning Continuum

The *learning continuum* is an articulation of a progression of skills and understandings inherent in learning goals. It helps us plan multiple aspects of our assessment, instruction, and intervention by *anticipating* stages of learning. Recognizing these stages allows us to make instructionally agile decisions, both during planning and instruction. We form learning continuums for our learning goals by using a backward planning process in which we unpack individual goals and anticipate what incremental progress should look like for each. We design learning events around the skills and knowledge we want students to develop as they work toward achieving the learning goals. This process provides numerous benefits for teachers and students and creates an experience for students that honors their individual learning needs.

Backward Planning and Unpacking

Clarifying the learning continuum requires that we deeply examine learning goals and imagine how learners may engage with them as they progress from building readiness through exploration and learning to reaching proficiency and beyond. This thinking is reflective of planning with the end in mind, which Grant Wiggins and Jay McTighe (2005) articulate in *Understanding by Design*, and unpacking standards that Larry Ainsworth (2003) describes. Their works state that truly effective and responsive teaching can only happen when we first explore the destination—the very reaches of where we imagine heading with our learners. Once we have visited that place through deep reflection and planning, we are poised to meet the needs of the learners and invite them into truly effective and engaging learning spaces. In this planning process, indicators of proficiency for the broad learning goals are considered in addition to the more short-term markers on the journey. This process can be done in conjunction with other unpacking processes (such as formulating "I can" statements for students, placing targets on a ladder in order of complexity, identifying key vocabulary, or determining knows, dos, and understands) and certainly isn't the end of our planning. Rather, the process builds a solid foundation for designing authentic, accurate, and reliable assessments and robust and creative learning experiences.

When we clarify key criteria for a learning goal within the learning continuum, we are affording ourselves the time and space necessary for anticipating student needs. This allows learning to unfold in a wide variety of ways, and allows us to provide differentiation and activate targeted intervention—all to increase the chances students will engage in a way that advances their learning and supports their emotional safety. This kind of planning is necessary because, as Wiggins and McTighe (2005) note:

> To put it in an odd way, too many teachers focus on the *teaching* and not on the *learning*. They spend most of their time thinking, first, about what they will do, what materials they will use, and what they will ask students to do rather than first considering what the learner will need in order to accomplish the learning goals. (p. 15)

By considering the learning continuum, we are thinking first about the depth and breadth of our learning goals and how we will travel alongside students in an attempt to have them demonstrate proficiency. Second, we are thinking deeply about our students, the knowledge they bring to the content, and the ways they may develop their understanding of the learning goals over time and through practice. In essence, we bring both the goals and the students to the planning process.

Learning Events With Clear Purpose

It is important to know that the learning continuum is neither subjective nor prescriptive. It is an articulation of what proficiency looks and sounds like in relation to learning goals and then what the journey looks like from readiness through exploration to proficiency and beyond. The learning continuum is about the knowledge and skills that lead to deeper understanding. Activities and assignments don't drive the continuum. The activities and events emerge from clarity about how student understanding develops along a continuum. The continuum and the students drive classroom experiences. When we create learning activities or events and then try to fit them into the kinds of learning our systems expect or, even worse, we decide its purpose after the activity and assess that, we can place ourselves and our learners in a very precarious position. For example, if we decide to ask learners to engage in a book project or to create a poster without being crystal clear about the skills and knowledge we are attempting to develop, we may end up with products that completely miss the mark in allowing practice and demonstration of proficiency on any of the areas required by our learning goals. This can lead to a hard edge of a lack of efficacy for learners and stress for educators when asked to explain learning and growth in our classrooms.

Instead, one of the best ways to facilitate and later explain learning is to clarify the purpose behind the learning experience as it relates to the learning goals. To be clear, this learning experience can take a multitude of forms: inquiry, small-group work, independent composition and creation, problem-based learning, play-based learning—the list is endless. However, in order to help students imagine new ways of understanding, processing, and applying their learning, we have to be clear about these possibilities ourselves. This requires a significant amount of advanced consideration by the teacher, which translates into planning that focuses on both clarity and possibility.

Certainly, this is the premise behind all planning, but, traditionally, planning has often meant devoting a great deal of time to thinking about what students would be *doing* and not nearly enough time thinking about *why* they would be doing it and *what they would be thinking and learning*. I certainly recall sharing "teaching ideas" with colleagues and scanning educational periodicals for games and projects that would be engaging for learners. However, investigating the purpose of these activities or the learning that was going to be developed was secondary to engagement. I could not have clearly stated the criteria for success for students beyond participation. Further reinforcing this disconnect was the placement of the topic of assessment in university methods courses and within curricular documents themselves. Assessment always seemed to be relegated to the back of the book or the end of a course. As a result, it became the thing to think about after the learning was done.

If we want to reconnect with the learning goals, with assessment, and with achievement, then we have to begin with the goals themselves. Clarifying the learning continuum ensures that our planning, instruction, assessment, and reporting are all based on a solid understanding of the learning goals. This is a powerful shift that has tremendous implications for both teachers and students.

Student Experience

The learning continuum is important to both teachers and students. For teachers, it is instrumental in ensuring that our planning attends to both the learning goals and the learners who will interact with them through classroom experiences. It helps us plan and assess in ways that inform our practice and allow us to be prepared for multiple possibilities as learning unfolds for each student. The learning continuum serves a different purpose for the students. By being familiar with the continuum, students are able to monitor their own progress as they develop skills and understanding. The continuum reflects the individual experiences of each learner and this experience may be a little "messier" than the teacher-generated continuum suggests. For example, students may begin exploration of a learning goal quite confidently and then encounter a specific concept or target that gives them some difficulty. They may move back in the continuum in order to build readiness and then more forward again as they practice their newly acquired skill. Despite this back-and-forth expression of learning, recognizing where students are on their own learning continuums allows us to be responsive to student needs.

Teachers work through stages for clarifying the continuum, but how learners experience these stages is unique to each learner. Prior to instruction, a teacher will clarify what proficiency looks and sounds like as part of their planning. However, achieving proficiency is a stage in a student's personal learning progression. The students' stages in experiencing learning may differ from the teacher's stages of mapping the learning. However, the work a teacher does to articulate the various stages of the learning continuum readies them to respond when the learners step into the learning and reveal the stage they are working through.

Using the continuum starts with the belief that all students can learn and that all students deserve learning experiences that invite them to develop proficiency of learning goals. Carol Ann Tomlinson and Marcia B. Imbeau (2010) state:

> The degree to which a teacher melds respect for the individual and belief in the capacity of the individual to succeed with the intent to know each student as individuals determines the likelihood that the goal of maximizing the capacity of each learner is operational. (p. 37)

This means when we determine that some students need support to build readiness, we can develop these supports through targeted small-group instruction. At the same time, those students who are exploring the targets within a goal can spend time independently practicing while peer assessing and self-assessing against strong criteria and exemplars. Meanwhile, students who have already reached proficiency may be working together to solve a real-world problem that invites further synthesis and application of the skills within the learning goal. Every student is engaged in learning experiences that honor where they are in their own learning continuum. This supports their needs as whole people by clarifying possibilities for learning that place them at the center of this consideration. Student learning flourishes when it emerges out of positive and purposeful interactions among the context (elements may include the environment, resources, purposes, or peers), the student, and the teacher. Each part is essential and, together, what results is compelling and empowering learning for everyone. Developing and nurturing this relationship is the most important thing we can do to soften the edges of classroom decisions, which flow out of this relationship.

Benefits

Using the learning continuum allows us to do the following.

- Imagine various ways each learner may experience the continuum.
- Ensure we develop student readiness in order to increase deep learning.
- Design preassessments that honor students' prior knowledge and skills before beginning a learning experience.
- Create differentiated and responsive learning experiences that anticipate a variety of needs.
- Equip our students with a shared understanding of growth and proficiency so they experience efficacy and confidence in their learning.
- Increase the validity and accuracy of assessment events to determine learning progress.
- Open up our search for resources that support each student's journey toward proficiency and beyond.
- Plan learning experiences for students who need enrichment, so they are not just doing more of the same things.

The continuum allows us to differentiate in meaningful ways for students. For example, if the learning goal is product based (for example, write a narrative essay), then the processes used to develop understanding and get to the written product can vary (for example, brainstorm topics, collaborate with others to develop the story, design an outline using a digital tool). If the learning goal is process based (for example, analyze relationships), then the product that demonstrates proficiency can vary (for example, a Venn diagram, T-chart, or debate). We have the autonomy to be flexible with how students will move through each stage and how we will meet their individual and collective needs. Karen Hume (2008) notes, "This is the art of teaching: our ability to hold expectations constant, but to pitch our instruction, based on evidence, to the right degree of challenge and the right amount and kind of support for each individual" (p. 5). We can expand when needed, support when needed, challenge when needed, and cheer when needed.

The continuum invites both teachers and learners to open to the possibility that learning happens in different ways, at different times, and with different amounts and types of practice. This is important because, as Kochhar-Bryant (2010) explains, "Assessment and grading must recognize that students learn at different rates and show growth in many ways. This more encompassing and informative system honors all the ways humans grow" (p. 176). A classroom where differences are embraced creates a climate where learning will flourish. This is just one way to work toward the larger, lifelong goals of accepting diversity, showing empathy, and practicing patience.

Exploring the Stages for Creating the Learning Continuum

The learning continuum is composed of four stages: (1) building readiness, (2) exploring the learning goal, (3) clarifying proficiency, and (4) enriching understanding. Each stage includes questions that clarify the purpose of the learning and provide a catalyst for deeper investigation. These questions support the need for purposeful engagement and intellectual challenge, creating soft edges. See table 2.1 for a brief summary of each stage's main objectives.

While students generally move through the learning process in the order of these stages (sometimes returning to earlier stages to review or clarify content), actually creating the learning continuum requires backward planning. For this reason, we will first discuss the proficiency stage, which is the goal we want students to reach, followed by the preceding stage, exploring, and the initial stage, building readiness. We will then examine enriched understanding after exploring the first three stages.

Table 2.1: Stages of the Learning Continuum

Building Readiness	Exploring the Learning Goal	Clarifying Proficiency	Enriching Understanding
This stage identifies the readiness that needs to be developed so students can *approach the learning goal*. This can include skills and knowledge gained in previous years or it can simply articulate the readiness to be developed in a learning goal when the topic is brand new. Activation questions guide this stage.	This stage articulates the various steps a student could take to explore the learning goal in a robust and meaningful fashion. It maps the *specific skills and knowledge a student needs to develop* to understand the intent of the learning goal (not to be confused with activities). Exploration questions guide this stage.	This stage states the *indicators of proficiency* for the learning goal, including a demonstration of independence, confidence, and consistency. Essential questions guide this stage.	This stage suggests *possibilities for enrichment* when students are ready. Enrichment questions enhance exploration.

Clarifying Proficiency

While enrichment is part of the continuum and will be discussed later, the best way to ensure absolute clarity in our assessment practices and ready ourselves for planning is to begin developing the learning continuum by clarifying proficiency. This stage focuses on the *indicators of proficiency* for the learning goal. It also includes a demonstration of independence, confidence, and consistency. Essential questions guide this stage.

Identifying indicators of proficiency allows us to very clearly define what it looks like when students produce artifacts of learning that demonstrate the learning goal. Because thinking happens internally, we must rely on (and invite) outward indicators of learning to infer the degree of proficiency.

It can be helpful to think of this stage as a door—call it the *doorway of proficiency*. This is the door a student walks through when he or she shows the understanding and skill named in the learning goal. The student must be able to independently place his or her hand on the doorknob, turn it, open it, and walk through (an exception to this may occur in the primary grades, where proficiency could occur with assistance). As educators, we do our very best to prepare students to walk through the doorway of proficiency but, in the end, we need them to be able to do it on their own. This is our shared destination, and it represents the proficiency stage of our continuum.

When working through the process of clarifying indicators of proficiency, there are three steps that will help guide us in our work: (1) identify and explore key verbs, (2) clarify the context of the verbs, and (3) explore essential questions. By engaging in these first two steps (clarifying the key verb or verbs and their context), we are essentially articulating the indicators of proficiency. We must have a strong sense of both the content and the processes to reveal the content. These kinds of considerations are important because they invite a deep understanding of the intent or purpose of the learning goals and the ways they could be lived in our classrooms. This clarity leads directly to responsive instruction and contextual assessment practices. Without clarity, the edges of our planning and subsequent assessment will harden.

Identify and Explore Key Verbs

To clarify what proficiency means for learning goals, we begin by identifying and exploring the key verbs in the learning goals (Ainsworth, 2003; Vagle, 2015; Wiggins & McTighe, 2005). This allows us to consider and then clarify the *types of learning* our students will demonstrate at the proficient level. Let's explore this stage by using an example from the sixth-grade English language arts (ELA) Common Core State Standards (CCSS):

> Analyze how a particular sentence, paragraph, chapter, or section fits into the overall structure of a text and contributes to the development of the ideas. (RI.6.5; National Governors Association Center for Best Practices [NGA] & Council of Chief State School Officers [CCSSO], 2010a)

In this example, the students are being asked to *analyze.* Identifying and focusing on this verb is helpful in ascertaining how students will engage in the content that follows. It also allows us to be very clear about the type of assessment opportunity we offer students when it is time for them to show understanding. Consider another example from the fifth-grade mathematics CCSS:

> Recognize that in a multi-digit number, a digit in one place represents 10 times as much as it represents in the place to its right and $\frac{1}{10}$ of what it represents in the place to its left. (5.NBT.A.1; NGA & CCSSO, 2010b)

Here, students are being asked to *recognize.* This requires quite different processes and skills than analyzing, and it is vital to be clear about these differences from the outset. In analysis, students need to understand two or more ideas fully and then be able to explain the relationship between those things, supporting their explanation with details and examples. When students are, instead, being asked to recognize, it means understanding the attributes of something enough that it could be identified in an unfamiliar context. Sorting out the different processes and skills required for each standard or learning goal is the first step in clarifying proficiency.

Clarify the Context of Key Verbs

It is equally necessary to examine all information that follows the verb in a learning goal because this provides the context. Verbs, in and of themselves, do not portray the entirety of depth and breadth. Analyzing the causes of two world conflicts in social studies will require different kinds of knowledge and skill than analyzing game tactics in physical education. The context allows us to explore the depth of thinking required by the verb in each learning goal. We can ask ourselves, "Analyze what?" In the first ELA standard example, the answer is *analyze the ways sentences, paragraphs, sections, or chapters fit into the structure of a text and contribute to idea development.* Now that we understand what students are being asked to analyze, we can begin sorting out the parts of the standard that students must attend to. They will need to be able to recognize pieces of a text in various forms (sentences, paragraphs, and so on). They will also need to comprehend the text, identifying key ideas. They then need to consider the ways those smaller structures of a text develop the overall message; in other words, they need to consider how the text's meaning is impacted by the way it is written.

In the mathematics standard, students are being asked to *recognize the relationship between the value of the numbers in a multidigit number and their placement within the number*. So, when a number is given, a student will be able to recognize the value of each digit in relation to the digits next to it. As soon as we explore the deeper intention behind a standard, we can begin to imagine how this will look as it is being introduced, explored, and eventually fully understood. In other words, the continuum begins to unfold.

Whether we use Bloom's taxonomy (Anderson & Krathwohl, 2001; Bloom, 1956) or Norman L. Webb's (2002) Depth of Knowledge model, it is important to understand the kinds of thinking required of students and what that thinking will look and sound like when it is lived in our classrooms. By considering this ahead of time, we are affording ourselves the confidence to design strong learning experiences and assessment events for our students that invite the practice and exploration they will need to reach proficiency.

Explore Essential Questions

To truly ready ourselves for planning, a valuable third step is to explore some of the potential essential questions we may use to frame our lessons and formative and summative assessments (McTighe & Wiggins, 2013; Wiggins & McTighe, 2005). These essential questions help us determine the purpose behind the learning goals. While it is optimal to design essential questions alongside our students, we can also plan some of these questions prior to teaching as we plan our lessons. We can create essential questions while planning *and* we can refine them when working with students. Both options lead to empowerment.

Strong essential questions often (although not always) start with *how* or *why*. These kinds of questions invite students to synthesize and consider the purpose behind the learning experiences they engage in. They can also prepare students for inquiry and open-ended exploration. A compelling essential question (for example, Why are questions as important as answers in science? How does where an artist lives impact the art he or she produces?) can serve as the backbone for strong assessment and instruction and can frame several days of focused discussion, exploration, and inquiry.

One of the most heartbreaking hard edges for teachers occurs when we engage in processes that never impact our day-to-day classroom life. We may spend hours or days unpacking learning goals or designing assessment plans, only to leave them on our shelves because we cannot integrate them into our actual teaching context. This indicates a disconnect between what we are being asked to do as educators and what we actually believe and do. This disconnect can occur when essential questions are posted in our classrooms but never discussed or revisited, or worse, when they appear in our unit plans but are never raised with students. This signals a process in which teachers, who were initially invested in the consideration and creation of essential questions, ultimately lack the skill or investment to know how to integrate them into actual learning experiences. As a result, the questions and the continuum they represent end up being owned solely by the teacher and not by the learners, which can result in reduced potential for engagement by everyone.

For the ELA and mathematics standards examples introduced earlier, once we have determined what indicates proficiency, we can begin to craft some essential questions to springboard planning and learning (see tables 2.2 and 2.3, pages 39–40). As we examine each indicator of proficiency, we can consider questions we might ask in order to invite thinking that will allow students to explore learning and eventually demonstrate the understanding and skill expressed in the indicator. What do these indicators accomplish in relation to a deeper understanding of the goals? How do these indicators invite students to make sense of the concepts and skills within the goals?

Table 2.2: English Language Arts Standard, Proficiency Indicators, and Essential Questions

Standard	
Analyze how a particular sentence, paragraph, chapter, or section fits into the overall structure of a text and contributes to the development of the ideas (RI.6.5; NGA & CCSSO, 2010a).	
Proficiency Indicators	**Essential Questions**
• Recognize text structures by name and attribute. • Engage in texts for meaning.	• How does the structure of a text contribute to its overall meaning?
• Analyze the relationship between text structure and the development of ideas to communicate meaning.	• Why do authors make the structural choices they do?
• Support analysis with details and examples from texts. • Engage in analysis independently.	• How do their choices impact a reader's understanding of their message?

Table 2.3: Mathematics Standard, Proficiency Indicators, and Essential Questions

Standard	
Recognize that in a multi-digit number, a digit in one place represents 10 times as much as it represents in the place to its right and $\frac{1}{10}$ of what it represents in the place to its left (5.NBT.A.1; NGA & CCSSO, 2010b).	
Proficiency Indicators	**Essential Questions**
• Recognize the value of all digits in a multidigit number.	• How can I determine the value of a digit in a multidigit number?
• Recognize the relationship between the value of a digit in a multidigit number and the value of the digit to the right side or left side.	• How does the value of one digit in a multidigit number relate to the value of the digit next to it? • How does knowing the pattern of the values of digits in multidigit numbers help when working with numbers in various ways?

Exploring the Learning Goal

After identifying what will constitute proficiency, we can consider how to explore the learning goal and ensure our students develop proficiency over time. This stage states the various steps a student could take to explore the learning goal in a robust and meaningful fashion. In this stage, we map the *specific skills and knowledge a student needs to develop* to understand the intent of the learning goal (which is not to be confused with activities). Exploration questions guide this stage.

Imagine that in front of the doorway of proficiency is a *hallway of learning*. This hallway is why schools exist; it is where much of our good work happens. This is where we formatively assess and offer feedback. This is where we scaffold and differentiate. Sometimes we hold student's hands as we lead them down the hallway. Other times, students are almost at the door and ready to be released to turn the handle themselves. This hallway is where the learning happens, and there is no shame in being here. In fact, it is a celebration, because it means we have work to do and our students are learning. On our continuum, this is exploring the learning goal.

As we engage in this stage of the continuum, it is important to soften the edges for ourselves by honoring any work we may have done in previous attempts to plan with our learning goals. This stage is not new. In fact, teachers have been exploring ways to help students learn specific skills or concepts for years—this is the nature of teaching. This exploration often manifests in our daily lesson plans, pacing guides, and other processes that invite us to think about how learning will unfold. The difference here is that this process asks us to consider *key* understandings and skills that learners need to develop on their journeys toward the doorway of proficiency. These key skills and understandings may occur in many ways and in a variety of orders, but they are the essential pieces that will ultimately result in proficiency for everyone. Sometimes our students already possess some or all of these individual skills and simply need the opportunity to synthesize them in a demonstration of the learning goal. Our preassessments and formative assessments will tell us which students fall into this category, but having clarity about these pieces is essential for effective planning.

Identify Skills and Knowledge That Lead to Proficiency

We begin the process of articulating the exploring journey by identifying the steps that lead to proficiency. It is helpful to refer back to our proficiency work and ask ourselves these questions.

- "What skills will students need to develop as they explore and develop proficiency?"
- "What knowledge do students need to acquire as they explore and develop proficiency?"
- "What kinds of connections among content, skills, and processes do we want students to make?"
- "What questions are students exploring?"
- "What kinds of reasoning are required?"
- "What are the pieces we need to build together?"

As we answer these questions, we begin to make decisions about the key markers on the path to proficiency. We may find that the exploring the learning goal stage looks somewhat like the clarifying proficiency stage, except the proficiency indicators are actually being *developed* as opposed to synthesized and demonstrated.

In some literature (for example, Moss, Brookhart, & Long, 2011), the exploring stage results in the formation of learning targets or "I can" statements. This great work is very informative as we plan our learning experiences. An additional aspect of clarifying the learning continuum is considering which of our learning targets (or "I can" statements) are actually indicators of proficiency and which may, instead, be part of the building readiness, exploring, or even enriching stages. We need to be sure we are not requiring targets at the proficient stage that go beyond proficiency. For example, if the learning goal requires students to *identify* performance cues when throwing a ball, it would be extending beyond the goal to require learners to *assess* which cues are most essential. (We will explore enrichment later in this chapter.) To ensure our targets represent a continuum, it is helpful to consider how one may lead to the next in developing deep understanding. This invites strong formative assessment practices and instruction that supports meaningful growth, as well as clarity about proficiency, when the target is attained.

Targets are the building blocks of learning, and it is our responsibility to track their development in our students and offer feedback, correction, and practice when necessary. We clarified the proficiency indicators in the previous stage, and this is what we measure when the students are ready for verification through a summative assessment. However, our work in the exploring stage is focused on readying our learners for these measures of proficiency through practice, inquiry, and feedback.

Form Questions for Exploring the Learning Goal

As with the proficiency stage, questions are helpful for creating clarity about where learning may travel. Questions are also effective in eliciting student investment and guiding both structured and open-ended exploration. By revisiting the key skills and knowledge we have identified for this stage, we can then form exploration questions.

Continuing with our ELA and mathematics standards examples, tables 2.4 and 2.5 illustrate what this stage may look like.

Table 2.4: English Language Arts Standard, Key Skills and Knowledge, and Exploration Questions

Standard	
Analyze how a particular sentence, paragraph, chapter, or section fits into the overall structure of a text and contributes to the development of the ideas (RI.6.5; NGA & CCSSO, 2010a).	
Key Skills and Knowledge	**Exploration Questions**
• Recognize and identify key text structures (sentence, paragraph, chapter, section, stanza, and so on).	• What are some of the key structures in literary texts?
• Engage in and comprehend the main idea and supporting details of literary texts.	• What is the message in this text? • What are the supporting details that help in understanding the author's message?
• Analyze relationships between various elements and ideas in literary texts.	• How do authors structure their texts? Why do they make the decisions they do? How do their decisions affect readers?

• Compare parts of a text to the whole text, and analyze the relationship in terms of both structure and meaning.	• How does part of a text connect to the whole? How would the meaning change if that part were missing or structured differently?

Table 2.5: Mathematics Standard, Key Skills and Knowledge, and Exploration Questions

Standard	
Recognize that in a multi-digit number, a digit in one place represents 10 times as much as it represents in the place to its right and $\frac{1}{10}$ of what it represents in the place to its left (5.NBT.A.1; NGA & CCSSO, 2010b).	
Key Skills and Knowledge	**Exploration Questions**
• Recognize the place value of a single digit in a multidigit number.	• How do I know the value of a digit in a multidigit number?
• Show understanding of and be able to calculate multiples of ten.	• How does the value of one digit relate to the value of another digit in a multidigit number? Why does this matter? • What is a multiple of ten? What does a multiple of ten mean?
• Be able to accurately use the phrases *ten times more than* and *ten times less than* when comparing digits in a multidigit number.	• How do I know if one number is ten times more or less than another number?
• Understand how fractions can be used to explain relationships between digits in a multidigit number.	• How can a fraction explain how one digit is related to another in a multidigit number?

You will notice that the key indicators at this stage do not contain isolated bits of knowledge (for example, define a sentence or know numbers in sequence from one to one thousand), nor do they include the assessment strategies teachers could use to arrive at and measure the desired learning (such as complete a problem or work in a group). Further, this stage does not contain the instructional strategies the teacher will utilize in order to "get at" the learning—*how* the learning will be experienced (such as be able to use manipulatives, be able to use a graphic organizer, or be able to engage in focused conversation). All these additional items will develop as a result of clarifying the learning continuum. As mentioned previously, the continuum is not a unit plan—it is a catalyst for a unit plan.

Building Readiness

Once we understand the best ways to explore learning goals, we can work backward to identify the foundational skills and knowledge we may need to build in students to ensure they are ready to engage in those learning goals. Without this stage, students are asked to engage in learning they may not be prepared for. This stage identifies the readiness necessary for students to approach the learning goal. This readiness can include skills and knowledge gained in previous years or simply articulating what has to be developed when the topic is brand new. Activation questions guide this stage.

Sometimes students need to develop skills and knowledge that prepare them for engaging in and exploring a learning goal. This need can occur for a wide variety of reasons. Perhaps students were absent for portions of the previous year and missed some necessary concepts and skills; perhaps students need the opportunity to review vocabulary that will enable them to use a shared language with the teacher; perhaps students have cognitive difficulties that necessitate extra time spent building readiness; perhaps the topic or content the teacher is introducing is brand new for students and everyone needs to activate knowledge and develop readiness. Whatever the reason, it is important to consider some of these initial building blocks because when we fail to do so, we can leave students behind from the very outset, challenge their intellectual and emotional safety, and harden the edges of everything that follows. This stage ensures a strong foundation to build the learning goal. Without it, students can falter.

Imagine that at the beginning of the hallway of learning is a set of stairs called the *building readiness stairs*. When students are on these stairs, it means they need to build skills and knowledge that ready them for entering the hallway with confidence. This stage is where greater scaffolds and interventions may be needed. This is where front-loading vocabulary and practicing basic skills may be necessary. It is vital to know when students are on these stairs because this knowledge equips educators with the ability to provide needed supports. A preassessment before learning begins or a targeted formative assessment early in the learning process can identify students who need to build readiness for the learning goal. When students are not in the hallway and haven't been able to climb the stairs even after support and learning opportunities, they are likely deeply struggling or disengaged. This is important information to know in order to soften the edges for both our students and ourselves before our learners fall further and further behind and become irreparably disengaged and we are faced with a student who has stopped attending school.

Building readiness is about building capacity. It is part of the growth and learning process and there is absolutely no shame in standing on the stairs. Anytime we encounter brand-new contexts, we all step back onto the stairs for a while. The first time I moved out of the classroom and began to work with adults as a professional developer, I stepped right into the building readiness stage. I needed to spend time exploring the traits of adult learners. I had to work on skills like projecting my voice and fully utilizing the space. Building these foundational skills was critical before I could even begin developing my content. Schimmer (2014) explains, "Readiness is about each student's starting point, which has very little to do with what a student will eventually achieve. Teachers most effective and efficient with differentiated instruction are usually quite clear about the difference between ability and readiness" (p. 78). When a student is standing on the stairs, we are able to celebrate each step they take. Like in any other stage, we can soften the edges and respond to their needs through formative assessment.

Consider Foundational Skills and Knowledge

We begin our work with this stage by considering foundational skills and knowledge—the very beginning steps learners may take as they approach the learning goal. It is akin to learning anything for the first time. Think of when you first learned to drive. Before you started the vehicle and practiced driving, you needed to familiarize yourself with the vehicle parts and function of those parts. You also needed to learn what road signs indicate and how to respond. Driving could not happen without this knowledge. This is what building readiness is about. There are things we need to explore before we can even engage in the key parts of the goal. These may include vocabulary, basic concepts, and foundational skills. Sometimes, students may have been exposed to this information in previous years but failed to retain it. Sometimes, it is simply the initial information essential to explore before undertaking the complexity of the learning goal.

It is critical to keep in mind that how we describe each stage of the continuum to students, particularly the building readiness stage, could make or break student investment and student-teacher relationships as a whole. If we portray this stage with deficit language (*lacking skill*, *missing knowledge*, *struggling*, *failing*), we will misrepresent the importance of this stage in the learning continuum. Furthermore, when we include families in discussions about the continuum, how we explain this stage will affect whether they feel optimistic and hopeful or distressed and anxious. The intention is to celebrate growth and articulate how continued learning will lead to proficiency. There is optimism in the continuum, not finality. It is a means for conversation about learning, not a judgment.

It is important to note that sometimes when determining interventions, we may have to go further than the continuum. The stages of the continuum are the start of an assessment and response conversation, not the end. Building readiness highlights the foundational skills and knowledge of learning goals, but once we see that challenges exist even after targeted and sustained time and practice, we may need to dig deeper and explore more specific interventions. In these cases, the building readiness stage can be used to activate supports if a student fails to make timely progress. Individual program plans, success plans, intervention plans, supports from consultants and paraprofessionals, and so on may be activated when a student is finding it difficult to build readiness. Setting smaller goals within this stage is vital for celebrating growth and nurturing emotional safety for these students. Sharing success in relation to these smaller steps is a great way to communicate with families and soften the edges of our reporting practices.

Consider Activation Questions for Building Readiness

Once we have identified foundational skills and knowledge, we can consider questions that activate learning to build readiness. These questions may invite all kinds of thinking and position learners to explore key foundational aspects of the learning goal to ready themselves for more complex learning experiences. Tables 2.6 and 2.7 illustrate how this may look for our two standards examples.

Table 2.6: English Language Arts Standard, Skills and Knowledge, and Activation Questions

Standard	
Analyze how a particular sentence, paragraph, chapter, or section fits into the overall structure of a text and contributes to the development of the ideas (RI.6.5; NGA & CCSSO, 2010a).	
Skills and Knowledge for Building Readiness	**Activation Questions**
• Understand the use of vocabulary (within a sentence, paragraph, chapter, or section) and the text structure (main idea, supporting details or ideas, message, author, and meaning).	• What is the vocabulary I need to know? How can I develop my understanding?
• Know how to analyze, support an analysis, and track idea development throughout a text.	• What is an analysis? How do I best support my ideas?

• Identify strategies for improving comprehension.	• How can I be sure I understand what I am reading? How will I know when I don't understand?
• Recognize text forms and structures.	• What is a text form? What is a text structure? How do text form and structure help the author develop the message?

Table 2.7: Mathematics Standard, Skills and Knowledge, and Activation Questions

Standard	
Recognize that in a multi-digit number, a digit in one place represents 10 times as much as it represents in the place to its right and $\frac{1}{10}$ of what it represents in the place to its left (5.NBT.A.1; NGA & CCSSO, 2010b).	
Skills and Knowledge for Building Readiness	**Activation Questions**
• Recognize a multidigit number. • Know right and left.	• What is a multidigit number? What is a digit? What do digits represent?
• Isolate a digit in a multidigit number, and identify the place value of a number.	• What are place values in a multidigit number? Why are place values important? • What is the relationship between ten and one hundred? Between one hundred and one thousand?
• Multiply numbers by ten. • Divide numbers by ten.	• How do I build confidence in multiplying and dividing by ten?
• Recognize a fraction and explain what it represents.	• What is a fraction?

These tables illustrate the kinds of foundational understanding students need to develop to explore the standard. Sometimes our learners surprise us and we realize there are additional foundational pieces we hadn't considered when mapping our continuum. In cases such as these, we can remain flexible enough to simply add them to our continuum and then address the needs of our learners. By considering the readiness needs of a learning goal and of our students, we can plan to differentiate and formatively monitor progress before we run into trouble. Furthermore, building confidence in the beginning increases the chance that confidence will continue as the student engages in increasingly complex learning. This confidence indicates a soft edge.

Enriching Understanding

We have now worked through the process of planning to develop proficiency by establishing readiness and exploring the key skills and understandings reflected in our learning goals. Often, this may be the end of our planning, but it is essential to consider one final stage because when we don't, we create a very hard edge for those learners who are ready and need to explore learning more deeply. A fourth stage in the learning continuum is the enriching understanding stage. This stage states the indicators of enrichment or extended exploration of the learning goal. It also includes a demonstration of independence, confidence, and consistency. Enrichment questions frame this stage and invite learners to explore the learning goals in new and more complex ways through interaction with provocative questions. They ask learners to consider new applications, methods for creating content, or strategies for exploring more challenging concepts as they relate to the learning goals.

This stage has been called a number of things (extension, exceeding, gifted), but the premise is to consider the learning needs of students who have demonstrated proficiency on a learning goal before their peers. This stage of learning presupposes that learning is never finished and that all students deserve to be challenged and to continue growing. Enriching understanding involves engagement in the learning goals in ways that invite more complex thinking in increasingly varied contexts.

This stage of the continuum represents what we find beyond the doorway of proficiency once students have opened it on their own. This is the *landscape of enrichment*. When students reach this stage, it means they are ready to explore the vistas beyond proficiency. This landscape is vast and does not support doing more of the same, but rather doing different things and exploring further. It also does not call for moving to the next grade's learning goals (although we have to remember that these goals can be pretty broad and sometimes impossible to avoid in their entirety). There is no set road a student must explore when he or she is travelling through this landscape. Learning can continue in so many ways, and this should be embraced and communicated.

When we expect some students will reach proficiency early, we should be ready with opportunities to explore goals more deeply and in new ways. Nicole Dimich Vagle (2015) agrees: "For those learners who come to us already knowing a standard, or who achieve quickly, our instruction needs to push their thinking and learning"

(p. 82). Sometimes this means students explore with greater complexity (for example, more difficult data, expanded vocabulary, or more difficult texts). Sometimes it means they explore applicability in a meaningful and deeply contextual way (for example, building models, engaging the community, or designing a product). Sometimes enrichment means exploring adjacent topics that expand knowledge of the learning goal more fully (for example, when studying worldview, explore worldviews of societies from the past or across the world; when studying ecosystems, study sustainability of a particular ecosystem when variables are introduced).

Articulate the Criteria for Enriched Exploration

We begin our consideration of enrichment by asking ourselves how we can deepen our students' exploration of the learning goal. This invites us to articulate the criteria for enriched exploration so we keep it from becoming vague or cumbersome and creating a hard edge. We have to acknowledge that when we ponder this question, we are investigating our goals in new ways which may not be explicitly articulated and which we may not have previously considered. This distinction is important to understand and explain to students and families. This discussion will grow even richer when we invite students into the conversation. This is critical for student investment and a softened edge. However, it is helpful to consider enrichment even before we dive into instruction, so we are ready to respond when students demonstrate proficiency before their peers.

For example, many people are proficient with using a portable device, driving a vehicle, and cooking a meal. Their proficiency is indicated through actions they have taken consistently and independently over time. Now, imagine a person has five hours to improve his or her chosen skill—five dedicated hours to this very specific skill. What would the student work on? How would he or she get better? Would practice driving a different kind of vehicle help? Trying new apps? Cooking a dish that requires a specific process not tried previously?

Our work at the enrichment stage invites us to consider the ways the learning goal could be deepened, expanded, or stretched. How can we invite students to further develop their understanding? Do we need to engage them in more complex data sets? Do we adjust their audience and purpose? Do we invite them to create a product based on their analysis? It is helpful at this stage to return to the verb in the learning goal and remind ourselves of our decisions around proficiency.

Next, we can begin to imagine how those proficiency indicators would look if we had more time to spend exploring them. Where could a learner go, and how could we address holistic needs through this deeper exploration? Sometimes they could engage in the same type of learning (analyzing, for example), but the context or details may become more complex. Or, perhaps, the students are introduced to a real-life application of the skill in the learning goal—one that is new to them. Another alternative is to have the students engage in the learning goal, but engage in it using a different kind of thinking—instead of analyzing, maybe assessing or creating the content. The possibilities are endless. The key is that the learning we are inviting the students to do at this stage is different learning—not more of the same. Otherwise, students will learn very quickly that enrichment simply means doing more work than everyone else, which does little to address their needs.

Identify Questions for Enrichment

As with the other three stages, it is helpful to next consider *enrichment questions* to engage and empower students. These questions, posed to students, are different from those noted in the preceding paragraphs that we ask ourselves as part of instructional planning. We remind ourselves of what it means to be proficient, and then we craft questions that could ignite further exploration of this learning. These are questions to guide enriching understanding. Tables 2.8 and 2.9 offer possibilities for this stage, using the examples we have been exploring.

Table 2.8: English Language Arts Standard, Possibilities for Enriching Understanding, and Enrichment Questions

Standard	
Analyze how a particular sentence, paragraph, chapter, or section fits into the overall structure of a text and contributes to the development of the ideas (RI.6.5; NGA & CCSSO, 2010a).	
Possibilities for Enriched Understanding	**Enrichment Questions**
• Assess how sentences, paragraphs, chapters, or sections impact the message within a text, and determine which parts have the greatest impact on ideas in various texts.	• Which parts of a text have the greatest impact on the development of ideas?
• Craft alternative portions of a text to alter the development of ideas.	• What happens to the message when the structures are changed? How can students show this?
• Analyze increasingly difficult texts with unique text structures, and explain how the parts impact the whole.	• How do some authors utilize unique structures to develop their ideas? Why did they do this?

• Compare texts with similar messages, and examine their structures to determine the impact of structure on message.	• How do texts with the same message use structures differently? What is the impact? Does it change the way the ideas are developed?

Table 2.9: Mathematics Standard, Possibilities for Enriching Understanding, and Enrichment Questions

Standard	
Recognize that in a multi-digit number, a digit in one place represents 10 times as much as it represents in the place to its right and $\frac{1}{10}$ of what it represents in the place to its left (5.NBT.A.1; NGA & CCSSO, 2010b).	
Possibilities for Enriched Understanding	**Enrichment Questions**
• Explore larger numbers and smaller numbers and test whether the same logic holds true.	• Does this logic hold true in larger numbers? In much smaller numbers? In numbers less than one?
• Explain the relationship between digits that are farther than one digit apart in a multidigit number.	• How are digits that are two apart in a multidigit number related?
• Create a visual representation of this relationship to help someone to understand it without words.	• How can you show someone this relationship without words?

Considering enrichment possibilities during the planning process softens the edges for teachers because it satisfies our need for preparation and confidence. We are ready for and know how to respond to the student who, fifteen minutes into the class, declares he or she is done, and we check his or her understanding and find it to be proficient. Considering enrichment also softens the edge for learners because it offers them challenges and supports them in continued intellectual development. This, in turn, builds confidence and curiosity, which nurture emotional and, depending on the context, physical stability. Learners who receive enrichment can share in decision making about their learning, which may involve the choice of working in a group or working alone, depending on their emotional and social needs. They may be able to choose learning that is kinesthetic in nature if activating their bodies is a good fit for them. Reciprocally, they may seek learning contexts that limit physical movement and allow them to devote mental resources to solving complex problems.

By engaging learners in crafting contexts that support enrichment, we can increase our chances of meeting the needs of the whole learner.

One of the greatest disservices to students who are ready for enrichment is to ignore this need and give them more of the same or ask them to sit quietly until others are finished. Students who have observed that reaching the enriching understanding stage will simply result in doing more of the same work or helping other students do their work are likely to become disengaged very quickly. For too long, this kind of learning has appeared to be more punishment than opportunity. These decisions then become *compliance decisions* because we are not offering these students a compelling or purposeful task, so they either comply or they rebel. Neither choice is an adequate alternative. Furthermore, these students rarely feel complexity and challenge, which means they come to expect learning to be easy. In those instances when they meet a challenge, they are ill-equipped to respond with confidence and stamina. We need these students to develop a belief in themselves and their ability to overcome challenges. If we are going to change this, we will need to deeply consider what enriching learning could mean.

One of the best ways to determine what comes next is to involve students in the conversation, but we must be prepared for some pushback. Many students have come to believe that the secret to high grades is to comply with teacher requests, work quickly and efficiently, and complete all tasks required of them. Thinking more deeply and in increasingly complex ways, as opposed to simply complying, can elicit frustration at first and may create a hard edge. In order to soften the edges for these learners, we have to look carefully at how these students are positioned in their classrooms and how challenging them impacts their understanding of who they are and what their schooling is about. The problem with the traditional paradigm is that if we don't address their enrichment needs, we run the risk of having these students complete the same work year after year with the only difference being a new teacher. Conversations about learning and support during a changing paradigm will be critical for these students, in both the short and long term.

Putting the Stages Together

Once each stage has been carefully considered in relation to the learning goal, it is time to bring everything together. Examining the continuum in its entirety allows us to see how the stages connect to each other and also allows us to anticipate, once again, how learning may unfold. Do we think many students will be beginning in the building readiness stage, or do we expect learners to come equipped with substantial background knowledge? Do we believe there may be learners who will already be able to demonstrate proficiency, or is this topic so new that we would be surprised if this were the case? How might we structure a preassessment, and how can the building readiness and exploring stages inform our design? When do we imagine a formative assessment might be critical? How might a summative assessment look when the times comes? Because we measure progress toward the learning target in the context of the learning continuum or progression, the stages on a continuum are presented in the order of a general trajectory (building readiness, exploring the learning goal, clarifying proficiency, and enriching understanding), although students may move around within or revisit early stages as needed. The completed learning continuum invites deep consideration of our instructional choices and assessment decisions before we begin to map out a learning plan. It positions us to anticipate student needs and craft methods for gathering the evidence critical for being truly responsive. Table 2.10 (page 54) offers an example of a complete learning continuum featuring the mathematics standard and questions we have been exploring throughout each stage in the preceding sections. To access additional examples of how each stage fits together to develop student proficiency and enrichment of learning goals in a variety of subjects and grade levels, see the appendix (page 197).

Anticipating Challenges

If we are going to effectively craft and utilize learning continuums, we have to avoid making the continuum something it isn't. For example, it is not about point tallying or creating a to-do list. It is also not the same as creating a rubric, although the information sequenced may be developed into one later. The learning continuum is not structured around *kind of good*, *more good*, *really good*, and *super good*, which are unhelpful qualifiers. It is also not based on 1, 2, 3, or 4; 25 percent, 50 percent, 75 percent, or 100 percent; or A, B, C, or D. This is simply not the intent and can be incredibly discouraging for students—not to mention miscommunicating the value that building readiness and engaging in exploration holds for developing understanding. Placing numbers anywhere on the continuum makes it mean something entirely different to students. Students are preconditioned to be assigned a numerical value, and when we assign a number (even 1–4), we are confusing the intention and hardening the edges of a practice intended to soften challenges by meeting the need for clarity and optimism.

That being said, if we choose to adapt the continuum into a rubric to use with students, it can become a communication, reflection, and growth tool that holds opportunity to clearly and specifically share important information about where learning is headed—if it is done in a way that keeps in mind the need for softened edges. Another way to think about it is that the work of clarifying the continuum is initially serving the teacher. Once educators are clear about learning goals, then they

Table 2.10: Mathematics Standard and the Complete Learning Continuum

Standard				
Recognize that in a multi-digit number, a digit in one place represents 10 times as much as it represents in the place to its right and $\frac{1}{10}$ of what it represents in the place to its left (5.NBT.A.1; NGA & CCSSO, 2010b).				
	Building Readiness	**Exploring the Learning Goal**	**Clarifying Proficiency**	**Enriching Understanding**
Skills and Knowledge	• Recognize a multidigit number. • Know right and left. • Isolate a digit in a multidigit number, and identify the place value of a number. • Multiply numbers by ten. • Divide numbers by ten. • Recognize a fraction and explain what it represents.	• Recognize the place value of a single digit in a multidigit number. • Show understanding of and be able to calculate multiples of ten. • Be able to accurately use the phrases *ten times more than* and *ten times less than* when comparing digits in a multidigit number. • Understand how fractions can be used to explain relationships between digits in a multidigit number.	• Recognize the value of all digits in a multidigit number. • Recognize the relationship between the value of a digit in a multidigit number and the value of the digit to the right side or left side.	• Explore larger and smaller numbers and test whether the same logic holds true. • Explain the relationship between digits that are farther than one digit apart in a multidigit number. • Create a visual representation of this relationship to help someone understand it without words.

	Building Readiness	Exploring the Learning Goal	Clarifying Proficiency	Enriching Understanding
Questions	• What is a multidigit number? What is a digit? What do digits represent? • What are place values in a multidigit number? Why are place values important? • What is the relationship between ten and one hundred? Between one hundred and one thousand? • What is a fraction? • How do I build confidence in multiplying and dividing by ten?	• How do I know the value of a digit in a multidigit number? • How does the value of one digit relate to the value of another digit in a multidigit number? Why does this matter? • What is a multiple of ten? What does a multiple of ten mean? • How do I know if one number is ten times more or less than another number? • How can a fraction explain how one digit is related to another in a multidigit number?	• How does the value of one digit in a multidigit number relate to the value of the digit next to it? • How does knowing the pattern of the values of digits in multidigit numbers help us work with numbers in various ways?	• Does this logic hold true in larger numbers? In much smaller numbers? In numbers less than one? • How are digits two apart in a multidigit number related? • How can you show someone this relationship without words?

can adapt the information to support the students in a wide variety of ways, one of which may be through a rubric in student-friendly language.

Another challenge occurs when the continuum is dependent on compliance. It is not a checklist (for example, write a title, include a cover page, and so on) but rather explores a goal in its fullness—namely, to borrow from Michelle Goodwin (2009), "to arrive at clear statements that show teachers and students how the standard will translate into student work" (p. 91). We have to be agile within and between each stage. This is the art of teaching. Oversimplifying the learning through the continuum simply frustrates both teachers and learners. When the continuum becomes a chore list, learning is neither creative nor flexible; it is the opposite of the intent. It should empower, not restrict. Furthermore, when our descriptors are dependent on quantity rather than quality (for example, list three supporting details versus strengthen development of the main idea with supporting details), we increase the need for compliance and decrease the need for understanding.

Using the continuum doesn't imply that learning is linear. Sometimes we are moving toward proficiency and have to return to building readiness (for example, to add vocabulary to students' understanding). Sometimes when our class is exploring the learning goal, we find ourselves making a really strong connection that catapults us into enriching understanding. The purpose of the continuum is to think ahead and anticipate where learning might go. It is not to move students lockstep through each phase; that would ignore the need for flexible intellectual growth and create a hard edge.

Another hard edge can form when we use varied language and processes—this is confusing to students and families alike. In order to ensure transparency in our communication with both learners and families, we must consistently use the language of the continuum (for example, *building readiness*, *exploring the learning goal*, *clarifying proficiency*, and *enriching understanding*). We can use the language of the continuum when we offer feedback and celebrate growth. We can develop consistency in how we share a vision for learning that supports the holistic needs of our students and families.

Lastly, it is empowering to know that we can make choices about how to explore our learning goals and craft our learning continuums. We may choose to do this work on our own and ensure powerful learning experiences for our students. We may also choose to engage in this work with colleagues. Richard DuFour (2015) explains, "It is not the product—the actual test—that leads to greater adult learning, it is the *process* of exploring together the question of how to gather the best evidence of student learning that leads to greater insights" (p. 186). Alone or with others, the power lies in the continuum itself and the degree to which it is experienced by our learners.

Final Thoughts

In order to soften the edges of our assessment practices and build a sense of celebration and control for ourselves and for our students, we have to continue to invite students into the conversation about their learning. These stories are theirs—not ours. We are the teachers who have the privilege of walking alongside students as their learning stories unfold. We can hold up mirrors and ask students to tell us what they see. We can help them construct the next part of their stories. But the stories are theirs, and they need to be involved throughout. As Kathleen Kryza, Alicia Duncan, and S. Joy Stephens (2009) note, "We want to create a space for our students where they feel safe making mistakes, safe being different, safe knowing they are accepted without condition" (p. 17). We can use the continuum to develop and support a classroom climate where it is safe, and even necessary, to take risks. We can build an understanding that learning develops over time and practice counts.

Exploring the criteria within the continuum is important so we can engage in quality learning through questioning, exploring, and uncovering misconceptions. The process must be the focus. A strong process leads us to strong products, but if our language always focuses on the product, we lead students to believe that the end is all that matters, when, in fact, the journey may be the most important thing of all, as Marnie Thompson and Dylan Wiliam (2007) note:

> Teachers cannot create learning—only learners can do that. What teachers can do is create the situations in which students learn. The teacher's task, therefore, moves away from "delivering" learning to the student and towards the creation of situations in which students learn. (pp. 5–6)

To do anything else is undermining the development of the whole student and neglecting to communicate that our students are capable and responsible for their own learning.

Questions for Reflection

The following questions for reflection have been divided into three sections: (1) architecture, (2) student response, and (3) personal response. The architecture questions invite consideration of how we design our assessment processes to ensure our assessment choices reflect learning accurately and reliably. The student response questions prompt us to consider assessment choices from the perspective of the learner. The personal response section asks us to reflect on our own beliefs about assessment and consider these beliefs in relation to decisions we may make. Each question is intended to act as a catalyst for deeper thinking and may lead to new questions. Taking time to reflect on one or two at a time, through journaling, conversation, or as part of a group discussion, can help determine aspects of assessment that may have a hard edge and those that we have successfully softened.

Architecture

- To what degree have you given yourself the time and opportunity to clarify the learning continuum for your learning goals? How often do you start here?
- How clear are you about what proficiency looks and sounds like for each learning goal? Have you thought deeply about the verbs within the learning goals? Do you have clarity about what they mean for students within the context of the goal?
- How much time have you spent developing understanding of the steps students will need to take to explore the learning goal fully? Have you considered which steps could be explored first?
- How confident do you feel in identifying and addressing the readiness skills and knowledge needed for your learning goals?
- Have you developed essential questions for your learning goals? How do you use them in your classroom context? How do students use them?
- How often do you plan for enriching understanding ahead of instruction? How do you know when learners are ready for enrichment? How do you respond?
- How do you use the continuum for planning? For instruction? For assessment? For intervention?

Student Response

- How comfortable are students with the continuum language? How comfortable are their families?
- To what degree do students associate intelligence or ability with where they are on the continuum? What are the emotional responses of students when the continuum is discussed? Why is this students' response?
- To what degree do you feel students are engaged as opposed to compliant? How do you know? How can you support the need for efficacy?

- How often do students who need enrichment get it? How often are these students doing more instead of different?
- How much time are students given to develop readiness for a learning goal? Is it enough? Too much?

Personal Response

- Do you feel comfortable using the continuum as a tool to design assessment and units?
- How often do you quantify the continuum? Does this work for you and your students?
- How much time do you have to make sense of your learning goals? How could you find more time if you need it?
- How often do you have the chance to work with your colleagues?
- Do your planning processes support your intellectual, emotional, social, and physical needs?

CHAPTER 3

Preassessment

I clearly recall times in my teaching career when I opted out of preassessments. Sometimes I was too pressed for time. Other times, I wasn't sure what I wanted to know. Most often, I simply assumed I knew what my learners knew and didn't know. I didn't need to preassess them because I already knew where they were. I had taught this grade and content before.

I can most certainly connect these instances to challenges that cropped up later. Often, I would sequence my lessons into units only to discover my students were unable to engage in skills I assumed they had learned the previous year. I would then have to double back and, in many ways, lose any progress I thought we were making. At times, I would attempt to group students only to discover that the group members were so diverse in their prior understanding that one student was inevitably stuck helping everyone else catch up, much to his or her frustration. I would later catch these same students rolling their eyes and sighing as I asked them to engage in something they could already do and had done "a million times." Occasionally, I would sit at my desk at the end of the day, trying to decide which resources to use with my students the next day, realizing too late that I didn't really know what they were interested in or what they had done in past years.

Through these experiences, I learned about the necessity and power of a strong preassessment. Had I preassessed in each of these instances, I would have known which skills students had not fully developed, which they had proficiently developed, and which they would find the most engaging. I would not have been left guessing because I would have involved students in the conversation about their learning; I would have discovered what they brought to the learning before trying to decide where to go next. In this chapter, we will review foundational information to gain an understanding of the concept of preassessment and examine steps for designing preassessments.

Understanding Preassessment

When we think of teaching, as Carol R. Rodgers (2002) states, as "a response to students' learning rather than the cause of students' learning" (p. 250), we realize we must facilitate opportunities to measure student learning at each step on the journey to respond appropriately. Because learning doesn't start or end within the walls of our classrooms, we have to acknowledge that students possess understanding and skills we may not be aware of. Furthermore, when they leave our classrooms at the end of the day, they continue to interact with a whole wide world. This means that the students who left us yesterday are not the students who greet us today. Responsive instruction—assessing student needs at critical times and offering targeted instruction that specifically meets these needs as they emerge—is dependent on our ability to capture student understanding in a wide variety of ways on topics and skills that will have meaning for the learning experiences we design.

When we ignore the stories of our students, we are limiting their potential. Bateson (1994) notes:

> If teachers were to approach their classes with an appreciation of how much their pupils already knew, helping to bring the structure of that informal knowledge into consciousness, students would have the feeling of being on familiar ground, already knowing much about how to know, how knowledge is organized and integrated. (p. 205)

Preassessment provides insights into a student's learning story and allows us to acknowledge the whole person and the understanding and previous experiences he or she brings to our learning spaces. It is also one of the most effective ways to plan for differentiation and ensure we are supporting soft edges by addressing diverse student needs.

The information we gain from a preassessment can offer us a clear view of learner needs in relation to the learning goals. The literature on differentiation is clear—if teachers establish student readiness, preassess student skill and knowledge, and differentiate instruction to meet the varying needs of students in a class, increased student learning will occur more consistently (O'Connor, 2007; Stiggins et al., 2004; Tomlinson, 2005a; Tomlinson & McTighe, 2006). The ultimate purpose of preassessment is to solicit immediate, timely information about what students already know and can do, so we can plan responsively and engage them in learning from the very start. Hume (2008) notes:

> All the evidence you gather about your students informs and deepens your knowledge of those students, allowing you to refine the next round of evidence collection so that you have an increasingly rich understanding of what your students know and can do. . . . Preassessments help you determine: the content, skills and strategies you need to teach; the misconceptions students may bring to the unit (whether misconceptions of content or of themselves as learners); how to group students for instruction; the kinds of activities that will support various students." (pp. 7, 134)

Preassessments can hold many forms and can serve multiple purposes. They can be used to determine what students don't yet know or reveal what they may already know. They can be used as a tool to track and celebrate learning throughout the process. Further, preassessments can be used to measure student interests and dispositions, enabling us to facilitate learning experiences that optimize engagement.

Some preassessments help us know when we need to help our learners build readiness. These kinds of preassessments are *diagnostic* in nature. The building readiness stage of our learning continuum can assist us in targeting a preassessment to measure the skills and knowledge essential for beginning the journey toward accomplishing a learning goal. We may choose to preassess essential vocabulary or measure a student's ability to perform a prerequisite skill before additional skills are added. For example, if students are going to be giving a persuasive speech as part of mastering a learning goal, we may choose to measure their abilities to organize an argument, adopt multiple perspectives, or speak loudly and clearly. In order for this diagnostic preassessment to be effective, we must be clear about our learning goals and the kinds of skills or prior knowledge essential for exploring the goal fully.

Some preassessments measure skills and knowledge we know students will most certainly acquire over the course of exploring the learning goal but that some students may already have. Measuring upcoming knowledge, skills, and even understanding before we begin allows us to determine where particular students may have already demonstrated proficiency on parts of the learning goal (targets) or even on the entire learning goal. Lamb (2001) reminds us:

> The educator has to recognize that the child has a personal history that she brings to the learning situation and for that reason the continuity of her memory should be respected, because the capacity to learn what is new is vitally connected to the liveliness of that memory. (p. 212)

When students have already acquired the knowledge and skills the learning goal requires, we can offer enrichment immediately instead of forcing students to repeat practice intended to develop understanding they already possess.

Preassessment results can be used as a way to track and celebrate learning as it develops. When students are finished with a preassessment event, they can keep a record of the targets (skills and knowledge) that were assessed and use it to monitor their own growth. For example, if students have taken a math preassessment, with the questions clearly connected to individual targets, they may keep this preassessment in the front of their notebooks and refer to it before each lesson as a way to guide the learning and allow them to track their growth over time.

Inviting students into this assessment conversation and using the information gained to celebrate learning enhances the potential for student investment and for nurturing a positive classroom environment, both of which indicate a soft edge. The teacher can use the same assessment to highlight the day's learning target. At the beginning of class, a teacher could invite the learners to turn to their preassessment and find the questions that measure their understanding on the applicable target. Those students who show proficiency can immediately receive enrichment opportunities, while the other students can identify the intended learning by revisiting the questions they were asked on the preassessment. This group can celebrate their proficiency by redoing the preassessment questions at the end of the class or once they feel ready. Ideally, teachers share the responsibility for learning with students and invite them to identify individual goals and markers of progress. Students define their success, and this builds clarity, efficacy, and optimism. When we use preassessments in this manner, we are using assessment as part of the learning process. The lines between instruction and assessment fade, and the learning cycle becomes organic.

Preassessments allow students to become part of the learning conversation by giving them a sense of the content they will be exploring and what understanding they already possess. Students can track their own growth alongside teachers and together begin a learning relationship. This is an essential component of using assessment information to support instruction and address learner needs. Without preassessments, students become frustrated when they already know the content and possess the skills we are attempting to teach. Reciprocally, they become frustrated when they lack readiness for the learning goal, which we may have overlooked if we did not preassess applicable knowledge and skills. Our instruction no longer meets students where they are, which hardens the edges for us as teachers because we are immediately not reaching students through our attempts at instruction, which undermines our confidence.

Preassessment can soften the edges for teachers because its practice and the information we gain allows us to be more efficient and effective in leveraging our instruction to meet student needs. The edges soften when our practices align with our needs and values—in this case, the need to experience efficacy and gain understanding about our learners. This, in turn, softens the edges for our learners because through preassessment we can honor their need to be seen and heard—challenged and supported. Embedding preassessment into our assessment architecture can even lead to the possibility that some of the steps in the exploring the learning goal stage may not need to be built into the actual learning plan because they have already been mastered by the learners. If we are aware of our students' foundation of understanding, we are able to more efficiently build on that foundation instead of starting from scratch.

Designing a Preassessment

There is a series of steps to help guide us as we design preassessments: (1) consider the learning goal, (2) determine the purpose, (3) determine the method, (4) decide how to use data, and (5) act on the data. We discuss these in the following sections.

Consider the Learning Goal

We can begin to consider what we might include in a preassessment by revisiting the learning continuums for our learning goals, reviewing the destinations and possible steps along the way. The continuum is the basis for assessment decisions and ensures all decisions connect to the learning goals. Often, in the day-to-day business of planning and teaching, we can lose sight of where we are headed. There is no shame in revisiting the continuum as a way to re-familiarize ourselves with the complexity of the learning goals and our path for meeting learner needs.

Determine the Purpose

Next, we determine the purpose for our preassessment. It is critical to allow ourselves the space to really think about why we might preassess and what information we really need to acquire. Within this consideration is a caution that even though we may have taught a student previously and even though we may have taught a particular age group or subject for years, the nature of continual learning means that the preconceived notions we may have about where learners are in relation to the goals may not, in fact, be true. We have to check, very precisely, if we are going to address our students' intellectual needs.

We can start our exploration of purpose by asking ourselves the following questions.

- "Is our purpose for preassessing to measure readiness?"
- "Do we need to take stock of the degree to which we already share with our students a domain-specific language that relates to the learning goal (for example, the language of experimentation, the language of nutrition, the language of mathematical reasoning, or the language of cellular respiration)?"

- "Do we need to know if students remember processes and skills they may have been introduced to last year (for example, how to serve and return a volleyball, how to reduce a fraction to its simplest form, or how to write a strong thesis statement)?"
- "Are we curious to discover whether students are able to engage in the kinds of reasoning the learning goal is asking of them (for example, critical analysis, interpretation of data sets, or proposing solutions)?"
- "Are we wondering whether learners can engage in the kind of product generation we plan to assign to them (creating a brochure, building a website, or constructing a model)?"

All of these kinds of questions invite preassessments to ascertain the direction instruction should go. There are two main factors that influence our decisions about the direction we take our instruction: students' learning goal proficiency levels and students' dispositions and interests.

Preassessments That Measure Learning Goal Proficiency

Are we interested in discovering which students are already well into the hallways of learning? Do we want to determine which students are already poised to demonstrate proficiency? This is when we may engage in a preassessment that measures students' understanding of the building blocks of the learning goal and the synthesis of these parts into a whole demonstration of proficiency. Wiggins and McTighe (2005) recommend this type of preassessment to celebrate growth and recognize proficiency early on. They recommend making the first and last assessment of a unit the same so the learning path for the entire unit of study is clear to both the students and the teacher. This type of preassessment allows us to ascertain which skills and understandings learners possess before the learning begins. As a result, our instructional planning can specifically target areas where focused instruction and practice is needed and avoid instruction in areas where proficiency is already present. Differentiated lesson plans may emerge from this type of assessment, giving teachers more lead time in designing flexible groupings based on a higher volume of questions measuring a higher volume of skills and understanding. The main consideration of this type of preassessment is ensuring learners understand the purpose of attempting challenging questions before learning and practice have occurred. Students have to experience the benefits of this type of preassessment by witnessing their teachers attend to their learning needs the very next day.

If we remain concerned about diminishing student confidence through this practice and creating a hard edge for our learners, we may choose to seek a compromise and craft our preassessment to ask students to attempt the skills and knowledge they will need to explore the learning goal (the smaller pieces, like the targets or "I can" statements). By doing this at the front end of learning, we can decide how to group students to meet learning needs and also decide whether students may actually be ready to demonstrate proficiency and move into the enriched understanding stage. Again, our learning continuum can help us design a strong preassessment that measures exploration and proficiency because we have already considered the steps that lead to this end.

Preassessments That Measure Disposition and Interest

By asking about students' previous experiences related to topics and skills we anticipate building into our learning plan, we can glean an idea of what may be most engaging, relevant, and challenging for our learners. For example, in English language arts, it may be useful to learn which novels and stories our students have read that share themes or genres with content we will be studying. It also may be helpful to know when students have experienced trouble or a lack of confidence in the past. If a student believes that balancing equations was difficult in the past, it could be helpful to hear this story, so we can plan engagement in a way that builds confidence, interest, and even presents the skill in a way that is unfamiliar (and thus bypasses a student's preconditioned response). This type of preassessment may simply be a journal entry or a questionnaire—any method that invites learners to safely express their feelings and preferences. For example, I once asked students to write me a letter explaining their relationship with mathematics, and I was astounded at their stories. The information I gathered from that single preassessment allowed me to be far more responsive and sensitive than I previously would have been.

Determine the Method

A third step in our design of strong preassessment is to determine the method we will use to gather information. Preassessments do not have to resemble a test, although they certainly could. Clarity about our assessment purpose and the learning goals will help us make strong decisions about how we will invite students to share their current understanding and skill. There is no real limit to how we can preassess, although it is always important to consider how long we want to spend gathering initial information and how often we intend to revisit that data. If we are planning to have students place a preassessment in their binders and revisit the questions each day as a way to track learning, then a more robust assessment may be in order. The format will also have to enable easy referencing for both our students and ourselves. If, however, we are curious about a specific skill we plan to introduce, then a quick entrance card that day or an exit card the previous day may be enough.

If we are interested in activating prior knowledge while gathering information, we may want to engage the students in a brainstorming activity. This could be done individually or as a whole class as long as we can get a clear picture of the knowledge *each student* brings to the table. Combining independent reflection or journaling with whole-group sharing can be a way to get a sense of each student's knowledge, skill, or disposition while still honoring the collaborative process of group discussion. The brainstorming session can activate understanding for the group as a whole, and inviting students to individually reflect or build a quick response can ensure we get a sense of individual strength. For example, in physical education, students may gather as a group to discuss the rules of the game of soccer, followed by individual written responses or video clips in which learners share their best tactics and strategies for obtaining an offensive advantage. This helps us see the more refined skills and understanding each student brings to the activity before we begin instruction.

There are times when individual conferring is the best method for preassessment. It is through conversations that we can come to deeply understand the stories of our learners. Finding time to connect with students prior to a learning experience can serve as a way to gain an understanding of their dispositions, while at the same time, preparing them for the learning to come. This type of preassessment may not be necessary for every student in your class, but if you believe a learner may have difficulty connecting with the content or skills you will be exploring (for example, a student who is reluctant to engage in physical activity during a wellness class), this may be the best way to assess misconceptions, hesitations, or resistance. If the topic is sensitive (for example, an English language arts context about family dynamics or a health unit about terminal illness), then a one-on-one conversation will be an important way to get information about the learner's needs and build the trust essential for engaging in learning that honors the whole student. These types of preassessment conversations may occur during class time, when other learners are engaging in an independent task, or it may be best suited for a discussion in a private setting. In the end, conferring can serve as a preassessment and the beginning of a response all at the same time. When learners are unsure or reluctant to take risks, we can engage in a dialogue about how we might approach their risk taking while protecting their social and emotional safety. We can plan how learning can occur and under what conditions.

Decide How to Use Data

Next, we will decide how we will use the data. The actions we take as a result of the information we gather will indicate our *instructional agility* (an intentional maneuver a teacher makes in response to evidence of learning; All Things Assessment, 2016b). Considering the following questions invites us to create strong *assessment architecture* (a layout of the plan teachers will use to monitor learning throughout a unit of instruction).

- Will we give students the preassessment results as part of engagement in tracking growth over time? Or is the assessment a quick check that will serve to simply help us make responsive, flexible groups?
- Will we record the data for future reference, feedback, and celebration?
- How will we demonstrate to our students that the preassessment will serve to improve their learning and engage their interests?
- How will we communicate the purpose of the preassessment to learners and reassure them that this is only the beginning of their learning stories for this goal?

Considering our answers to these questions will go a long way to ensuring the edges of our preassessment practices are soft.

Act on the Data

Once we have made a decision about how we intend to use the information we gather through our preassessment, the final step is to act on our decisions. It is critical that we take this action and that our students are able to clearly see our action so they come to understand the purpose of a preassessment. Otherwise, the purpose is lost on them and they will be reluctant to authentically engage in the practice the next time it is introduced. Being explicit about the connection between the preassessment data and their learning experiences is important. We may use phrases like, "I am grouping you today based on what I learned from your preassessment yesterday. I am making sure that each of you is getting the exact practice you need to grow your learning." Connecting the dots is critical.

If we decide to engage our learners in the data, we may ask them to place the preassessment in the front of their notebooks. Or we may decide to graph their collective progress on a chart in the classroom (individual charting of progress may create a hard edge for learners if they feel they are being compared to each other). Whatever approach we take, consistent monitoring of growth will go a long way in making preassessment valuable and part of the learning process.

If we decide to use the data to create flexible groups based on learner needs, we can prepare our learners for this approach and reassure them that flexibility means all learners are getting exactly what they need to succeed. We may need a method for tracking our groups, according to the targets our preassessments measured, and any variety of tools are available to help us organize this work.

We may decide to celebrate individual and class growth following a preassessment. A class cheer may suffice, or we may decide to privately communicate celebration, depending on the comfort of the students. Regardless of the method, celebration is an essential aspect of assessment and a preassessment is the benchmark we need to recognize growth as soon as it happens, letting us know when celebration is in order.

Final Thoughts

Preassessment is part of the contract we have with students to make sure that each learner gets exactly what he or she needs to be successful. It is our way of showing our students that we are serious about meeting their needs and a way of honoring the experiences a learner brings to the learning space. It can be incredibly empowering for students to have an adult ask them what they know, because that question has the built-in assumption that they know something. Students are not told this often enough and, as a result, can begin to feel trapped in a system in which they are simply one piece of a puzzle that doesn't really seem to be about them. We do not want to create a hard edge and neglect a need for efficacy for any student. Furthermore, we do not want to waste valuable class time assuming our students know too much or too little, only to have to backtrack and repair misconceptions and unrefined skills. We also want to avoid spending time on instructing students who already know the very things we are trying to teach.

Questions for Reflection

The following questions for reflection have been divided into three sections: (1) architecture, (2) student response, and (3) personal response. The architecture questions invite consideration of how we design our assessment processes to ensure our assessment choices reflect learning accurately and reliably. The student response questions prompt us to consider assessment choices from the perspective of the learner. The personal response section asks us to reflect on our own beliefs about assessment and consider these beliefs in relation to decisions we may make. Each question is intended to act as a catalyst for deeper thinking and may lead to new questions. Taking time to reflect on one or two at a time, through journaling, conversation, or as part of a group discussion, can help determine aspects of assessment that may have a hard edge and those that we have successfully softened. See the reproducible "Recognizing Hard Edges in Preassessment" (page 72) for an additional resource to help identify preassessment practices and circumstances that can create hard edges, and see the reproducible "Softening the Edges of Preassessment" (page 75) for specific and practical recommendations of ways to ensure soft edges with preassessment.

Architecture

- How often do you preassess? How do you use the information you gather?

- How often do you differentiate instruction? How do you make decisions about how to differentiate?
- What kinds of information do you seek during your preassessments? Does this information help you plan? How does your continuum help?
- How often do you share the preassessment results with students?
- How do you identify student strengths before beginning a learning experience?
- How often do you seek information about student interest related to learning goals?
- How do you decide what form the preassessment will take? How do you make sure it is not too cumbersome?

Student Response

- How do students feel after a preassessment? Are these feelings constructive? Why do they feel this way? Are their holistic needs being met?
- Do students ever refer to a preassessment later in the learning cycle? Why or why not? Do your students understand the purpose of a preassessment?
- Does student learning increase as the result of your preassessment practices?
- How often do students use the preassessment to set personal learning goals? Class learning goals?

Personal Response

- How helpful are your preassessments? To what degree are they currently part of your learning cycle?
- How often have you assumed what your students knew and found you were incorrect? Why did this happen?
- What is your greatest frustration with preassessments?
- What has been your most successful preassessment?
- Are your preassessment practices supporting your needs as a whole person?

Recognizing Hard Edges in Preassessment

How do we recognize when our preassessment practices have hard edges and lack alignment with our own beliefs and values and the needs of the whole person? The following sections describe some indicators to watch for.

Basing a Preassessment on Something Other Than the Learning Goals

A hard edge for both teachers and students may occur when we design a preassessment without taking the time to clarify the learning continuum and deeply understand the learning goals. As with any assessment, if a preassessment is not aligned with the learning goals, then it can become an isolated event with little relevance. Preassessments in preexisting resources or programs must be examined carefully to ensure alignment with the learning goals. When a preassessment is not aligned with learning goals, it miscommunicates the destination and importance of our learning exploration in the long term and undermines emotional and intellectual safety.

Using a Preassessment Result as a Summative Score

When we treat a preassessment like a summative event, a hard edge is formed. In this case, we are stifling a learner's need to practice and make mistakes, which can create a lack of emotional safety and willingness to take risks. A preassessment comes *before* any opportunity to explore and practice and is in no way indicative of where learning will end up—it is the catalyst for learning and conversation. Treating every assessment event summatively removes accuracy and validity from our assessment architecture because we are not measuring proficiency at the conclusion of the learning cycle but are instead measuring (and holding students accountable for) learning *in progress*. This is not the intention of preassessment.

Failing to Take Action

Preassessment can feel like a waste of time if we never use the information we get from it. Some teachers may preassess because they feel they have to, but then never use the assessment to build responsiveness for themselves and hope for their students. It is essential to understand why we are preassessing, when it makes sense to do so, and what kinds of questions to ask. Too many times, I have witnessed preassessments that sit in a drawer and are never revisited and never impact future learning choices. This a hard edge—a waste of time and energy, and a destroyer of hope.

Presuming to Know Our Students

It is critical that we separate what is new to us, as teachers, from what is new to our students. It is human instinct to imagine our reality is the same others experience—to imagine the order and way we learn is the same for students. We know that our students are learning things differently than we did—at different rates, at different times, and in different ways. If we are truly going to be responsive to student needs, we must first take time to preassess students in our classrooms to discover their learning stories. Otherwise, we fall into the trap of assuming we know what students know and what they can do; we assume students have had the same learning experiences that we or the person sitting next to them had. D. Jean Clandinin and F. Michael Connelly (2000) explain that we cannot assume the student receiving the assessment message is neutral. They bring something to the interaction. The work we are doing is human work and we are always entering a student's story "in the midst" (p. 63). Remembering this can help us soften the edges for both ourselves and our students. It allows us to dig more deeply into the students' prior knowledge, into the ways of thinking they have developed over time and experience, and the attitude they bring to the learning space. Stephen R. Covey (1989) says, "Seek first to understand" (p. 235), and his words ring true for our work in building learning relationships with our students. We must seek first to understand our students. Only then can we hope to construct assessment and learning experiences that will truly support learning.

Using Preassessment Data to Refuse Learning Invitations

A hard edge forms when we deny students the opportunity to engage in high levels of thinking, inquiry, and exploration of the learning goal until they have mastered all parts of the preassessment. Again, learning is not a lockstep activity. It is organic, and the best way to learn skills and gain knowledge is often to practice them within a meaningful and rich context. Memorization, on its own, it not engaging, but memorization in an authentic context serves a greater purpose for students. Preassessments should not set up an if-then paradigm, where students only get to do the fun stuff after they have memorized thirty vocabulary words. This approach is sure to fail to engage students. Instead, engagement in vocabulary through a video, role play, or a discussion is much more likely to develop long-term contextualized understanding.

Making a Preassessment Too Complex

A preassessment so complex that it is impossible to diagnose how, when, and with whom instructional choices need to occur is a hard-edged preassessment because it removes our ability to respond to both our own and our learners' needs. Taking an assignment and calling it a preassessment does not work because we are asking students to synthesize when they are ill-prepared to do so. A strong preassessment provides specific information about students' challenges and existing knowledge. A preassessment that is too complex can do little more than frustrate students and set them up for disengagement.

References

Clandinin, D. J., & Connelly, F. M. (2000). *Narrative inquiry: Experience and story in qualitative research*. San Francisco: Jossey-Bass.

Covey, S. R. (1989). *The seven habits of highly effective people: Restoring the character ethic*. New York: Simon & Schuster.

Softening the Edges of Preassessment

A well-considered and well-constructed preassessment can help us create soft edges for both teachers and students when the following occurs.

Preassessments Serve a Clear Purpose

When we use preassessments to guide daily instruction, celebrate growth, and develop readiness, it reassures our students that the preassessments serve a purpose for everyone. Karen Hume (2008) notes, "Students will be watching to see how you make use of their preassessment information, and the effort they put into future preassessments will be influenced by your decisions" (p. 141). Using the preassessment as a springboard for future learning demonstrates a clear purpose. Inquiry can also follow a strong preassessment because the destination is clear and students are free to explore topics in ways that make sense to them. Clarity can often be a springboard for creativity and exploration, both indicators of a soft edge.

The Purpose Is Shared With Students

It is essential to be upfront with students about the preassessment purpose. Many teachers avoid preassessments because we fear we will set up students with a failure mindset and create a hard edge. This is no small concern. If students perceive the preassessment as something that "counts" or as something that assigns their intelligence a value, they may well end up feeling defeated. Creating a classroom climate that is growth oriented means being clear about how learning unfolds and how each step is to be celebrated. Identifying what we don't know is part of learning. Conversations like these are essential in our classrooms.

When students really seem to be struggling with the preassessment purpose, we need to recognize it immediately and make time and space to talk it through. Many of our students are preconditioned to believe all assessments count and that they define ability and potential. Jeffry Overlie (2009) observes, "As other students score low on assessments, they see themselves as unsuccessful and lose confidence. They feel embarrassed, and their motivation decreases" (p. 182). If we want to change this paradigm, we need to include students in the conversation at all stages. We want our students to feel confident and optimistic, not defeated before we even begin. When we don't talk to students about our assessment practices, we remove their sense of agency, which can be very discouraging. Tom Schimmer (2014) suggests approaching the very first assessment in a way that ensures all students can demonstrate success, explaining, "A way of serving *all* students and of ensuring the best possible *first impression* for how students feel is to over-prepare them for their first evaluation" (p. 21). When we follow up the first preassessment with an immediate response and celebration, we can begin to nurture this cycle of optimism. Kathleen Kryza, Alicia Duncan, and S. Joy Stephens (2009) assert, "It is essential to create an interdependent community where students feel safe to grow and learn, question and experiment, overcome failure and enjoy success" (p. 16).

We Really Notice Our Students in All Their Complexity

Preassessment also allows us to *notice* our students and recognize when aspects of a foundation we assume exists, in fact, does not. Some students may have missed or failed to retain key ideas and skills that ready them for the learning goals we are about to explore. Recognizing these foundational gaps at the outset allows us to address misconceptions and a need for additional instruction and practice before we dive into learning experiences that may provide more challenge than learners can handle. This attention to readiness creates an environment that supports learning rather than simply measures it. It also invites students into the learning conversation in a way that offers them the exact right amount of challenge. Lev Vygotsky (1978) refers to this "just right" challenge as *the zone of proximal development*, and Karen Hume (2008) builds on this concept, explaining:

> The zone of proximal development is the zone of instruction—where learning takes place. This is the point where the student combines existing knowledge and skill with the right amount and type of assistance to meet the achievable challenges of the lesson. (p. 218)

Preassessment offers us the opportunity to make sure our instruction is designed to meet students right where they are and invite them to stretch just enough to ensure learning occurs in the best way possible.

References

Hume, K. (2008). *Start where they are: Differentiating for success with the young adolescent.* Toronto: Pearson Education Canada.

Kryza, K., Duncan, A., & Stephens, S. J. (2009). *Inspiring elementary learners: Nurturing the whole child in a differentiated classroom.* Thousand Oaks, CA: Corwin Press.

Overlie, J. (2009). Creating confident, capable learners. In T. R. Guskey (Ed.), *The teacher as assessment leader* (pp. 181–201). Bloomington, IN: Solution Tree Press.

Schimmer, T. (2014). *Ten things that matter from assessment to grading*. Boston: Pearson.

Vygotsky, L. (1978). *Mind in society: The development of higher psychological processes*. Cambridge, MA: Harvard University Press.

CHAPTER

4

Formative Assessment and Feedback

Imagine you have found a suitcase belonging to someone you don't know. Imagine opening this suitcase and taking out a single item—a book about drums. What might you think about the owner of the suitcase based on this single item? Likes drums? Is planning on visiting a music store or is taking a class? Now, remove another item—an umbrella. What now? Maybe the person is going to attend a concert in a rainy climate. Maybe the person is simply planning for various weather eventualities. Maybe this person is organized? A third item—a map of Nashville. Now you are piecing together a story—this person is travelling to Nashville to attend a percussion concert and he or she is bringing the umbrella for protection in case it rains. You are making inferences based on artifacts in the suitcase. The more artifacts, the more robust and accurate your story becomes.

This act of piecing together a story based on artifacts is the same inferring process we use when assessing students. We collect samples—papers, posters, oral presentations, problems, observations—and use them to put together a story of student learning. The more samples we have, the more robust and accurate our inferences are about student understanding. Sometimes we get it wrong—maybe the owner of the umbrella was going to use it for protection from the sun. Maybe the person borrowed the drum book for a friend and doesn't enjoy drums. Similarly, maybe the student doesn't understand a concept as well as we thought. Or maybe the student understands it better than we thought. This is why it's important to remember that assessment facilitates making an inference, but it isn't foolproof. We might need to collect more evidence, change our opinion, or replace old evidence with new.

We should replace evidence because learning continues to change and shift over time. Students' knowledge today will not be the same knowledge they have tomorrow. So, we have to keep checking. We do this by re-evaluating evidence from formative assessments and by engaging in conversations about what the data reveal, allowing opportunities for students to clarify their understanding and for teachers to provide feedback to students to encourage improved understanding and new learning. In this chapter, we will review foundational information to gain an understanding of the concept of formative assessment and examine steps for designing formative assessments. We will then review the importance of strong, constructive feedback and explore steps for creating effective feedback processes.

Understanding Formative Assessment

As Kryza et al. (2009) explain, *formative assessment* is "the continuous process of gathering data about our students before, during, and after learning. This ongoing assessment keeps us, and our students, informed of progress, which allows for more efficient and effective use of instructional time" (p. 170). It requires us to continually capture moments of learning in all its complexity to help us *infer* a student's level of understanding *and take action* based on what we learn. When we do not take action on this information, the assessment becomes summative and signals an end for the opportunity to grow and develop. Understanding these differences is critical to softening the edges of our assessment practices.

Assessment is how we make inferences about our students' learning stories as they develop over time. A student's story is constantly evolving, both in and out of school. When we assess students, we are asking for information at a moment in time in order to positively impact their learning stories. Through the use of strong assessment, we can structure experiences to develop skills and knowledge in students that support higher levels of learning both now and throughout their lives.

We can never fully know what is inside another person's head. And yet, teachers are tasked with measuring student understanding and reporting learning accurately. We must take the information we gather and adjust our instruction accordingly. Considering assessment as the act of making learning visible and then making inferences about degrees of understanding helps us think about how we can do this as effectively as possible to ensure we meet learner needs.

When we help our students make their learning visible, we can turn this visible learning into a recursive dialogue that becomes the catalyst for future learning. Visible learning means looking at learning through the eyes of a learner and helping our students see how they are thinking and how that thinking can be shifted and enhanced over time (Hattie, 2009; Ritchhart, Church, & Morrison, 2011). The key understanding when engaging in formative assessment is that the information we gather will impact learning through actions that both we and our learners take in the short term. Inviting students to show their thinking regularly allows us to see individual progress on those targets that make up the larger learning goal, and to address needs before students develop too many misconceptions and miss too many concepts, and before both teachers and students lose confidence. Portfolios, photographs, videos, reflections, observations, work samples, and rough drafts are all ways of capturing learning and making it visible to both the teacher and students. Settling for data from a single, final product is like accepting the drum book as the entire story of the suitcase owner. It simply isn't enough if we are going to make strong inferences about student learning.

Making an inference becomes easier when artifacts are supported with dialogue. Assessment shouldn't be one-way communication in which we collect the test and try to figure out what the student knows. Teachers and students need to feel comfortable asking questions. We need to embrace the idea that learning should be a conversation that continues all the time; in fact, it is through this conversation that learning continues to happen. Coming to know the suitcase owner is much easier when we can ask questions of the owner: Do you like drums? Are you going somewhere sunny or rainy? And asking those questions is much easier when we have artifacts in front of us: What did you mean by this? How can you expand your thinking a little on this point? Where could you go to support this idea further? It is this conversation that is the crux of formative assessment and feedback and pivotal in addressing the needs of whole learners. Through conversations about learning, we know how to adjust, enhance, and correct learning experiences so our students take learning further. This conversation brings students into the process and invites a learning partnership that does not exist when we simply assign and assess.

Engaging in Formative Assessment and Feedback

Formative assessment and feedback go hand in hand. Formative assessment allows us to gather important information about our learners and their engagement in the learning goals so we can make instructional decisions. When we use this information to engage in a conversation with our learners and invite them to reflect, set goals, and move forward, our entrance point for initiating this conversation is often in the form of feedback. Feedback allows us to enter into a dialogue with our learners about decisions they make, their understanding of the content, and their developing skills. There is a series of steps to help guide us as we design formative assessments that lead to feedback: (1) commit to the process, (2) utilize the learning continuum, (3) determine the purpose, (4) identify the method, (5) capture artifacts, (6) plan how to use data and take action, and (7) ensure accuracy and reliability. We discuss these in the following sections.

Commit to the Process

The first step in engaging in formative assessment is to commit to its importance. Teachers are pressed for time, and we may find it difficult to commit to a rich formative assessment practice. It can feel like it is taking valuable time away from the learning process. We may feel like we have to choose between promoting learning or measuring learning. This is another unneeded either-or paradigm. Well-designed formative assessment practices are, in fact, *part* of an effective learning process. DuFour (2015) proposes we need to move away "from viewing assessment as taking time away from instruction to recognizing good assessment is a vital element of good instruction" (p. 181). Committing to formative assessment is committing to learning.

Utilize the Learning Continuum

The learning continuum is the basis of strong formative assessment design. As explained in chapter 2, attending to the verbs in a learning goal as well as the specific skills related to targets students will practice to develop proficiency is important for increasing confidence that our formative assessments actually measure the specific learning required to the intended degree. This knowledge positions us to stay focused on the destination. The readiness stage of the learning continuum will provide the information we need to craft strong preassessments to build scaffolds and design interventions when students show need. The skills and knowledge we identified in the exploring stage give us a solid basis for crafting our formative assessment plan. Whether we format them as learning targets, "I can" statements, or indicators, we can begin to imagine how learners might demonstrate these skills and this knowledge.

Some of the indicators may naturally occur early on in the learning journey while others may develop later. As always, it depends on the prior knowledge and skills students bring to the learning space and the kinds of experiences we invite them to engage in. If students are going to make inferences while reading literary texts, for example, they will first need to be able to make predictions, identify the main idea, and then connect this understanding to their own personal knowledge. Our formative assessments for this learning target, therefore, will need to measure the skills of predicting, identifying the main idea, and developing personal connections before we summatively measure the skill of making inferences in literary texts. Many students will require the opportunity to practice these skills in isolation before bringing the skills together and applying the broader understanding and application often required in learning goals. Depending on the students (and our preassessment), some may be engaging in a wider variety of texts or increasingly complex texts, but all students will be developing the ability to make strong inferences and support their inferences fully with details and examples.

Consider another example, this time in mathematics. If the learning goal asks students to apply area and perimeter formulae for rectangles in real-world and mathematical problems, students will need to develop an understanding of the formulae and what they represent, identify the characteristics of rectangles, understand the difference between area and perimeter (what they represent and how they are calculated), plus know how to approach mathematical and word problems, devise a plan for solving the problem, check answers, and so on. Learning goals as expansive as these require many stops on the learning journey to check for understanding and skill development. Ultimately, when the time comes, we will use a summative assessment to measure the more complex skill of applying formulae. In the meantime, we need to give students opportunities to practice and engage in feedback through the use of formative assessments that measure individual skills and knowledge. Through all of this, we are creating a soft edge for ourselves by allowing us the chance to shift instruction, activate interventions, and teach strategies that will help students with their learning in the long term.

Having a strong sense of the processes, reasoning, and skill development involved in our learning goals is essential to developing an accurate formative process. By engaging in the learning continuum, we can anticipate the pieces students will need to explore and be ready to check their development in a timely manner so we can adjust instruction for additional practice and learning. This is necessary whether we teach first grade or twelfth grade. Working collaboratively with our colleagues to sort out what the learning goals mean, how they develop, how we will measure them, and how we will invite students to practice the skills they contain can build our confidence in designing formative assessments, softening the edges before we enter a learning space with our students.

Determine the Purpose

As with preassessment, determining the purpose a formative assessment will serve for us, as teachers, is critical to making decisions about format, timing, and response. For example, the purpose of a formative assessment may be to learn how well students understand yesterday's lesson on infectious diseases so we can decide who needs a targeted minilesson to revisit information and who is ready to dig deeper. Or, we may need to check whether our learners are self-monitoring for comprehension when they read aloud to us so we can group them and focus on the self-monitoring strategies they may be missing. Being clear about our purpose helps guide our instructional decisions.

In addition to serving our own needs as teachers, purpose is tied closely to the needs of our learners. When the intent of our work is to equip students for future learning, we have to consider their learning needs in the short term (for a specific course or school year) and in the long term (for lifelong learning and career readiness). Formative assessment supports both short-term and long-term needs. First, it ensures students are practicing and developing their skills and knowledge to become proficient and move beyond proficiency. Second, a balanced assessment approach also equips our students with the confidence and strategies to face future learning challenges *on their own*. Therefore, formative assessment coupled with feedback serve the double purpose of equipping students with the skills to show proficiency on the learning goals *and* the confidence and strategies to face any learning challenge in the future.

As we assess students and respond to gathered information, we must also think about how to shift responsibility, over time, to students so they feel efficacy for their own learning. Modeling, support, and guidance are all parts of good teaching. However, it is equally important to know when it is time to release some of the responsibility to students and meet their need for autonomy, responsibility, and self-regulation. The best way to support a timely release is to engage in conversations (or a feedback process) about learning with students from the outset. We will know when to gradually release responsibility because our formative assessments and conversations that result will help us make timely decisions.

Our commitment to understanding the learning continuum for our learning goals and sharing this continuum with learners helps us with the feedback conversations that emerge out of formative assessment. The descriptors within each of the four stages are great starting points for our constructive conversations. We may begin by identifying the target or stepping stone the learner is currently practicing or developing. We can ask questions about the decisions our learners made while engaging in the learning experience. We can monitor the strategies they use and their feelings of success or challenge. Our learning continuums can frame our feedback and help us develop a shared language about criteria for proficiency and the things we need to learn and develop along the way. By considering learning needs before engaging in learning experiences, we are setting up feedback and instruction that honor student needs in the moment and honor our ability to address these needs with confidence.

Identify the Method

Once we have determined the purpose of the formative assessment for both ourselves and our learners, we are ready to identify the method that best suits this purpose. We may choose a quick problem or two at the end of class if we are trying to make flexible groupings for the following day, or we may decide to engage in a longer, more robust formative assessment to measure more than one concept so we can plan stations that will anchor lessons for the next week. Perhaps a quick entrance card with three prompts will tell us what we need to know in order to offer feedback. Or maybe we need to meet with colleagues and map the key concepts that will get learners to the goal of using a complex concept with purpose. We may opt to share our assessment tool with colleagues so we can gather helpful information and analyze it together. When our method is tightly aligned with our purpose, we can invest time wisely and ensure the value of formative assessment is clear to our learners.

Capture Artifacts

Once we are clear about the smaller indicators of growth toward proficiency and have considered the order we introduce the learning and practice, we are ready to consider how to best capture artifacts of student learning so we can make strong inferences about their understanding. There will be times when it is most appropriate to engage in smaller formative assessments, so we can adjust instruction in real time. Some of these kinds of assessments include exit cards, small quizzes, practice questions, and journal entries. Anytime we invite students to make their learning visible, we are engaging in these smaller formative assessments. We can then be clear about how the next learning experience is a response to the formative assessment. In this way, students will understand that learning involves trial and error, risk taking, and constant monitoring and feedback.

At other times, we may decide it is essential to engage in larger-scale formative assessments. Often, these take the form of common formative assessments, designed by collaborative teams, to focus on measuring the essential skills and knowledge needed to eventually develop proficiency on the learning goal (DuFour & Eaker, 1998). These larger common assessments invite us to soften the edges for ourselves and our students by collecting information on a wider number of indicators to more significantly alter our instruction and structure supports for students who need them. Erkens (2015) explains the value of larger common formative assessments:

> Instructional agility develops when teams work to write their assessments and attending tools before they begin instruction. Once the desired end goal is clear, the formative pathway is illuminated. At that point, teachers can be flexible yet precise in their choices to support learners along the way.

If we return to our mathematics standard example from chapter 2, we can imagine how smaller formative assessments or a larger-scale formative assessment may look, depending on the information we are hoping to collect in a single event and what we intend to do with the information. For example, if we have just taught a lesson on multiples of ten, we may decide to ask students to show their understanding by responding to three questions at the end of a class period. Based on student responses, we can then plan the next day's lesson to provide (1) feedback and practice opportunities for some students, focusing on calculating multiples of ten, (2) a targeted minilesson using using manipulative materials to attend to specific misconceptions for those learners who are really experiencing challenge with the concept, and (3) enrichment for other learners who grasp the concept well.

In this example, we could engage in smaller formative assessments each day or every few days to check for key skill development and understanding students need to reach proficiency on the learning goal. We would assess students' understanding of place value, their ability to work with multiples of ten, their ability to use the language of place value to describe relationships, and their proficiency with using fractions to express relationships. Students would explore and practice each target within the exploring stage and perhaps even some within the building readiness stage (depending on the results of the preassessment), and we would formatively assess them to identify difficulties and provide supports. These formative assessments may include quick quizzes, daily practice assignments, entrance cards, mathematics journal entries, demonstrations, or any other method that allows a teacher to clearly see the degree to which proficiency is being developed and the misconceptions that still exist. Based on the results of an assessment, instruction the following day may call for revisiting this skill for some or all students, or the class may be ready to move on to the next target. Our work with the enrichment stage ensures that when we have some students who are proficient and some who are not, we are ready with possibilities for engaging the proficient students in enrichment while others continue to practice.

A different possibility may exist for formative assessment using this example. Together with our colleagues, we may decide that this learning goal is especially challenging and we need to work together to determine student needs before digging into daily instruction and collaborate ahead of time on solutions and strategies for approaching what we know is traditionally a diverse set of challenges. Therefore, we look at the continuum as a whole and plan a larger formative assessment that measures student skills not only on determining the value of a digit in a multidigit number but also each of the other skills listed in the exploring and even the readiness stages. In this case, our activation questions and exploration questions can really help guide the assessment planning process. We could ask ourselves how best to measure student understanding of the relationship between digits in a multidigit number. Do we invite short explanations? Fill in the blank? Diagrams and concept maps? By collaborating, we can work together to ensure our questions get the precise information we need to engage in responsive planning. Next, we decide how to measure student ability to work with multiples of ten and express relationships as fractions. Each point in the exploring and building readiness stages of the continuum helps us create common formative assessments that accurately measure the targets.

Once we administer the larger formative assessment, we can meet with our colleagues to plan next steps. We can share instructional strategies and design supports. We can plan to engage students who are already proficient. We can plan further assessments that measure the skills as students begin to synthesize them and apply them in increasingly complex contexts. This kind of formative assessment and collaborative work ensures teachers are able to respond with greater instructional agility.

The size of the formative assessment is dictated by our purpose for gathering the information. If we want to be instructionally agile in the moment, we will engage in formative assessments that capture bits of understanding as they are practiced. If we want some lead time to our responsive planning, we will engage in larger formative assessments that are given at intervals when it is essential to see how much progress is being made on synthesizing some of the isolated skills we have been working on. As long as our assessment events specifically measure what they are intended to measure, we can be assured of their accuracy in informing us of the progress being made by a learner.

Plan How to Use Data and Take Action

The very nature of formative assessment is to support growth, and growth emerges from purposeful action. Just as with preassessment, developing a plan will ensure the information we gather and the action we take moves learning forward. For example, after looking at a set of exit cards, we may recognize that four of our students completely misunderstood the steps for analyzing a work of art, five students understood and could apply some of the steps but were missing others, and twelve students could analyze art work well. We could then respond the next day by working directly with the four who missed the skills needed for analysis. The five students who were on their way could work as a group and compare and combine their analyses into a strong collaborative analysis and explain their choices. We could ask the twelve students who could already analyze to work in pairs and compare and contrast two works of art based on the characteristics we just learned. This kind of purposeful decision making based on formative assessment data allows us to maximize learning time and target our instruction and feedback responses.

Ensure Accuracy and Reliability

Our next step in designing a formative assessment is to increase reliability by removing any factors that may reduce the accuracy of the measure. *Accuracy* refers to clarity about what we are assessing (goals or targets), why we are doing so, and how best to ensure that we are actually measuring what we intend to; it means that our measurement represents the degree of understanding or skill a student holds in relation to a target (Chappuis et al., 2012). *Reliability* is "the consistency with which any assessment provides a picture of proficiency or the degree of consistency between two measures of the same thing" (Mehrens & Lehmann, 1987, p. 38). In terms of accuracy, as mentioned in the previous sections, aligning our assessments to our learning goals is the most important thing we can do. In addition to following the general steps described here for designing formative assessments that lead to feedback, there are three specific ways we can accomplish accuracy and reliability: (1) be mindful of students' interests and experiences, (2) provide multiple formative assessment opportunities, and (3) ensure we include observation.

Be Mindful of Student Interests and Experiences

Student interests and experiences can affect the accuracy and reliability of our assessment practices. We want to be sure students are expressing their very best learning, so activating their interests is optimal. Prompts or tasks that invite learners to make choices and personal meaning can invite the kinds of deep thinking we hope to see. For example, when measuring a student's ability to connect to a text, by inviting them to choose a personally meaningful text to demonstrate this skill, we are accessing their interests and assessing the skill we hope to see.

Learning in a social context is necessary and effective in developing deep engagement, greater productivity, and overall understanding. Engaging in a formative assessment following a highly engaging experience is another way to invite great thinking by our students. We can ask our learners to share the understanding and skill they developed in a group context by completing an independent journal entry that expresses individual understanding.

We may need to attend to cultural bias if we are inviting students to demonstrate their developing proficiency in ways that are not culturally sensitive. As described earlier, bias can occur when we assess learners using contexts and language with which they are unfamiliar. For example, students who are English learners may have deep understanding of concepts but may not be able to access the prompt because of a language barrier. Or they may be asked to connect their learning to an experience they have not had (for example, riding a bicycle, traveling on an airplane, or celebrating a particular holiday). Assessment must truly reflect a learner's skill and understanding, and we may have to remove barriers or shift our assessment approaches to do that. Tammy Heflebower (2009b) asserts, "Teachers must be aware of how assessments that include offensive content, stereotyping, unfair representations, unfamiliar situations, or poorly written items can cause a student to perform poorly" (p. 104). Allowing students to practice in ways that honor their individual interests, experiences, and skills give us the best sense of students' growth and their need for continued learning.

Provide Multiple Formative Assessment Opportunities

We should also plan to engage in formative assessment as often as student learning requires. Not only do we want to be sure our assessment is accurate but we also want to make sure it is reliable. Simply put, we want to be sure students are actually developing proficiency. In order to do this, our assessment plans may need to include more than one formative assessment opportunity during practice and exploration. Granted we have limited time, but it is equally important to be sure our learners are developing the skills and knowledge we think they are. I have, from time to time, been caught believing an entire group of learners had developed understanding when, in fact, one or two students had spoken on behalf of the rest, and I allowed myself to be misled.

Ensure We Include Observation

One of the best ways to ensure reliability is to combine formative assessment events with our own observations to be sure that what we hear matches what we see lived by individual students. Claude Bernard (1999) notes, "To have our first idea of things, we must see those things; to have an idea about a natural phenomenon, we must, first of all, observe it. . . . All human knowledge is limited to working back from observed effects to their cause" (pp. 32–33). Teachers understand the importance of observation at a visceral level; it is how many decisions are made on a daily basis. However, accepting observation as a valid method to gauge learning occurs less often. Many educators are hesitant to acknowledge their own observations as a form of formative assessment and the foundation for professional judgment, often because they don't feel their observation of a learning experience counts as an assessment event. Many wonder if observation is enough to conclude that learning has occurred.

Certain subject areas, including physical education, industrial arts, drama, and music, depend on observation. In areas where performance is the mainstay, observation is deemed vital, and everyone accepts a teacher's judgment as sound and reasonable. Teachers design moments when performance will be assessed, and they document their observations certainly, but this is *enough.* Teachers in these areas are not expected to ask students to write down each step for completing a lay-up or for performing a monologue. Instead, students perform these actions, teachers observe them as they do it (formative assessment), and instructional decisions and feedback follow without question. Observation is also widely accepted as part of the documentation of learning in preK and kindergarten; the play-based environment lends itself beautifully to observation. Pair this with strong invitations or provocations to learn (materials, resources, and environments designed to stimulate curiosity, inquiry, and student-directed exploration) and effective verbal engagement between teachers and students, and you have a recipe for growth and development. No one questions whether the teacher has the *right* to observe and make instructional decisions; this is how primary grades educators formatively assess. However, the same cannot be said for all subjects or grade levels.

If physical education, drama, or kindergarten teachers use observation of learning as a formative assessment event, why can't a middle school mathematics teacher? As students move through our education system, it is tempting to require students to record their thinking through writing all the time. We may feel that by asking students to write during a formative assessment, we are honoring the importance of the skill of writing. Granted, we must develop and assess literacy. It is critical that students learn to express themselves in a variety of ways, including through the written word. However, when writing is the *only* way students are invited to show their understanding, some students' intellectual and even physical needs are not being met and edges can become very hard. This forces students to express their understanding in a single way, and it forces teachers to mark written assessments even when they may have seen an expression of the learning half an hour earlier during an activity. Sometimes the most efficient and powerful way to capture assessment information so we can take action (formative assessment) is by watching and listening. This is the power of observation as formative assessment.

If we are going to consider observation as a method of formative assessment, we need to address possible concerns. There may be a fear that if a parent or administrator questions a decision or judgment, we won't be able to support our actions, so we want to have tangible evidence for our decisions about student learning and, eventually, grading. This is a valid concern and may signify a hard edge for us. In this case, we may need to learn how to make learning visible and document what we see and hear. If we document learning (with photographs, anecdotal records, or videos) as part of our observation and keep track of our observations during learning experiences (write them down, date them, and assign them to specific students), we will have plenty of *evidence* to support our decisions. In fact, the evidence will be stronger and certainly more compelling than a single worksheet would, for example. Another reason we may be reluctant to use observation is a lack of trust in our own professional judgment. It may seem easier to fall back on mathematics calculations as justification for a decision than it is to assert our training, education, and experience with children and learning. The truth is we are always making professional judgments, even when we assess a mathematics paper. It is just that those judgments are often superseded by a score.

It is the responsibility of teachers to teach and assess learning. We need to become comfortable with ourselves as professionals. We need to trust our observations. Once we do, we are free to experiment with learning experiences. We can move beyond paper into a three-dimensional world. Using observation regularly allows us to be highly responsive in our instruction. It allows us the freedom to walk alongside students as they construct meaning, engage in inquiry, experiment, take risks, and experience new things. No longer would we have to think: *Wow, you really understood that. I sure hope you do well on your test next week!*

We must reflect on what strong observation looks and sounds like if we are going to use it effectively in our assessment practices. Pete Hall and Alisa Simeral (2015) clarify:

> The first step in gaining awareness is to pay attention to what's going on. On the surface, this sounds simple enough. However, the devil is in the details. You must be intentional about looking for, and noticing, different components of your classroom. (p. 52)

This is often easier said than done in a busy classroom. We must structure learning experiences that engage students and require complex thinking, so we allow ourselves time to step back from the action and notice students practicing, refining, and creating. Just as physical education teachers invite students to play a game, we should engage students in moments of application to observe how well they are synthesizing and making sense of the building blocks they develop. This meets students' need to explore, solve, create, and imagine while serving our need to see learning in action and infer degrees of understanding and skill.

Next, we must structure learning experiences that allow students to voice their thinking. If we are going to observe students, we are dependent on them expressing their learning aloud or demonstrating it through their actions. Students cannot choose to sit passively during a performance task or sit silently during a brainstorming session. They cannot opt out of participating in classroom dialogue. We must create environments where students perceive safety when they take risks and express their thinking, even when it may not yet be fully developed. This kind of environment flows out of assessment practices that are strongly formative and where feedback and goal setting are part of everyday life.

Anne Davies (2011) refers to the effective use of COP (conversation, observation, and product) to triangulate our information about learning development. Using three sources of information, we increase our chances of assessment accuracy and effective response. As Hall and Simeral (2015) note, "To be a better observer is to be a better teacher" (p. 105). Observations, combined with discussions and learning artifacts, allow us to make strong inferences about degrees of proficiency and respond with confidence.

Observation is both a professional gift and a professional responsibility. It allows us to investigate human behavior and the manifestation of learning in a manner that honors the whole student. By building multifaceted opportunities to witness and support intellectual development and emotional safety, we soften the edges of assessment. When we engage in observation and make it *count*, we utilize a powerful tool for supporting the whole student while engaging in formative assessment.

Understanding Feedback

My seventeen-year-old daughter and I were discussing a poetry analysis she was working on for the following day. She had written it and was looking for feedback because she wanted to take her writing to another level. We had been brainstorming transitional phrases when the words tumbled out of her.

"I feel like we are cheating," she said as we sat side by side at the table.

"What do you mean?" I asked.

"I feel like when we talk about my writing, it isn't fair."

Her worrying confused me. When a learner is afraid that experiencing learning, feedback, and growth is cheating, it means she has spent much too much time in a system where everything "counts." I reminded her that she was still trying to get better, and that she had asked if she could talk to me about her writing. I explained that learning should not feel like cheating. When she wrote her final exam, I wouldn't be there to offer her feedback. But she was nine months from her final and had only begun the year. My feedback was purposefully reflective and questioning. I was trying to coach her into more descriptive and precise language. This is the purpose of reflection—to get better. I felt sad that this made her feel shame.

This scenario illustrates the hard edges that can form for students in an education culture that emphasizes grades and points rather than learning. For my daughter, making mistakes, working through drafts, and seeking help was not permissible because everything she had been doing seemed to count. She had grown to expect that her education meant getting it right on her own, the first time through. She had come to believe that receiving support from anyone meant she was receiving an unfair "advantage." Collaboration, exploration, discourse, and revision were signs of a lack of strength and skill. She was caught between wanting to grow and wanting to conform, and this was a very hard edge for her.

This episode also illustrates that sometimes learning and vulnerability go hand in hand. Assessment can empower, but it can also open us to the possibility that we have not yet reached our goals—that we still have work to do. The emotions associated with this aspect of assessment must be acknowledged so we can ready ourselves and our learners to handle the implications of this reality. When we find ourselves in an environment where this vulnerability is embraced as part of a strong learning cycle, we equip ourselves with an attitude that positions us to embrace these challenges and, most importantly, move forward from them. Tan Ai-Girl (2004) explains, "Teaching is thus beyond delivery of content knowledge. Teaching engages the teacher's willingness and competence to co-construct spaces of learning to cultivate children's meta-learning skills and competence" (p. 91). Creating a safe space to learn, where emotions are acknowledged, is vital to establishing a strong formative assessment and feedback cycle and softening the edges of our assessment practices.

When students engage in formative assessment and receive feedback frequently (verbally or in writing), they become accustomed to using these practices to improve their learning outcomes. When successful learning and higher engagement are the results, learners come to understand the importance of formative assessment and feedback and begin to depend on this type of rich learning experience. Furthermore, the responsibility for learning is clearly shared between teachers and learners, and students can see how their engagement in formative assessment, feedback, and reflection is essential for growth. When we trust students to be part of assessment and feedback, we empower them. John Hattie (1992) confirms the importance of this decision: "The most powerful single modification that enhances achievement is feedback. The simplest prescription for improving education must be 'dollops of feedback'" (p. 9). Our job, then, is to take this advice to heart and ensure that the kind of feedback we offer moves learning forward.

Whether it is us or others giving feedback, we need to plan feedback opportunities frequently and for every student. Conferencing and feedback can be offered digitally, between the teacher and the student, between pairs of students, through group feedback sessions (students take turns, in groups of three or four, asking questions about each other's work and offering options for refinement), or even from a guest. If teachers don't offer students the chance to reflect on their thinking and their processes, students can't change the ones that aren't working. Feedback does not have to be lengthy. In fact, targeted feedback is much easier to respond to. Relating feedback to the learning criteria is important, and connecting that criteria to the overall learning goal is vital for establishing a broader context.

Not only helping students understand where they are headed but also suggesting multiple ways to strengthen learning must be part of our feedback processes. It is not enough to be told we are not at our destination yet when we aren't sure which steps to take to get us closer. Often, we assume students know how to improve. We ask them to do more or better, forgetting that this information can be frustrating when the students perceive their initial effort as their best. We empower our learners when we equip them with the strategies needed to re-engage.

Establishing a Strong Feedback Process

As with the other forms of assessment discussed in previous chapters, we can follow a number of steps that will help guide us as we create effective and constructive feedback processes. We must (1) consult the learning continuum to ensure feedback clearly responds to learning goals, (2) reflect on processes to ensure they support learning goals, and (3) develop a strong learning partnership with students.

Consult the Learning Continuum to Ensure Feedback Clearly Responds to Learning Goals

Building an effective and constructive feedback process begins with the learning continuum. It is impossible to ask questions to guide growth when we are unclear about the destination. For our feedback to be specific enough to invite reflection, we must be clear about the criteria by which we are measuring progress and verifying proficiency. Being timely relies on an equally clear understanding of the kinds of knowledge and skills we are exploring and the order in which those building blocks need to be acquired and practiced for the next layer of learning. Returning to our learning continuum work, we can revisit the readiness we want to develop, the skills and knowledge we plan to explore, and the indicators of proficiency and enrichment that will guide our feedback.

By attending to the continuum, we can ensure our feedback will help students where they most need it. If they are still building readiness, our feedback will focus on processes for building knowledge and foundational skills to support the learning that follows. If students are in the exploration stage, we can direct our feedback to processes that will further develop automaticity and deeper connection making and problem solving. When students are in the enrichment stage, we can help them develop interests and refinement. The continuum targets our feedback.

Reflect on Processes to Ensure They Support Learning Goals

We will also want to spend time reflecting on the processes that support growth over time. These processes must be part of our feedback because they help students understand *how* to improve. When processes are new to students, we should be more explicit in our feedback, offering additional instruction when needed. For example, if feedback for a student relates to the skill of drawing conclusions in a science lab, it is often not enough to tell a student that his or her conclusions are not fully supported. This is a good start because it refers to specific criteria for making strong conclusions. However, if a student believes his or her support is strong enough, we may need to guide the student further in his or her processes. Perhaps the student is making conclusions too early and not considering the experiment in its entirety. Therefore, our feedback may suggest revisiting the lab procedure, observations, and hypotheses before drawing a conclusion to ensure attention to all potential factors. Or it may be that a student drew a strong conclusion but needed practice organizing supporting details and examples. Refining the student's organization process will help him or her develop conclusions. A student may, in fact, have a strong conclusion and support; in this case, our response shifts to enrichment. We may suggest bringing in supports from other sources or assessing the importance of our conclusions by engaging in the processes of prediction and analysis. This is the art of offering strong feedback—developing ways to work alongside students so we can help them discover increasingly effective ways to strengthen their work and increase their independence.

Develop a Strong Learning Partnership With Students

The next step is to develop a strong partnership with our students—to walk alongside them on their learning journeys. We start by understanding the nature of feedback. Feedback isn't advice or correction. When advice is given, the learner is not engaged in the thinking and is not a partner in the learning. Correction, too, tends to involve much work for the corrector and little for the student. Instead, feedback at its best is a conversation between a learner and someone who is willing to become invested in the learning of another person. This second person often acts as a mirror, reflecting back choices and outcomes to be analyzed by the learners themselves. The person acting as the mirror can vary from task to task and day to day, and the more varied the sources of the feedback, the better. When feedback is just between the student and the teacher, it is possible that students may resist their own thinking and decision making in favor of doing what they think their teacher wants. If, during a feedback session, the teacher is directive about changes the student should make in his or her work, the learner may internally question the advice or want to explain his or her own reasons for making those choices but may choose to not raise these questions in favor of complying with the teacher (in hopes of pleasing him or her or getting a higher grade, for example).

Feedback is optimal when ownership for the processes and the final product that emerges from those processes rests with the learner. One approach that nurtures this ownership involves a learner receiving feedback from more than one source (the teacher and a peer, or a friend and a mentor, for example). Multiple feedback sources can invite multiple perspectives and impressions. In cases such as this, the responsibility for making a decision shifts back to the learner. Students are invited to reflect on which opinion aligns with their goals and move forward with autonomous purpose. Learners may take the feedback they receive and blend it into a direction that matches their intent. This kind of rich process meets learners' need to make decisions for themselves and set personal goals.

Feedback focuses on specific criteria and invites further thinking and problem solving. The most effective feedback can often be in the form of questions (for example, Did this presentation have the impact you hoped it would? How can this paragraph more clearly reflect your thoughts? Why is this part unclear? How did you solve that problem? Did anything give you difficulty, and what did you do?). Our questions should invite students to engage in deep reflection and give us a window into their processes, which allows us to offer alternate approaches and strategies. Creating a shared space where conversations about learning occur naturally requires asking our students about *their* perceptions instead of expressing our own. This involves releasing control back to the students, which is essential to the development and support of the whole student. The give and take of strong feedback softens the edges for both teachers and students.

Final Thoughts

Any practice can either harden or soften the edges of assessment and learning. We must be vigilant by examining our purposes for engaging in practices and equally as vigilant about examining and reflecting on the impacts for ourselves and our students as whole people. Engaging in any form of assessment simply because it is what we think we should be doing is not good enough. We must reclaim our professional responsibility to make decisions based on what is best for the students in our classrooms. We need to honor the whole needs of our students and ourselves any time we embark on an assessment process. We must ask ourselves: Does this tell me something I need to know? Does this give me enough information? Will it result in further student learning? Will it help me instruct more responsively tomorrow? Is it respectful of students' time? Is it respectful of my time? Does it nurture my learners and me emotionally? Physically? Socially? Formative assessment and feedback are about creating hope. They are about imagining a future with optimism. They are about believing in the gifts and potential of our whole students.

Questions for Reflection

The following questions for reflection have been divided into three sections: (1) architecture, (2) student response, and (3) personal response. The architecture questions invite consideration of how we design our assessment processes to ensure our assessment choices reflect learning accurately and reliably. The student response questions prompt us to consider assessment choices from the perspective of the learner. The personal response section asks us to reflect on our own beliefs about assessment and consider these beliefs in relation to decisions we may make. Each question is intended to act as a catalyst for deeper thinking and may lead to new questions. Taking time to reflect on one or two at a time, through journaling, conversation, or as part of a group discussion, can help determine aspects of assessment that may have a hard edge and those that we have successfully softened. See the reproducible "Recognizing Hard Edges in Formative Assessment and Feedback" (page 99) for an additional resource to help identify formative assessment and feedback practices and circumstances that can create hard edges, and see the reproducible "Softening the Edges of Formative Assessment and Feedback" (page 104) for specific and practical recommendations of ways to ensure soft edges with formative assessment and feedback.

Architecture

- How do you know what to assess formatively? When do you make those decisions?
- How often do you assess formatively? How do you determine what learning needs to be addressed and when?
- How do you decide the form of your formative assessments? How purposeful are your decisions?
- What do you do with your formative assessment information?
- How do you plan for feedback? How well are you able to offer feedback to every student? What is the most challenging aspect of offering feedback for you?
- How often are formative moments graded? Why does this occur? Is homework ever graded?
- To what degree do students understand criteria? How do you know?
- How often do you assess students in groups? How clear are you about who knows what?
- To what degree do standardized tests determine what and how you teach? How do you feel about this?

Student Response

- How often are students invited to practice skills and knowledge before engaging in an assignment? Is it enough? Too much? How do you know?
- How do your students respond to formative assessment? What language do they use when discussing it? What does this indicate about the edges?

- How often do you explain the connection between formative assessment results and shifts in instruction? How involved are students in the process?
- Does student learning increase as the result of your formative assessment practices?
- How well do students respond to feedback? Do they understand what to do with it? Why or why not?
- How often are learners involved in giving feedback to others? How often have you discussed the attributes of quality feedback? How often does feedback guide further practice, investigation, and revision?
- How clear are your students about their strengths? How do you share or discuss strengths?
- How comfortable are your students in revising, revisiting, and relearning? Why?

Personal Response

- How often do you feel like you are working harder than your students? How could you address this?
- How connected are your formative assessments and feedback?
- How do you offer feedback?
- Do you have enough opportunities for one-on-one conferring? How do you know?
- How comfortable are you with observation as a form of assessment? What are the challenges? How can you overcome those challenges?
- How often do you engage in common formative assessments with your colleagues?
- How comfortable are you in responding to different needs at the same time?
- How often do you seek feedback from your students? What do you do with the information you gain?

Recognizing Hard Edges in Formative Assessment and Feedback

How do we recognize when our formative assessment and feedback practices have hard edges and lack alignment with our own beliefs and values and the needs of the whole person? The following sections describe some indicators to watch for.

Failing to Take Action

The key factor in whether an assessment is formative is the degree to which it impacts future actions and decisions. When we formatively assess students and never do anything with the information we gather, we fail to meet both our own needs and those of our students, and the edges become hard. Formative assessment with no action taken or feedback given implies that the opportunity to continue to grow and learn, to observe and respond, has ceased. Furthermore, it creates a climate of purposeless assessment for both teachers and students.

Turning a Formative Event Into a Summative Mark

Grading formative assessments assigns a value to students' practice, which can reduce their emotional and intellectual safety. The opportunity for improvement and continued growth is halted the moment a formative assessment is treated as a summative assessment. Feedback becomes meaningless because a decision has already been made. Scores trump learning.

Treating a formative assessment as a summative event may occur for reasons other than by specific design. If we have not considered our learning continuum, we may create a summative assessment that should be formative because we have not clarified for ourselves what the learning goal is asking students to demonstrate. As mentioned previously, the smaller steps we take to practice and explore pieces of the learning goal should not be assessed summatively. These steps are part of the exploring stage. It is only when students are asked to synthesize these pieces into the complexity of a learning goal that we should be assessing summatively.

Grading Homework

Homework is the topic of much debate. Arguments for and against homework abound, and discussions flourish in relation to the definition of *quality homework*. Alfie Kohn (2006) and Sara Bennett and Nancy Kalish (2006) argue against the practice of homework in general, while authors such as Robert J. Marzano and Debra J. Pickering (2007) contend that homework has a place in our schools, but the instructional quality of homework needs to improve. The hard edge being discussed here is not so much about the decision of whether to issue homework (although our decisions around this may or may not foster hard edges) but rather in how that homework is used in the name of assessment.

If we accept the idea that when the purpose of our homework is to allow learners time to practice and refine their skills and knowledge, then we have to conclude that homework falls under the category of formative work. To assign it a summative grade would be a premature act. Among Ken O'Connor's (2007) arguments to support this statement is the following:

> When homework assigned as practice is scored and included in grades, what becomes most important to students is that it be done because it "counts," not because of any learning that might occur. It becomes an issue of compliance so it really doesn't matter who does the homework—the student, a parent, a sibling, or a friend. If we want homework to be about learning, we need students to understand that it is for practice if they need it, not compliance or grading, because then the person who benefits from the homework is the learner. (p. 100)

A further argument can be made for the hard edge of assigning homework a summative score. Homework, when treated as a summative event, advantages students who have the time for extended practice outside of school while creating a hard edge for many students who have commitments such as part-time jobs and child care responsibilities. Furthermore, learners who do not have a quiet place to work at home, who do not have technology available to them after school, and who do not even have basic supplies like pens and pencils at their disposal are at a distinct disadvantage when homework is brought back to school and graded. This causes the gap in achievement to widen between students who have the required resources and those who do not. This does not nurture the whole person.

Practice is essential, and when students are highly engaged in learning, we find them making time for practice in any way possible. We may offer tutorial or homework times during the school day (lunch, for example), or designate a half hour, one or two days a week, when students can work on practice for their classes. We may decide to build practice more fully into our class time so we can monitor progress as it develops. We may even shift our homework to include practice that can be done easily and with minimal materials (for example, sending home a set of playing cards so students can practice multiplication tables through games or in short periods of time). Engaging in practice in ways that are accessible and meaningful can be a soft edge of homework, but we have to acknowledge all parts of each student and face the reality that homework is a luxury some students cannot afford.

Added to the need for practice to be accessible to all learners is the importance of our need to verify proficiency. When educators make a professional judgment about student learning, they have to be certain who has been doing the learning and under what circumstances. Homework invites variables that make it next to impossible to verify independent learning.

Homework is an effective tool because it offers exceptional opportunities for reflection and feedback. However, using homework in any other way creates a hard edge in our assessment practices.

Lacking Clarity About What Needs to Be Assessed

When assessment serves little purpose and we are not sure what we are measuring, completing the work is all about compliance and no longer about the learning goals. If we are unclear about the learning continuum, we are unclear about growth. If we are unclear about what we hope to learn from an assessment, we are setting both ourselves and our students up for frustration and disengagement.

Using Data From a Few Students to Determine the Needs of Many

Asking students to work in groups invites them to develop skills like collaboration, communication, consensus, problem solving, and empathy—all important to the development of the whole student. However, when we are assessing understanding, it is important to avoid the trap of collecting information from a few students and taking that as a sign that understanding has been developed in all students. For example, in a group discussion about a new concept, it is easy to ask one or two students to respond to formative-type questions to gauge understanding. However, just because some students show proficiency, it does not mean all students are proficient. We also have to consider that very early in the year, students develop an understanding of who in their classes will be answering most questions and representing the class's collective understanding. This pattern is set up quickly in some classrooms, and students understandably take advantage of it. Strong formative assessment collects evidence of understanding by *all* students, not just a few.

Letting Standardized Assessment Dictate What We Teach and Assess

Giving a standardized assessment the power to define the kind and depth of learning in our classrooms creates a hard edge for teachers because it denies teachers' agency in making decisions for students and can even challenge teachers' beliefs about what should drive learning in schools. The work of Dylan Wiliam, Clare Lee, Christine Harrison, and Paul Black (2004) reassures us that our focus on learning goals does not limit our students' success on standardized tests. Their comprehensive study provides evidence that using formative assessment produces improved results on externally mandated tests. When we use formative assessment and feedback to help student learning develop in relation to broader learning goals, we can ensure long-term success and understanding, while at the same time students develop the skills and knowledge that will serve them well on a short-term test. We have to trust our own teaching as well as the ability of our students to demonstrate proficiency in multiple contexts. Letting standardized tests dictate what we teach and assess limits the potential of both our teaching and student learning.

Expressing Feedback in Terms Too General or Too Specific

When we use phrases like "Great work!" or "Lacking insight," we offer students nothing in the way of feedback. They cannot relate statements like these to either their learning goals or to the processes they engage in to strengthen their learning. These kinds of comments can nurture an overdependence on praise and remove efficacy for learners. Instead, comments that refer to criteria are much more helpful, such as: "Your hook was highly engaging through your use of dialogue" or "You have supported your opinion with a few details, but more references to the research would strengthen your argument." Reciprocally, when we return student work after correcting every error and making an exhaustive list of suggestions at the end, we do two things. First, we do most of the work—correcting student errors completely removes all responsibility for learning from students. Anyone who has done this with essay after essay knows this is emotionally and physically draining and is a hard edge for teachers. Second, we overwhelm students and remove any confidence they have in reaching a goal. By understanding our learning continuum, we can be crystal clear about where a student is on the journey and offer feedback about the next step. For many students, this seems more attainable than a fully documented list of every single step they need to take.

Failing to Return Formative Assessments in a Timely Fashion

Simply put, students cannot learn from their mistakes and celebrate growth if they have nothing to examine and reflect on. This means staying current in our assessment work so students can receive immediate information and refine their knowledge and skills before they add new learning. When they are forced to build walls on a potentially unsteady foundation of understanding, they have a greater chance of building a house that collapses in the long term.

References

Bennett, S., & Kalish, N. (2006). *The case against homework: How homework is hurting our children and what we can do about it.* New York: Three Rivers Press.

Kohn, A. (2006). *The homework myth: Why our kids get too much of a bad thing.* Philadelphia: Da Capo Press.

Marzano, R. J., & Pickering, D. J. (2007). The case for and against homework. *Educational Leadership, 64*(6), 74–79.

O'Connor, K. (2007). *A repair kit for grading: 15 fixes for broken grades.* Portland, OR: Educational Testing Service.

Wiliam, D., Lee, C., Harrison, C., & Black, P. (2004). Teachers developing assessment for learning: Impact on student achievement. *Assessment in Education: Principles, Policy and Practice, 11*(1), 49–65.

Softening the Edges of Formative Assessment and Feedback

How do we soften the edges of formative assessment and feedback? Here are a few suggestions.

Share Criteria for Successful Learning With Students

When we clarify and share the learning continuum with our learners, we invite an immediate shared responsibility for learning. Students benefit immensely from knowing the destination and key markers along the way. Every time we start a class or learning experience, we must be explicit about where we are going and how it will look, both as we travel and when we approach the destination. We need to share the criteria *every time*. Even better, co-construct the criteria for proficiency with students. Work together to examine work samples, craft assessment tools, and imagine the story of learning. No surprises, no ambiguity. Even when we are engaging in inquiry and the process is less linear and more organic, we need to share the criteria for strong inquiry (the process).

Start With Strength

It is nearly impossible to determine the next steps on the learning journey if we don't take time to acknowledge the skills and knowledge learners are developing as they explore each target in their journey toward the learning goal. It is tempting to focus on the steps that remain, but first we must celebrate the steps we have already taken. Formative assessment allows us to acknowledge these steps every time they happen. The preassessment will have identified the skills and knowledge learners possessed even before the goal was introduced. Targets needing instruction are identified and those already mastered are acknowledged. After that, each day is filled with practice, questions, and discussions. Each target that students explore and master is added to the list of accomplishments to celebrate. First, this act honors the learners and their efforts. Every learner brings something to the learning conversation, and this must be acknowledged. Second, it allows us to determine where we go next, in what manner, and how growth will be recognized and celebrated. A strength-based approach is not just a catchphrase. It is an integral part of educating the whole student. Every assessment and feedback experience must start with strengths.

Equip Students With the Strategies They Need to Experience Successful Learning

It is not enough to give feedback about where a student is on the learning continuum. Students may also need clarity about *how* to move to the next step. This means equipping them with the strategies that will help them make better sense of their learning goals. Without explicit teaching followed by practice in applying these strategies, students often cannot grow.

When we talk about learning strategies, we are talking about *thinking*. Learning strategies are those strategies humans apply to make sense of their world and their responses to the world, and to formulate an action or feeling. So, when we respond to challenges during a lesson, we are not responding to the activity itself or even the product; we are responding to the *thinking* that occurs before, during, and after students engage in the learning experience. This is difficult because thinking happens inside a person's head and may not be shared verbally or visually. We have to design ways to make this thinking visible or engage students in a conversation about their thinking processes.

When we don't see or hear these processes, we can make assumptions about where a student may need support with little evidence to back our assumptions. For example, we may assume a student knows that making strong predictions is a great way to begin the process of identifying the main idea or that organizing numbers is important before beginning a computation. When these assumptions are wrong, however, they can be frustrating for both our students and ourselves. When we ask students to get better and don't help them to know how, we are ensuring a repeat performance.

Involve the Students

Feedback is ineffective without student investment, and formative assessment is useless if it doesn't inform future actions for learners. Our students must become consumers and users of formative assessment information. This asserts their role as partners in their learning. Students and teachers engaging in dialogue that serves learning will help create soft edges. This dialogue has to involve two or more parties and focus on strengths and next steps. Carol R. Rodgers (2006) clarifies this further:

> It is not an evaluation of good and bad but an exploration of what helps and hinders learning and why. In all, feedback gives everyone the chance to slow down, to breathe, to make sense of where they've been, how they got there, where they should go next, and the best ways to get there together—a decision made with students, rather than for students. (p. 219)

We have to remind ourselves to speak *with* students, not *at* them. In fact, there is some research to suggest that delaying our feedback in favor of self-reflection and assessment on the part of the learner may reap greater rewards. There is even more conclusive evidence that both delayed and immediate feedback are better than no feedback at all (Thalheimer, 2008).

Involving students is also an investment for teachers because, in the end, it can save us time. When students become proficient at reflection and feedback, they can begin to offer it to each other, freeing us to focus on other things. Furthermore, strong formative assessment allows us to stop practices that no longer serve our students and, in return, gives everyone time to focus where it is most beneficial for them, softening the edges of assessment.

Use Formative Assessment to Guide Differentiation

When we engage in timely formative assessment, we are offered insight into our learners' strengths and the specific steps needed to help students reach the next phase on their learning journeys. Furthermore, strong formative assessment supports flexible grouping by need, which leads to learning experiences tailored to each student. This kind of flexible response to student needs is called *differentiation*. Carol Ann Tomlinson and Marcia B. Imbeau (2010) clarify the role of assessment in differentiated instruction: "[Assessment is] a data-gathering and analysis process that determines the degree to which students have achieved essential outcomes and informs decisions about and planning for instruction" (p. 21). Once we know how each student is doing in relation to proficiency (for example, in which stage of the learning continuum they are currently engaged), we can design lessons that invite different learning experiences intended to address different targets based on learner needs, all within the same class period. Pete Hall and Alisa Simeral (2015) explain, "Planning intentionally now shifts from using this instructional practice because it's a good thing to do to choosing this instructional practice because it's what's best for students at this moment in time" (p. 106). When students see that the outflow of a formative assessment is a new learning experience that supports their growth very specifically, it renews hope in all assessment processes. Students want to be noticed, supported, challenged, and trusted. When formative assessment leads to differentiated instruction, student receive these outcomes and their needs are met with a soft edge.

Utilize Both Smaller and Larger Formative Assessments

When we have clarity about the formative assessment purpose, the information we will gather, and how we will respond, we can make precise decisions about the type of formative assessment we will invite and the range of information it will address. There is room in a balanced formative assessment practice for both in-the-moment assessments and robust formative measures of larger pieces of the learning goals. Quick formative assessments each day allow us to be responsive and instructionally agile and, as a result, are often the bread and butter of effective teachers. However, there is also room for larger formative assessments. When we measure multiple pieces of a learning goal, and we capture several stages on the learning continuum all at once, we notice students' needs and build in smaller scaffolds or more intensive interventions early.

Make the Feedback Cycle a Two-Way Street

Receiving feedback from students is just as important as giving it to students. If assessment is a conversation, then there has to be an exchange of information between parties. There are times when we are too quick to respond to formative assessment. We assume we know what students need, when, if we continued the conversation just a little longer, we would gain some additional insight.

However, receiving feedback from students is not an easy task, and acknowledging the challenges feedback presents to us as educators is part of softening the edges of this practice. We need to be prepared for the honesty of our learners. At times it can feel like they have been restlessly waiting for someone to ask them what they think. Once we give students a much-needed voice, we may get more honesty than we bargained for at first. For example, after engaging in a lesson in which students worked in groups, we may ask them how they felt the experience helped them learn. They may share a lack of enjoyment or engagement in the group process. This is a great moment to continue the conversation and try to determine the reasons for their comments. Was it the process itself that was difficult? Was it their relationships with group members that was challenging? Did they learn less than they should have or did they just experience less enjoyment of learning? Is there a way to increase enjoyment and engagement? What needs to be addressed tomorrow? These are rich conversations that only emerge out of relationships built on honesty and inquiry. It would be easy to dismiss the feedback, but getting at the root of it can help us develop our learning experiences alongside learners. This does not mean we always do what students want; it means we are interested in their perceptions of the learning experiences they are having.

We also need to be prepared for contradictory feedback. Some students may see great benefit to our approaches while others may not. Even more complex, there may be a juxtaposition between favorable student learning outcomes and their feelings about the learning experiences themselves. For students who are accustomed to achieving early and easily, engaging them in enrichment and deep thinking, while good for them intellectually, may destabilize their confidence and create a hard edge. Students who traditionally either opt out of fully engaging in learning experiences (refuse to participate, sit back during collaborative learning) or achieve solely by minimal compliance may perceive our approaches as inconvenient to their understanding of how school works. To soften these edges, we must be prepared to return to these conversations over and over and help students create new stories of successful learning. A hard edge for learners can be softened when they come to deeply understand that learning involves risk taking and mistake making. It can feel uncomfortable and unmanageable at times. The edge of these lessons can be softened when they occur in a classroom filled with formative assessment, feedback, reflection, relationships, and trust. Resilience can be built in an environment where the edges are soft in our assessment practices and where we communicate a belief in our students' capabilities, even in tough times.

As teachers, we know that people do not always feel good about the journey through new and challenging learning. Happiness is not always directly correlated to growth and change. When I think about my own personal experiences, I know I am often very uncomfortable during times of rapid growth, but it is through these challenging experiences that growth happens. By partnering with students in the process, we can strive to work together better and even open up to our students' ideas of what learning looks, sounds, and feels like. Learning about learning is important, and two-way feedback facilitates an exploration of this goal.

Stay Curious

A typical learning experience (lesson, activity, and so on) is filled with complexity. When we plan learning experiences for students, we consider outcomes, criteria for success, ways learning could be lived, and environments that support and enhance learning. We consider a great deal when we teach. It is this very complexity that makes it challenging to identify exactly where difficulty occurs for students when they are having trouble experiencing success or growth. As a result, we have to stay curious to determine why and respond accordingly.

Staying curious takes a concerted effort. For example, when a student does not follow our instructions during a game in physical education, we may conclude *defiance* or *not listening*. However, as Mary Catherine Bateson (1994) explains, "Too narrow an attention to the obvious—can make one miss something essential going on at the periphery" (p. 100). Staying curious includes stepping back and looking at all of the parts of the learning experience. Some questions we may ask ourselves are, "Did the students hear my instructions?" "Do they understand the words I used to explain the game?" "Do they have visual or auditory challenges?" "Is the game too complex?" "Why didn't they pick up on social cues from their peers?" "At exactly which point did they show difficulty?" "Did they respond when I gave them a verbal cue?" Being curious means we ask many questions before determining possible responses.

Be Aware of a Student's Preconceived Notions About Assessment

How students perceive the assessment process impacts how they respond to our feedback. Our conversations with learners need to start with their previous assessment experiences and how our practices may or may not shift their beliefs. We may have to clarify the role of formative assessment in learning, articulate how feedback will be given, what actions will result, and how both processes will support increased achievement. There are many misconceptions about formative assessment, and we can soften these edges by including students in the conversation about how assessment will impact their learning.

References

Bateson, M. C. (1994). *Peripheral visions: Learning along the way.* New York: HarperCollins.

Hall, P., & Simeral, A. (2015). *Teach, reflect, learn: Building your capacity for success in the classroom.* Alexandria, VA: Association for Supervision and Curriculum Development.

Rodgers, C. R. (2006). Attending to student voice: The impact of descriptive feedback on learning and teaching. *Curriculum Inquiry, 36*(2), 209–237.

Thalheimer, W. (2008). *Providing learners with feedback—Part 2: Peer reviewed research compiled for training, education, and e-learning.* Accessed at http://willthalheimer.typepad.com/files/providing_learners_with_feedback_part2_may2008.pdf on November 4, 2016.

Tomlinson, C. A., & Imbeau, M. B. (2010). *Leading and managing a differentiated classroom.* Alexandria, VA: Association for Supervision and Curriculum Development.

CHAPTER

5

Self-Assessment and Goal Setting

A few years ago in a community art class, I introduced watercolor painting to a new batch of students. We had completed a day of exploring basic techniques and, on our second day, we were painting landscapes. Through instructions and modeling, I led the learners to create brief sketches with sky and land, practicing specific techniques. I noticed a couple of students seemed a little disappointed with their results. Some had experienced difficulty with some techniques, ending up with landscapes that reflected the need for further practice.

On the spur of the moment, I decided to try something I had not attempted before with my watercolor lessons. I asked everyone to set their landscapes on the table in the center of the room, and we gathered around to discuss the art. I invited the students, one by one, to tell the group one thing they were proud of and one thing they wished they had done differently. Interestingly, every student seemed to find this request actionable, and as we worked our way around the circle, the reflections became increasingly insightful. Sometimes, one learner would make an observation and others would agree that they felt the same way about their own art. Soon, we were talking about what we had tried, and the students became interested in making a second attempt at their landscapes. I encouraged them to try again, using what they had learned through our reflection. Each student had to set a goal for his or her new landscape, and then got to work. I was astounded at the engagement and confidence in the room. They dove into their new works with little discussion and much concentration. A student or two asked to be reminded of how to do a technique they knew they needed, but most moved through the steps entirely independently.

After they were done, we set the new landscapes beside their first attempts and reflected again on the strengths and challenges. Some noted that while their technique surpassed their first attempt, the second was lacking the spontaneity of the first. Others were very pleased with the changes they had made. Everyone agreed that doing it twice made them better artists. Engaging these students in the reflective process completely changed both their engagement in painting and their willingness to practice and revise. Bateson (1994) explains this phenomenon: "*Insight,* I believe, refers to that depth of understanding that comes by setting experiences, yours and mine, familiar and exotic, new and old, side by side, learning by letting them speak to one another" (p. 14). By giving students the space to explore their feelings about their creations, they were able to self-assess, come to conclusions, and set new goals on their own. This would not have been possible without the reflective process. In this chapter, we will explore the concept of self-assessment and subsequent goal setting, examine how to develop strong self-assessment practices in our students, and investigate strategies for supporting self-assessment.

Understanding Self-Assessment

Self-assessment is the act of noticing and remembering events, consequences, and actions in relation to choices and measuring the degree to which the desired result was met. It often results in planning for future actions based on our desired goals. In essence, when we self-assess, we are taking stock of where we are and want to be, and making decisions to address the gap. "When students set goals for themselves, make plans regarding those goals, and monitor how they are doing over time, learning becomes personalized" (Schnellert, Datoo, Ediger, & Panas, 2009, p. 34). Personalized learning allows the needs of each learner to move to the forefront. When students are in charge of setting goals and taking action based on their needs (a need to achieve proficiency, a need to make choices, a need to experience agency, a need to self-regulate), they are empowered.

Self-assessment invites introspection and insight to emerge from everyday experiences. We examine our own mental and emotional processes and give serious thought to how we can achieve future goals with the greatest chance for improving self-esteem and self-direction. All these processes fall under the broader category of *metacognition,* which is the "awareness or analysis of one's own learning or thinking processes" (Metacognition, 2016). John B. Biggs (1987) notes, "To be properly metacognitive, then, students have to be realistically *aware* of their own cognitive resources in relation to the task demands, and then to plan, monitor, and control those resources" (p. 75, emphasis in original). When students leverage an understanding of themselves, they can strive to achieve their personal and academic goals through purposeful actions designed to lead to a desired outcome.

In many ways, school is like a giant experiment. We *do* things all the time in our classes in order to meet a predetermined goal, and then we step back and determine the impact or results. Often, in the rush to manage both curriculum and students, we may forget to involve the very people who can offer us the greatest insight into success or challenge—the learners. This is an unhealthy system that depends on one person to decide whether learning is rich for all people. Ron Ritchhart et al. (2011), however, argue, "To the extent that students can develop a greater awareness of thinking processes, they become more independent learners capable of directing and managing their own cognitive actions" (p. 22).

To honor the whole person and soften the edges of assessment, we must invite students into the learning cycle. This includes daily reflection alongside teachers. Students should be able to discuss their progress as clearly as teachers. When criteria for growth are clear and feedback is a daily event, self-assessment will flourish. However, self-assessment and goal setting are skills, and like any skill, they must be learned. When they are done in absence of a strong purpose, without explicit instruction, and with too little practice or feedback, students may create oversimplified goals and not fully invest in the process, resulting in a practice that has little impact on learning. When students are not confidently self-assessing regularly, we are not maximizing their learning potential. Leveraging reflection, self-assessment, and goal-setting skills will result in a magnified learning process, which leads to both strong responsive instruction and visible student investment. As Jeffry Overlie (2009) asserts, "Student involvement through formative assessment, and in particular self-assessment, engages students as active participants in the education process" (p. 182). When students engage in this kind of metacognitive work in a meaningful way, the edges of our assessment practices become soft as learners work toward meeting their own needs.

Developing Strong Self-Assessment Practices

The key to developing strong self-assessment practices is to increase the amount of metacognitive work we do *every day* in our classrooms. Asking students what a text says is different from asking a student *how they know* what a text says (what strategies they use to confirm meaning) or even *how they know that they know what a text says* (self-monitoring and self-assurance). If students dwell on the latter questions, we can work with them to identify strengths and challenges. We can provide explicit instruction when needed both to help students make sense of the text in question and of how teachers will monitor comprehension of all texts. These metacognitive processes support strong self-assessment and long-term skill development.

It would be inaccurate to suggest that students are completely unaware of and completely lacking in self-assessment skills. In fact, students *are* setting goals and engaging in reflective practices. They *do* know how to consider where they are and where they want to go. They *can* figure out which steps they need to take to grow, learn, and expand their experiences in this world. However, these processes (which students engage in internally every day) seem very separate from the self-assessment we ask them to do in schools. Students aren't connecting the reflection we ask of them to the reflection they actually engage in when playing games, reading for pleasure, riding a bicycle, or navigating their very complex daily lives. This perceived lack of skill may, in fact, be a breakdown between real life and school life for them. The same students who will not set goals or design strong action plans are actually, privately, engaging in self-assessment continually.

Consider your own daily growth—you are assessing and setting small goals all the time. You think: *I have half an hour. I think I can get that load of laundry started after I wash the dishes.* You reflect: *That conversation didn't go so well. Maybe next time, I will refrain from telling him my opinion before asking what he thinks.* You assess: *I haven't compiled everything I need for this agenda. I will have to look for more documents to support the team's work.* It is natural to engage in this cycle of assessment and future action when we are engaged in a strong purpose (getting chores done, maintaining relationships, completing a task for work) for a clear audience (our families, our friends, our employers).

So, what does strong self-assessment look and sound like in our classrooms? The best versions occur when students are highly engaged in a task with a strong audience and purpose. In these instances, we will hear things like, "I am trying to develop a good argument against plastic water bottles, but I can't find research to support what I am saying." This shows clear articulation of a goal (adopting a position and offering a persuasive argument), understanding of where the student is in relation to a goal ("I am not offering enough support for my position"), and the beginning of an action plan ("I know I need to find more research"). From here, we can work together to strengthen the action plan. Maybe we can direct learners to some great data sources. Maybe we can connect them with an expert who can help them build their argument. Maybe we can examine their supports and celebrate that they do, in fact, have enough research to support their point of view. When strong self-assessment occurs *in the middle of learning*, it allows us to work alongside students to problem solve and take steps toward where they have identified needed supports. It does not mean students have assigned themselves a grade (this is our job as educators) or even that they have placed themselves in a rubric (which would be fine). It means that students have articulated a goal, established where they are in relation to that goal, and begun to imagine the steps to move their own learning forward.

Strong self-assessment can also occur with students not showing academic proficiency yet—or with students still in the readiness or exploring stages. These students can be quite adept at sharing where they are in relation to the destination. Where they may need support is in identifying their strengths and crafting a plan to address gaps. Previous experiences may have positioned these students to believe the gaps are larger than they are—that they are insurmountable. Past failures without the opportunity and means to experience growth and eventual success may cause learners to believe that not achieving on the first attempt means the lack of achievement is permanent. If students never have the opportunity to set goals, engage in further practice, ask questions, and try again, their perceptions about their potential skills and abilities may be severely diminished. Past experiences have the potential to undermine a student's belief in the power of setting personal goals. A lack of self-confidence can harden the edge of self-assessment, and softening this edge will require an explicit connection between setting a goal, taking a risk, and experiencing success. This is why learners need to first practice self-assessment in contexts where the possibility of success is very high.

When self-assessment is not strength-based and growth does not result from this practice, some students simply either give up or exaggerate their skills to hide their deficits. For example, a student may say, "I can't do this." When you probe further, the student may share, "I don't understand how to do these problems, and when you put us in groups, everyone gets it and I don't. They don't help me and I get left behind." To be clear, this is a situation that merits our attention. However, if we step back from the experience for a minute and examine this student's statement, we can celebrate the beginning of a self-assessment. The goal has been identified ("I need to solve these problems"). The student has clarified his or her current understanding ("I don't understand, and when working with a group, other students work too quickly for me to catch up"). We now support this student to determine the next steps. This student also needs help identifying strengths, not the least of which is the ability to share what has not been working for him or her. This is worth celebrating. This student has taken a risk in sharing difficulty, and risk taking is the foundation of a trusting environment where self-assessment is honored and ultimately leads to growth.

Supporting Self-Assessment

There are four strategies we can use to help students move through this process and develop their self-assessment muscles: (1) revisit the learning continuum, (2) facilitate key components of self-assessment, (3) clarify the benefits of self-assessment, and (4) consider subskills students may need to develop.

Revisit the Learning Continuum

As with other forms of assessment, the best place to begin engaging students in self-assessment is with the learning continuum for learning goals. The act of self-assessment requires students to focus on the learning goals and also on the processes that will help them develop proficiency. This dual focus can be challenging for students, especially when emphasis is traditionally placed on the final product and not so much on developing the building blocks needed to arrive at the final product.

Using phrases such as *step in* and *step out* with students can help them recognize when they have the opportunity to self-assess and can help them differentiate between reflection on the product and reflection on the processes leading to the product. The act of *stepping in* means being engaged in the learning goal content or context. For example, we may begin exploration of a new math concept by informing the learners that we will be *stepping in* to a mathematics problem in collaborative groups. Stepping in, in this case, means working through problem solving and possible solutions with peers. The act of *stepping out* means that students will be asked to think about their thinking and performance. So, after students work in groups for a while, they may be asked to *step out* and self-assess group processes. We may ask our students how well they felt they were able to collaborate. We may invite them to think about the degree to which everyone contributed to the solution. We may ask how their approach to the problem helped them and how it challenged them. For the edges of self-assessment to be soft, the act of assessing needs to flow in and out of the act of learning. Self-assessment is integral to growth, and it cannot rest outside a learning experience. Self-assessment can address the product and processes. Both kinds of self-assessment are important for enhancing learning experiences and meeting student needs. Ultimately, the questions we are asking students to consider are: How are you doing? Are you clear about the destination? Do you know how to recognize proficiency? Do you know what steps to take to move forward? Can you recognize your successes?

Facilitate Key Components of Self-Assessment

Whether we are asking students to self-assess their processes or their products, there are four key components of a strong self-assessment that learners need to engage in: (1) establish criteria for proficiency, (2) identify successes, (3) identify challenges and set goals, and (4) map strategies and actions to move toward the desired outcome. Table 5.1 explains how these components could be practiced and developed through the course of learning.

Table 5.1: Facilitation Possibilities for Key Components of Self-Assessment

Component	Explanation	Learning and Assessment Possibilities
Establish Criteria for Proficiency	Students are able to independently explain the criteria for proficiency on any given learning experience. In order to do this, students will have to develop a strong understanding of how learning looks and sounds as related to the learning goals.	• While discussing an upcoming learning experience, the teacher invites the students to write, state, or find examples of criteria for success. • Students work in pairs and generate possible criteria. They then select the top three needed to produce a strong product. • Students brainstorm, journal about, create videos about, or describe orally or in writing the qualities of effective learning goal demonstration. • Students locate exemplars of various degrees of proficiency and explain their choices based on criteria. • Students explain, draw, or act out what is expected of them and why this is an expectation.
Identify Successes	Students can examine their work, thinking, products, and actions and be able to identify things that went well. They can use specific examples to support their opinions.	• Students take a product that is either in development or completed and list the things they did well. They then identify an example in their work that illustrates this strength. • Students take pictures of themselves or each other while performing or demonstrating a learning goal and identify the aspects of their product or performance that illustrate strength. • Students highlight questions or sentences within their work in a certain color to indicate strength. • Students identify successes in their work by comparing it to exemplars, and support their ideas with evidence. • Students respond to the prompt "I am proud of . . . because . . . ."

continued →

Component	Explanation	Learning and Assessment Possibilities
Identify Challenges and Set Goals	Students can identify areas needing practice, improvement, or enrichment and set tangible goals for the future. They can justify their reasons for choosing the goal and can specifically explain how that goal will lead to future success. They understand the criteria for success and can explain how they will monitor their growth.	• Students highlight questions, sentences, or sections needing improvement or enrichment and choose one or two areas of focus for the next attempt. • Students discuss aspects of a learning experience they found challenging and identify how they would approach the same task differently next time. • Students identify more than one aspect of their learning they would like to improve and narrow a focus to a goal or goals, explaining how their goals will improve more than one area of learning. • Students videotape a performance and use it to illustrate a goal choice. • Students review the criteria they have identified or been given and choose one to focus on for growth. They can explain how success, growth, and learning will look and sound. • Students design ways of tracking their goals (charts, graphs, checklists) and explain how they will know when they are approaching their goal and when it is time to set a new goal.
Map Strategies and Actions to Move Toward Desired Outcome	Students can independently suggest ways they will work to meet their goals. Their strategies are sequenced, specific, and attainable. They can clearly explain why their chosen strategies and actions will	• Students brainstorm all the ways a goal could be reached and choose two they will try. • Students number the steps that lead to their chosen goal. • Students create a picture, collage, or storyboard identifying the parts or steps needed to achieve the goal. • Students develop a contract with themselves to reach a goal and invite friends, family, or mentors to cosign it as a demonstration of support.

	lead to growth. They can also identify necessary supports.	• Students verbally answer the question, How will you make this better (or more interesting, or stronger) in order to continue to work toward the learning goal? • Students choose strategies from a list that match their goal. • Students interview someone with a similar goal, discover how that person achieved it, and then develop their own plan.

Clarify the Benefits of Self-Assessment

The next step in engaging in self-assessment is to be clear about the benefits ourselves and then share these benefits with our learners. This helps us design self-assessment opportunities for students within the context of their daily learning. Some of the benefits of self-assessment include the following.

- **Self-assessment fosters an interest and investment in students' own accomplishments:** It supports active engagement in both the products and processes of their growth. By inviting students to self-assess, we are communicating a belief in them and their ability to impact their own learning processes—to make choices, set goals, and invest in themselves. Even more importantly, as students become more confident in their own self-assessment processes and the positive impact on their achievement, the act of self-assessing supports students' belief in themselves.
- **Self-assessment serves as a catalyst for purposeful discussions between teachers and students:** Conversations are a primary means for uncovering a learning story in the making to shift approaches and directions when needed. As Sharon V. Kramer (2009) explains, "The culmination of student involvement in the assessment process is the student's ability to articulate and have meaningful dialogue about his or her learning" (p. 242).
- **Self-assessment ties directly to continual growth, confidence, and clarity in relation to the learning goals:** The act of reflecting on proficiency criteria engages students in a deepened understanding of what proficiency looks and sounds like. In fact, self-assessment may have an even greater impact on the development of proficiency than

some other formative assessment strategies. It is a strictly formative process that has tremendous impact on growth and learning. Following a survey of students who had engaged in self-assessment, Heidi Andrade and Ying Du (2007) find that those students perceived they were more prepared, they produced higher-quality work, and they had a clearer understanding of expectations for their work. Further, students felt more motivated and were better at identifying strengths and weaknesses in their work. Self-assessment can be a catalyst for growth and learning, with the inherent question being, What next? and the answers directing tomorrow's efforts.

- **Self-assessment accommodates and supports diversity:** Students have diverse needs (intellectual, emotional, social, and physical), readiness, interests, and responses to learning experiences. Therefore, in order to soften the edges of assessment, engaging in assessment practices that can honor this diversity and support flexibility is important. Self-assessment is one such practice because it meets students where they are and invites personal reflection and goal setting, which allows for an element of self-determination in the actions that will be taken in the learning journey. The act of inviting self-assessment implies the importance of recognizing the needs of individual students and allowing the learners agency in making decisions and taking responsibility for their own learning.
- **Self-assessment builds responsibility and independence:** The dialogue around learning shifts from one-way (teacher to student) to two-way (back and forth between teacher and student) communication. When practiced over time, learners develop the ability to independently determine their own goals and assess their own growth. This is a primary goal in development of the whole student. As Hume (2008) explains, "If students graduate from our schools still dependent on others to tell them when they are adequate, good, or excellent, then we have missed the whole point of what education is about" (p. 254).

Consider Subskills Students May Need to Develop

Despite the clear benefits, metacognition—or thinking about our thinking—is a complex process. Applying this thinking to self-assessment requires practiced skill. When students are asked to reflect on reasons for making a decision or to design steps to improve a learning goal, they can find this task challenging even when the classroom environment supports risk taking and the proficiency criteria have been shared. Sometimes, despite our best efforts, students can still find self-assessment difficult. In times like this, it may be necessary to consider the *subskills* for successful self-assessment.

There are a total of seventeen subskills, grouped into six clusters as follows.

1. Noticing, remembering, and describing
2. Relating, comparing, analyzing, and connecting
3. Predicting, visualizing, and imagining
4. Empathizing and forgiving
5. Decision making and self-regulating
6. Organizing, revising, and revisiting

These subskills are grouped in clusters because they are rarely fully developed or used in isolation. The skills in each cluster share characteristics and may overlap when they are being accessed by learners. For example, noticing, remembering, and describing all invite learners to reflect on events as they are happening or shortly afterward, and shift them into memory by giving them focused attention. Often, when we work with learners to develop these skills, we are asking them to slow down or even pause, reflect back in time, and attach sensory details to those memories in order to enhance recall and allow learners to eventually link perceptions of past experiences to future decisions. In another example, empathizing and forgiving both involve emotional responses to events and require the connection to future decisions, risk taking, and feelings of success or failure. As students become increasingly proficient learners, they will become more and more adept at applying these skills intuitively, purposefully, and often simultaneously. Helping learners see the relationships among these skills within an actual learning context optimizes their application over time (Rog, 2014).

These subskills are essential for self-assessment. Without them, the process falls short for students. They are also important in contexts beyond self-assessment (reading, problem solving, and writing, to name a few). These subskills take time to develop, and many of them are strongly associated with other skills and qualities that reflect and support the development of the whole student. As students develop the subskill of making connections, for example, they can apply this skill in self-assessment when they connect their product to criteria, past experiences, or mentor texts (texts that model certain criteria, qualities, genres, effects, and so on). By developing and practicing the subskills, they can become more adept at self-assessment, which supports social, emotional, and intellectual growth. These subskills are essential to human development in the long term and, when practiced within the context of reflection and self-assessment, lead to stronger learning outcomes in the shorter term.

When addressing subskills, we should be sure to keep students' developmental capabilities in mind. It is useful to think of these introspective skills as learned over time and connected to each other as well as to the current context. As we work alongside students to nurture their ability to reflect, determine their strengths and their needs, and set goals, we must consider what is developmentally appropriate for various age groups. Children who are five years old need to practice *noticing* other people and *remembering* events in the near and distant past. These are developmentally appropriate subskills for a young child, which will support their ability to reflect and consider future actions based on past experiences. Adolescents, on the other hand, are ready to practice the subskills of *analyzing* their work in relation to detailed criteria and setting goals with multistep actions. Self-assessment becomes hard edged if we expect students to have skills that are simply not developmentally appropriate; assessment in this case can lead to diminished confidence and emotional safety. When a student is struggling to self-assess, consider whether the student needs to develop and practice these subskills.

Noticing, Remembering, and Describing

Before students can reflect on their learning, they have to *notice* their thinking and their actions as a result of that thinking. This is no small feat. We may have to teach noticing strategies such as marking a text while reading or stopping frequently during a task to describe what just occurred. It may also be helpful to record learning as it unfolds to develop awareness of students' choices through the course of their exploration. This invites discussion about why and how learning may shift from this point forward.

Helping students *notice* means developing their ability to remember and describe events from the near or distant past. Rodgers (2006) adds, "In a sense, description after the moment is practice for seeing in the moment" (p. 216). Asking students questions like, "Do you remember the last time you tried that?" or "Do you remember what your partner was doing during that activity?" can help students recall and describe important details critical to future decision making. Hall and Simeral (2015) explain the importance of reflecting and remembering: "We don't learn from experience. We learn from reflecting on that experience" (p. 80). The development of these subskills is essential to growth.

Sometimes, simply capturing learning as it happens is an important first step in developing these subskills. The act of documenting, important in the primary grades, is easily transferrable to all classrooms. Instead of always sharing finished products, documenting learning as it is developing is great for drawing attention to actions and choices in the moment and assessing whether they serve the larger purpose of supporting proficiency development. This can look like ongoing concept mapping in social studies, where new ideas and connections are made during each class, or filming or photographing a group activity to stimulate discussion the following day about what occurred and how to move learning forward.

Relating, Comparing, Analyzing, and Connecting

The ability to relate, compare, analyze, or connect concepts or skills can happen once students have become accustomed to noticing and describing their learning. This kind of complex thinking supports their ability to compare processes and products to specific criteria and self-assess progress toward proficiency. It is helpful for students to pause in their learning from time to time—to *step out* of the learning content or context and ask to what degree current learning experiences are moving them toward their learning goals. When students recognize and describe those experiences, they are ready to lay them alongside proficiency criteria and analyze the degree to which they support overall learning.

Helping students develop these subskills in increasingly sophisticated ways and in multiple contexts takes practice. At times, students will overgeneralize their comparisons, either prematurely identifying proficiency or failing to recognize it when it happens. This signals a need to continue to develop the subskills of relating, comparing, analyzing, and connecting in relation to more specific criteria. Our work in clarifying the learning continuum for learning goals can help students focus on relating their efforts to the specific building blocks of proficiency. The use of exemplars can further assist this subskill development. It is also helpful to have self-reflection flow out of informal discussions before applying it in more formal contexts (for example, written goals and action plans, or formally comparing work to criteria within rubrics). Communities of learners model the subskills with each other, spending time sorting out their thinking and showing vulnerability in a safe environment. Susanna Palomares and Dianne Schilling (2008) note that, for some students, being able to verbally express these skills assists in their development, stating, "During discussion, children translate experiential learning into cognitive understanding and commit concepts to long-term learning" (p. x).

Predicting, Visualizing, and Imagining

Can students predict how their learning may change when they change their strategies while practicing? Can they imagine possibilities in advance? Devoting time to predicting outcomes of decisions, experiments, games, and conversations helps students develop this subskill. This can simply mean teachers making time to pause and ask the student, "What do you think will happen if we change this rule?" "What will occur when we change this ingredient?" "How will the outcome shift if we add this prop?" Often, when our students seem unable to create action plans that will result in actual growth, it is because they have not considered how their plans may be lived based on what they already know about their learning processes and the content. Inviting students to consider future outcomes honors their current knowledge and asserts the teacher's belief in the students' ability to control their own learning stories.

To set goals and design action plans, as well as predict the possible outcomes of their plans, students must be able to imagine and visualize new ways of doing things. Relating these skills to real-life experiences is one way to make them part of a student's daily life. The following teacher prompts can help facilitate this reflection more deeply: Imagine your story really grabbed the reader's attention right in the introduction. How would it have changed? Visualize a way this experiment may have had different results. What would this look like? How would the process have changed? Predict the outcome of the rebellion if the Métis people had access to unlimited supplies. How could you capture this outcome more fully in your response?

Allowing students time to predict, visualize, and imagine in a variety of contexts and disciplines will help them design strong action plans for their imagined future learning stories—stories learners aspire to have because they will reflect their desired goals.

Empathizing and Forgiving

The ability to self-assess and set goals is intimately linked to the feelings students experience when faced with a gap between where they are and where they want to go. Empathizing with and forgiving both themselves and others is part of moving forward, growing, and learning. If students cannot forgive themselves for failure and relate current challenges to past challenges they have overcome, they cannot take risks and make changes. These subskills develop resilience and a belief in the students' own ability to improve, while accepting themselves as they are.

We can support growth in this area through honest discussions about owning our actions and decisions, facing difficulty, and exploring examples of others who have overcome challenges. We can also model our own challenges through think-aloud strategies. When students witness adult growth and change, it becomes easier to see that challenge is a part of every success. Showing vulnerability with our students is a tremendous asset in developing a culture of risk taking and resilience and supporting the needs of both ourselves and our learners. This happens, as David Culberhouse (2014) notes, "when you begin to understand that you can be strong and vulnerable simultaneously, that you can actually gain influence by letting go of power, or that you can lead and still be who you are at the same time."

Decision Making and Self-Regulating

Some students have a hard time making decisions because it ultimately involves taking a risk. When assessment consistently reflects high stakes, students learn very quickly that making decisions means ultimately winning or losing. As a result, self-assessment for growth and learning is not actualized, needs are not met, and the edges become very hard. Creating a classroom climate where students make decisions and the results of their decisions are consistently the basis for reflection, assessment, and future goal setting will result in greater growth and, ultimately, proficiency.

When students are unable to make decisions while attempting to set goals, they may be unclear about criteria for successful processes or products. They can't make a decision because they aren't sure where they are going or how they should be getting there. This is why the learning continuum is so important for students and teachers alike—it helps learners use the language of learning as they reflect and determine next steps. One-on-one conferring between teachers and students can help, too, because learners who are reluctant or unable to commit to a plan can be coached through the process until they gain confidence. When teachers and students share an understanding of how learning builds from readiness through exploration to proficiency and enrichment, students can develop the ability to clarify where they are in their own learning stories. This, in turn, helps them make decisions about where they need to go next and how to get there.

Strong decision making also invites students to self-regulate, when necessary. Learning is complex and sharing a learning space with others makes things even more challenging. Being able to address social, emotional, intellectual, and physical needs helps students believe they are positioned at the very center of their own learning stories. Making decisions that invite self-regulation lead to stronger learning outcomes. Helping students reflect often, not only on their learning needs but on the needs of their whole being, supports the whole student while developing the specific skill of self-assessment.

When students take risks, make their own decisions, and are responsible for their own learning environments, they become empowered and can affect their learning stories. Being responsible for their own needs and self-regulating to meet those needs is essential, not just for self-assessment, but for life.

Organizing, Revising, and Revisiting

Do students know how to revise their work? Do they know how to take an idea and look at it in a new way? Do they need help organizing their thoughts and ideas or sequencing the steps to make things clearer, stronger, or more proficient? Often teachers take these skills for granted. We assume because we have engaged students in these processes, they have internalized them into habits. However, students may need specific instruction and modeling for revisiting and revising a product effectively.

Allowing students the time and space to experiment with form and message is essential for developing these subskills. Cutting up written work and physically manipulating the parts can be very freeing and can show students that great thinking rarely emerges on the first attempt. Instead, ideas and products take reworking, revising, and multiple attempts before they become great. Taking finished art work and repurposing it into new pieces or revisiting any learning artifact can also communicate this message. Clarity about audience and purpose, plus a willingness to really dig into how these two elements impact their products, are important steps for students to develop a heightened understanding of how to approach revision. Walking alongside students as they experiment with organization and message is empowering to the learners in our charge.

Students come to believe very early in their schooling that *faster means smarter*. This misconception is further developed when time becomes a major discussion point when embarking on a new learning experience. Phrases like, "We only have two days to complete this project," or "Five minutes to finish!" communicate the importance of time over quality. Certainly, teachers feel the pinch of too-full curricula combined with too little time. This is clearly a concern. However, when we as teachers make time to deepen our understanding as opposed to always working a mile wide and an inch deep, we demonstrate to students the importance of revisiting our work, reflecting on the degree to which it demonstrates learning, and revising our ideas and products as needed. Without the space to do this, self-assessment becomes a too-rushed event in an already too-full day and meets the needs of no one.

Final Thoughts

Self-assessment is a critical skill in the growth and development of the whole student. Developing learners who can self-assess and set growth goals requires building their subskills for strong reflection, providing time for them to think deeply about learning progress, nurturing an environment where they are safe to take risks and make mistakes, and clarifying the learning continuum and criteria for achieving proficiency. When students struggle to self-assess, teachers may need to analyze the reasons for the challenges, predict possible outcomes if we change our instruction, and forgive ourselves for missing the mark. We can empathize with students and revisit self-assessment to get better results.

Providing time and space to invite self-assessment is investing in students' learning stories. This investment yields both short-term and long-term rewards and the softest of edges. The soft edges of self-assessment enhance learning by promoting creativity, ownership, and empowerment (Dueck, 2014). Learners who develop self-assessment skills exhibit confidence, investment, and intellectual growth. Allowing them to experience authentic engagement and efficacy through reflection and goal setting positions them for growth well beyond their school years.

Questions for Reflection

The following questions for reflection have been divided into three sections: (1) architecture, (2) student response, and (3) personal response. The architecture questions invite consideration of how we design our assessment processes to ensure our assessment choices reflect learning accurately and reliably. The student response questions prompt us to consider assessment choices from the perspective of the learner. The personal response section asks us to reflect on our own beliefs about assessment and consider these beliefs in relation to decisions we may make. Each question is intended to act as a catalyst for deeper thinking and may lead to new questions. Taking time to reflect on one or two at a time, through journaling, conversation, or as part of a group discussion, can help determine aspects of assessment that may have a hard edge and those that we have successfully softened. See the reproducible "Recognizing Hard Edges in Self-Assessment and Goal Setting" (page 129) for an additional resource to help identify self-assessment and goal setting practices and circumstances that can create hard edges, and see the reproducible "Softening the Edges of Self-Assessment and Goal Setting" (page 132) for specific and practical recommendations of ways to ensure soft edges with self-assessment and goal setting.

Architecture

- How often do you focus on self-assessment and goal setting? When does it happen most often? Least often? Why? To what degree do you think your students understand its importance?
- How do you ensure self-assessment is connected to strengths? How do you ensure students feel strengthened by the process?
- How often do you focus on the subskills of self-assessment? How do you know when students are lacking one of these subskills?
- To what degree do you think your students are familiar enough with criteria to use them in self-assessment and goal setting?
- Do your students know the difference between a goal and an action? Do they understand the connection?
- How do you use the results of self-assessment? How often do they impact grades?
- How often do you engage in conversation with students individually about their self-assessment? Is it enough? Too much? Why?

Student Response

- How do students respond to self-assessment and goal setting? Why do they respond this way? What does this indicate about edges?
- To what degree are students honest in their self-assessment? What does this indicate?
- To what degree can students connect self-assessment to their work using details and examples?
- How comfortable do the students feel when self-assessing? How can you increase their comfort? Do they take their reflections and apply them to future learning?
- How often do students refer to criteria when talking about their work?
- To what degree do students seem to understand how to improve or what actions to take? How do you know?

Personal Response

- How do you feel about self-assessment? Why? How does it meet your needs?
- To what degree do student goals impact your instruction?
- How comfortable are you in your ability to notice students in the act of self-assessment so you can reinforce this behavior?
- To what degree do you feel a shared responsibility with students for their learning?
- How do you actively support students with their goals? How do you track this to make sure it is happening?

Recognizing Hard Edges in Self-Assessment and Goal Setting

How do we recognize when our self-assessment and goal-setting practices have hard edges and lack alignment with our own beliefs and values and the needs of the whole person? The following sections describe some indicators to watch for.

Inviting Students to Self-Assess Just Because It Is What We Are Supposed to Do

Doing anything just because we have to (and not because we feel it holds value) creates a hard edge for everyone. Students will know immediately if we are engaging in processes that are inauthentic and we will feel frustrated both with ourselves and with how students self-assess. Before we engage students in self-assessment, we must be clear about its purpose and how it will look and sound when it is authentic. Practicing the subskills identified in the section "Consider Subskills Students May Need to Develop" helps us develop a shared language and recognize self-assessment successes when they emerge directly within a learning experience. We may need to spend time simply recognizing it in our classrooms, so we can begin a dialogue about when to do it and for what purposes. One-on-one conferring can be one of the most authentic entry points for beginning discussions around self-assessment. This may be where we need to begin.

Providing Unclear Expectations and Criteria for Success

Lack of clarity signals the death of strong self-assessment. Students need to be able to compare their own learning experiences to an articulated learning goal or target. They need to understand how learning develops over time and in what ways so they can ascertain where they are in relation to the goals and targets. When we as teachers do not share these goals with students, we are closing them out of their own learning stories. Learning then becomes an exercise in guessing what the teacher wants this time and deciding whether to attempt it. With little reassurance for success, it is no wonder many students opt out of the effort.

Setting Unclear Timelines

As long as students see that finishing quickly is more important than finishing well, they will hesitate to revisit their learning in order to improve. Checklists for completion and little reference to quality learning create learners who will march through tasks with little concern for whether the work reflects strong learning. When we accept less than our students' best, we communicate that finishing is more important than proficiency. Students need time to reflect, time to experiment, time to practice, and time to refine. Without time, self-assessment falters and quality learning falters with it.

Having Hidden Agendas

There are times when students just want to know what we really want from them. Sadly, our education system has created learners who can be suspicious of our choices and motives. For example, when we say we encourage self-assessment but we rush the process or insert it at the end of learning, students begin to wonder what we really want to accomplish. When we share the learning criteria and the learning continuum, but spend little time developing each piece, offering feedback, or formatively assessing, we communicate a false promise of proficiency. When we ask students to revise their work, but do not teach them how to do this effectively and deny them the time they need to do it well, we reveal a hidden agenda. Students begin to question the purpose behind their work and see that the only real audience is us at this moment in time.

Failing to Build a Classroom Culture of Trust, Risk Taking, and Optimism

Self-assessment is really hard when students don't feel safe to be honest and embrace their mistakes. In these circumstances, falling short of proficiency feels final. We need to create classrooms where there is time for reinforcement and practice and where everything is not always new. Moving too quickly with minimal attention to retention and application stifles a learner's ability to be reflective. In these instances, students may stop caring about what others think about the few choices they actually get to make, and they certainly won't take the time to consider how they, themselves, feel about their learning. They become used to success in a single paradigm, and the paradigms of trust, risk taking, and optimism have very different expectations and boundaries from what they are experiencing.

Neglecting to Set Goals, Establish Supports, and Take Action

When any form of assessment falls short of action, it is not formative. This certainly applies to self-assessment. Simply deciding how a learning artifact should be assigned a value is not true self-assessment for learning. It is not enough to know what is wrong if we don't know how to fix it and are not given the chance to do so. Self-assessment must result in the expansion of a learner's tool kit to address concerns and challenges. When self-assessment is authentic, students and teachers make decisions together about what background knowledge to develop (vocabulary, basic skills), what experiences need to unfold (field trips, interviews, community connections), what experiments students need to undertake (searching for examples of strong hooks in writing, exploring ways that substances combine in chemical reactions), and what enrichment is necessary (creating new solutions, using complex data sets). When students are part of this conversation, the opportunity to design learning and assessment that addresses learner needs increases tremendously.

Confusing Self-Assessment With Self-Evaluation

The responsibility for evaluation rests with teachers as part of our professional obligation to verify progress toward learning goals. Certainly, our conversations with students through the course of self-assessment and reflection can inform our judgments, but allowing students to assign a value to their learning hardens an edge for teachers (we can feel painted into a corner by promising students a say in how they are evaluated). It hardens an edge for students, too, because they may come to associate the act of self-assessment with grading, which increases the stakes and distorts the purpose away from formative growth, toward summative judgment. Students may become confused and reluctant to be honest about weaknesses and challenges. Their need for self-preservation may override any need to reflect honestly. In order for self-assessment to be truly formative, it must remain separate from evaluation.

Implying That the Only Reason to Self-Assess Is to Get a Better Grade

Teachers can find it difficult to explain to students who are proficient why they should self-assess and set goals. What do they have left to learn? How should they improve when they are already perfect? This is a strong misconception perpetuated by schools, and a primary reason why enriched understanding appears on learning continuums. Our work with these students is not only to help them recognize their strengths but also to identify areas for improvement. These students benefit in the long term from being challenged. We can tell these students that while they have demonstrated proficiency, their learning today should look different from the learning they do tomorrow. Their essay writing should continue to improve, their problem solving should become more proficient, and their thinking should become more complex. When school is simply about a grade, continual learning is taken off the table.

The solution is to be as explicit with these students as we are with all students about how they could approach the next task to improve areas they choose. We do not want students to believe their job is to complete a task and simply get a good grade. We want them to continue learning and become invested in their work. Resilience and stamina are key outcomes connected to self-assessment for all students.

Softening the Edges of Self-Assessment and Goal Setting

Softening the edges requires that teachers return to the learning continuum and consider how the whole student will interact with the learning and assessment experiences. When we invite students to be introspective, they offer us the gift of seeing the world through their eyes, knowing their learning stories, and witnessing them author the next chapter of their own growth and development. Here are some considerations for soft edges.

Establish a Clear Purpose for Self-Assessment

How learning experiences unfold after self-assessment will, ultimately, determine how well students engage in the process next time. If increased proficiency is the result, they will see a clear connection between formative and summative processes. Success breeds success. Stephen N. Elliott, Thomas R. Kratochwill, Joan Littlefield Cook, and John F. Travers (1996) explain, "By making students aware that they can 'think about their thinking,' you will also help them to improve those cognitive behaviours that result in better classroom performance" (p. 270). We must make sure students see how their own assessment practices lead to a more fulfilling classroom experience.

Build a Safe Environment

Students have to feel certain that taking risks will be supported and that personal reflection does not come with a penalty. When we foster open discussion and encourage vulnerability, we are rewarded with a more honest self-reflection. It is important that we never belittle a student's attempt to reflect. Instead, we reward students for their metacognitive journeys by ensuring their classroom experiences shift as a result of strong self-assessment. When we celebrate risk taking, supportive listening, active thinking, and problem solving, the edges of self-assessment soften because we are attending to learners' needs and supporting the development of positive beliefs about themselves as learners.

Ensure Self-Assessment Reflects the Learning Context

When self-assessment processes are connected to actual learning experiences, the results will yield far more authentic learning. Reflecting must be strongly connected to the learning environment and the kinds of learning experiences students engage in to foster growth. The best kinds of self-assessment happen in the moment, when students are working on an authentic learning experience and spontaneously consider the quality of their products or ask questions about the learning they are exploring. When this doesn't happen automatically, it may be necessary to design invitations to reflect. However, separating the process completely from the learning can seem contrived. When students view the process as an integral part of the learning cycle, they develop proficiency both with self-assessment and with the content they are exploring because the two go hand in hand.

Ensure the Needs of the Whole Student Are Supported

Students need to have a role in determining how self-assessment will be lived, and we have to attend to the whole person in the process. For example, students may be uncomfortable reflecting on their strengths aloud, so we need to negotiate how and when the reflection will happen. If we are truly nurturing the whole student, we must balance their need to self-assess with our need to support how they communicate. For some students, self-assessment may be most effective when spoken aloud, while other students may prefer to write down their reflections. Some students can reflect quite automatically, while others need time to process and think before committing to an assessment.

We also must remain attentive to the skills of identifying strengths and challenges which may prove difficult for some students because of an unwavering belief they hold about themselves and the degree of success they assume they will experience. In other words, they may be thinking, "Why are you asking me to identify successes when we both know there aren't any?" "Challenges? Where do you want me to start?" In these instances, we will have to be increasingly explicit in helping students identify growth in relation to a variety of criteria. This helps them move away from an all-or-nothing mentality and toward an understanding that there is strength in every product and process.

There may also be cultural factors we must attend to when approaching self-assessment. In some cultures, talking about or celebrating oneself is considered disrespectful, so we may need to find ways for students to identify areas for growth and celebration that are less direct (talking with a trusted partner, marking a checklist, or highlighting their work with colors indicating strengths and challenges). Another indirect way to help these students is to simply shift the conversation to future learning and away from current attempts by asking, "What would you like to try tomorrow that went well today?" Including students in decisions related to self-assessment invite us to support them appropriately.

Self-Assess During Learning

For the benefits to be most strongly felt by both teachers and students, self-assessment must be part of the learning cycle, not an afterthought. When it occurs at the end, students may perceive it as just another thing to do for the teacher. Again, self-assessment must be actionable. When students set goals and clarify strategies for growth, they need the opportunity to apply the strategies immediately. This is the only way they will experience a relationship between metacognition and increasing proficiency. Self-assessment during learning can also support connection making and cross-curricular thinking. It is important that students come to understand that goals and strategies can impact learning in multiple contexts. Their thinking, not the task in which they are engaging, is the pivot point. This is powerful knowledge for developing learners.

Invite Students to Think About Their Thinking and Feelings Often

Carol Ann Tomlinson (2005a) asserts that "students' attitudes about learning and about themselves as learners are of great importance in establishing, maintaining, and developing students' commitment to the learning process" (p. 263). Ask students questions about their thinking and feelings (students as young as five years old can share thinking and feelings), and make it part of your language every day. Ask questions about decisions students have made, their reasons for those decisions, what they are most pleased with, and what they would do differently next time if they could.

Work Toward Learning Experiences With an Authentic Purpose and Audience

Students who are engaged in what they are creating and exploring reflect naturally. This means students need choice in what they are doing and for whom they are doing it (someone other than the teacher when possible). The true sweet spot of self-assessment occurs when students are invested in their learning and the products they are creating. When we tap into their interests and share with meaningful audiences, learners buy into the idea of getting better and their learning becomes very personal. This is what learning should feel like as often as possible.

Invite Students to Reflect on Both Product and Process

Encourage students to discuss learning of both product and process (for example, "My bookshelf seems top-heavy. Next time before beginning construction, I will spend more time on my predesign and measurements to make sure it is balanced."). If a student is lacking an element, discuss it, and help him or her figure out *how* to develop that element next time. For example, if a student has a weak introduction to an essay, explore how to develop it through a template that organizes thinking or by asking strong questions before he or she begins to write. In this way, we help students understand that the way to grow is to employ new strategies for arriving at products and that a once-and-done approach rarely works for even the most experienced learner.

Let Students Choose Their Own Goals

If students do not set their own goals, they may slip into compliance mode, which rarely leads to meaningful learning. No one loves being told what they need to fix and how they should do it every time they try something new. Taking risks is directly tied to retaining responsibility for the outcomes. Make sure students discuss their goals and action plans using language they understand and relate to. For example, instead of engaging students in criteria like "Essay shows strong clarity of language," try "Your audience was able to get inside your head." This allows learners to really come to understand proficiency and its indicators.

Confer One on One With Students Often

Rich conversations about personal growth are most successful when they are with someone we trust. When teachers build a trusting relationship through one-on-one conferring, students will naturally build confidence and begin to develop similar relationships with their peers through strong modeling. When we hear students discussing learning with each other, we know we have facilitated a truly authentic experience!

Notice and Celebrate Moments of Self-Reflection Every Time

We may have to force ourselves to be on the lookout for these moments because they are easily overlooked. Teachers need to highlight and discuss moments of self-reflection with students. We need to make them part of our learning conversations. In effect, we are encouraging students to develop a learning relationship with themselves. As Hall and Simeral (2015) state, "If you realize you aren't so wise today as you thought you were yesterday, you're wiser today" (p. 68). We are teaching students that knowing what we don't know is a strong first step in learning. We are also teaching them that learning isn't always easy; difficulty and challenge are inevitable, but that doesn't mean they cannot overcome those challenges. In fact, we believe in them so much that we insist they exercise reflection, resilience, and drive in the quest to reach their goals.

References

Elliott, S. N., Kratochwill, T. R., Cook, J. L., & Travers, J. F. (1996). *Educational psychology: Effective teaching, effective learning* (2nd ed.). Madison, WI: Brown & Benchmark.

Hall, P., & Simeral, A. (2015). *Teach, reflect, learn: Building your capacity for success in the classroom*. Alexandria, VA: Association for Supervision and Curriculum Development.

Tomlinson, C. A. (2005a). Grading and differentiation: Paradox or good practice? *Theory Into Practice*, *44*(3), 262–269.

CHAPTER 6

Summative Assessment

In my tenth year working in education, I moved from teaching middle school to teaching elementary school. I was assigned a classroom of fourth- and fifth-grade students. I absolutely loved this teaching assignment. Every day I came to school with energy and passion for both the content we were exploring and for the inquisitive minds that greeted me when I walked in the door. I worked very hard to plan effectively, looking for similarities and differences in the learning goals at each grade level. Sometimes we spent time together as a class, and other times we would divide into grade-alike groups. I introduced projects and collaboration. We built a supportive climate and culture; we were a team. It was a great year.

Interestingly though, amid the enjoyment of this year, I also clearly remember the pain of report-card time. After months of well-considered instruction, I recall sitting at my computer, entering assignments and journal work, test scores, and project marks. At first, I was quite proud of myself for two reasons: I had designed a spreadsheet that completed wonderful calculations based on weighting and averaging. It was a new approach, and I loved the magic of watching student grades unfold before my eyes, much as I imagine a stockbroker loves the ebb and flow of stocks. I was also especially proud of the sheer volume of grades I utilized to calculate overall averages. In mathematics alone I had hundreds of scores and each one had the potential to affect a student's reported grade. Watching student grades appear on the spreadsheet was a little like gambling: I was never sure what would appear in the end, but I remained hopeful I wouldn't be completely surprised.

I tell this story to illustrate a couple of points. First, while recalling these days always sends a tiny shiver of shame through my heart, I know I was doing what I thought was right at the time. We have all engaged in practices that are less than authentic. Our work is a very human practice, and as such, error and change are inevitable. My *intent* was always to support my students. I forgive myself and so should anyone else in the middle of shifting philosophical beliefs. Second, there was a part of me that knew something about my summative assessment and grading system was flawed. My desire to accumulate masses of scores arose from a knowledge that no single assessment should be all or nothing. I also knew, going into report-card time, how each student was doing on the learning goals. If you had asked me, I could have described learning thoroughly for each student. I was spending a good deal of time watching my students wrestle with challenges and try new strategies. Together, we were talking about learning all the time. The problem was that I minimized this knowledge in favor of tabulation. I watched the scores populate, hoping they would reflect what I knew, instead of using what I knew to report learning. I was doing things backward. On top of it all, I was mixing everything together into a single score. Before student-led conferences, I remember gathering samples of various pieces of work to explain grades, if necessary.

In the midst of one of my best years of teaching were times when I dreaded having to talk about learning and assessing with students and families. While it was initially exciting to see how student scores would turn out, I found my grading system to be filled with uncertainty and an extreme lack of clarity. For those reporting periods, I felt I had to stop talking about what I loved (the students and their learning) and instead talk about what made me uncomfortable (marking, reporting, and defending).

It never occurred to me to organize my gradebook according to learning goals. It never occurred to me to be confident that what I was reporting was a reflection of student learning. It also never occurred to me that assessment could be part of learning, that it should reflect an ongoing conversation with students, and that it should never be a surprise. Learning was separate from grading. I would never have believed it could be informative and optimistic and that it could inspire hope. This wasn't how I had been assessed, and no one thought differently at the time. I didn't have a different model to follow. I know differently now.

I know now that summative assessment is about verifying degrees of learning in relation to learning goals. It is about celebrating growth and achievement after engagement in purposeful learning experiences and practice. It is not about generating grades. Certainly, verification of proficiency must be shared with students and families to foster essential partnerships. However, if summative assessment consists of compiling points, averaging attempts, or any kind of magic math, it is no longer grounded in learning or supporting a need for clarity and has developed a hard edge. As Robinson (2015) explains, "Ultimately, grading gets assessment wrong because assessment is not a spreadsheet—it is a conversation" (p. 202).

It is helpful when talking about summative assessment and the impact on the whole person to remember, "Grading is emotional for both the evaluator and the evaluated" (Vagle, 2015, p. 76). Emotional responses both during and after assessment have an impact on decisions we make about what we learn from the assessment process. When a number or score is attached to our efforts, we *feel* something, whether it be joy and pride, disappointment and frustration, or apathy and disengagement. Additionally, there is a broader cultural story of what it means to have our efforts assigned a value by our schools. Both the experiences in classrooms today and future opportunities for learners are tied to this act of assigning value, and our culture accepts that this is what schools are supposed to do. Changing the way summative assessment is perceived and then lived is no small task. However, honoring the whole student in our assessment practices requires that we reconsider how we engage in summative assessment—what it represents, how it addresses holistic needs, and how it is intended to be understood by everyone involved. In this chapter, we'll explore the concept of summative assessment, investigate strategies for designing strong summative assessments, build an understanding of the concepts of redemonstration and reassessment, and examine ways to approach these subjects with students and stakeholders.

Understanding Summative Assessment

Summative assessment is part of a multifaceted cycle of learning. It is neither the end nor the beginning. We start with preassessment and strong exploration of learning goals in ways that honor students' needs. We offer practice and learning opportunities to develop students' confidence and encourage deep understanding. We engage in formative assessment, feedback, and self-assessment regularly. Only after all this do we verify proficiency with summative assessment. It is at this point that we make professional judgments about whether to re-enter the learning cycle because proficiency has not been reached or to transition into enrichment or the next learning goal, connecting future learning to the knowledge and skills already gained. Viewing summative assessment as part of a larger continuous cycle frees us to make decisions that are right for our learners and right for ourselves. When we are clear about summative assessment's purpose and how it can support future learning, we begin to utilize it in ways that nurture the whole person.

Many great teachers spend hours combing through magazines or websites looking for great teaching ideas. Activating our thinking about teaching in this way is not wrong. It is just that when we do this without first clarifying our learning continuum, we run the risk of basing our summative assessments on criteria unrelated to the learning goals and building blocks for understanding. We want to retain the essence of *Understanding by Design* (Wiggins & McTighe, 2005)—first developing clarity about the destination and the ways we will know we have arrived, and then activating our creativity, crafting learning experiences that invite the focused development of essential skills and knowledge that nurture deeper understanding.

Designing Strong Summative Assessments

Defining a single method for creating a summative assessment amid this complexity would be next to impossible and ill-advised. However, a number of underlying strategies can help teachers design strong summative experiences, regardless of the context: (1) determine indicators of proficiency, (2) determine how to assess, (3) ensure reliability, and (4) ensure clarity when sharing results with students.

Determine Indicators of Proficiency

So how do we begin? Before planning either our assessment or our instruction, we should ask ourselves, "What would count as evidence of successful learning?" In other words, which tasks and evidence will validate degrees of proficiency? If we return to our learning continuum, we will find we have already spent time determining proficiency indicators. Further, we have clarified what students may be exploring when readying themselves for learning or when they are deeply engaged in the exploration stage. We have even proposed possible learning experiences that would invite enrichment. This means we are poised to consider how these indicators may be lived. The beauty of this approach to assessment design is it allows for much creativity in gathering evidence to infer the degree to which a student has internalized the intent of the learning goals.

Consider, for example, the fifth-grade English language arts learning goal "Summarize the points a speaker makes and explain how each claim is supported by reasons and evidence" (SL.5.3; NGA & CCSSO, 2010a). The actions in this example are *summarize* and *explain.* In essence, students need to demonstrate their ability to comprehend a text they hear and give a brief statement of the main points. They then must share details and examples that support the speaker's point of view and message. Interestingly, the words *reasons* and *evidence* in this learning goal seem to imply that the speaker is delivering an informational or persuasive text, not just a story. This is an important detail to attend to as we begin to craft a summative assessment.

In the process of clarifying the learning continuum for this learning goal, we will pose questions that reflect the intent of the goal. In this example, some questions may be: What is the speaker saying? What are the key points in this speech's message? How did the speaker support his or her claims? What reasons or evidence were given? These questions can form the basis of a summative assessment; when students answer them independently and accurately, we will verify their proficiency on the learning goal.

It is important for us to understand what summarization and explanation constitute for fifth-grade students. We can begin to ponder whether choosing summaries and explanations from a list (multiple choice, for example) qualifies as proficiency or if it is important for students to summarize and explain completely on their own (constructed response). These decisions can be, and often are, made by individual teachers; this is the professional responsibility of an educator. That being said, when we are first exploring learning goals (if the goals are new or if we are new to a particular grade or subject area), we may find that collaborative professional decision making is helpful. Professional conversations can result in individual summative assessment practices that are finely tuned to the learning goals and the developmental stage of learners. Working with others can help us figure out various ways to invite demonstrations of learning that are neither too simple nor too complex. Discussions like these lead to soft edges for teachers, generating confidence about what the learning goals ask students to know and how students could show what they know in classroom.

Regardless of whether we are considering summative assessment processes alone or with others, it is critical to remember that summative assessment is not a measure of the stepping stones (the individual targets, "I can" statements, or indicators within the exploring and building readiness stages of the continuum)—this is the purpose of formative assessment. Making the decision to ask students only stepping stone or target-type questions on a summative assessment is like never removing the training wheels from a bicycle. If students are never asked to synthesize or apply their learning, it would be like never really learning to ride a bicycle on their own. We have to believe that students are capable of high levels of thinking, complex skill development, and deeper understanding. Without this belief, our assessment processes will develop a hard edge for students in the long term.

Clarity about the actions within a learning goal allows us to determine how proficiency looks and sounds and how it will be revealed. For example, if the learning goal invites students to *analyze* a concept (for example, analyze the relationship between healthy eating practices and overall wellness), we know we must invite this analysis by presenting complex materials and asking students to make connections, look for similarities and differences, and determine purposes, key concepts, and criteria. When students are required to *solve* (for example, solve situational questions involving ratios), we know they must analyze key characteristics within a context, identify the pieces that are of greatest importance, manipulate or connect components of the problem, and arrive at an outcome that answers the key question. This kind of clarity allows us to design assessment experiences that invite the right kinds of thinking from students. If we were to simply measure a student's ability to *identify* (for example, identify healthy foods) or *calculate* (for example, calculate the value of *x* in the ratio), we would not be addressing the full intent of the learning goal. These skills can certainly be measured through formative assessment but would not be the right kind of thinking for the summative assessment. This kind of precision ensures that our summative assessments are accurate.

We may believe we are truly doing students a favor by including readiness or formative-type questions on a summative assessment. We may put these kinds of questions on a summative assessment because it allows all students to get some points for their efforts. Or, perhaps we view these kinds of questions as a warm-up for the more complex questions coming later in the assessment. However, I propose that this reasoning, while filled with good intent, does not support the whole student. It does not reflect a belief in our students' abilities to achieve proficiency or in our skills as professional educators. These practices are selling everyone short. Assessing these types of questions is certainly necessary, but should happen in the formative stage when feedback can be offered and practice can occur.

Determine How to Assess

Once we have clarified the intent of the learning goal by revisiting the learning continuum, we begin to imagine how we invite students to demonstrate their understanding. Will we provide students with a graphic organizer to support their analysis? Will we invite students to solve problems related to the real world or will the problems be more abstract? Will students be invited to utilize all the strategies they have come to depend on or will they be asked to hide these strategies from us? Will we be connecting their summative assessment to cross-curricular learning or will we narrow the focus to those we have specifically practiced? These kinds of questions are important to consider.

We can soften the edges by remembering our responsibility to verify the learning identified in the learning goal. What could we invite students to do that would enable us to make a strong inference? How will we know when they have learned? We often answer this question too quickly, with too little thought. Out of habit, we create summative events that look a lot like the events we undertook as learners. We craft tests that have the same components each time, with too little consideration of whether these types of questions actually measure the learning goals. We have to feel comfortable repeatedly asking, "How will I know?" Or even better, "How will *we* (both teachers and students) know?"

Returning to the verb (or action) in the learning goal is an effective way to generate thought about the method best suited for the goal. When the actions are *identify*, *define*, *choose*, *recall*, *label*, or *recognize*, selected-response questions are often the most efficient method for determining proficiency. We could offer multiple-choice, matching, or fill-in-the-blank questions. When the actions are *discuss, describe, analyze, summarize, compare, distinguish,* or *justify,* open-ended prompts are more appropriate. In this case, we will opt for short-answer prompts or open-ended journal writing, reflecting, video clips, or composing. When students are asked to *solve, plan, generate, invent, design, create,* or *construct,* we can nurture complex learning processes and, ultimately, measure proficiency through *performance tasks,* defined as tasks that use one's knowledge to effectively act or bring to fruition a complex product that reveals one's knowledge or expertise (Wiggins & McTighe, 2005). This requires that problems, projects, or creative tasks be aligned with the learning goals. Clarity about the kind of thinking students will be undertaking invites clarity about the form the summative assessment will take.

There is additional flexibility when we open up the learning space even further and consider the context in which students demonstrate learning. We may choose to offer a written test, but many learning goals do not specify written responses. We may, instead, decide to hold individual conferences with students where they are invited to orally express their understanding. For example, "Explain how the Pythagorean theorem can help with accuracy when building a house" or "Describe how your identity has changed over time." Or perhaps we plan a simulation or experience that requires students to make decisions illustrating their understanding. For example, "Based on your understanding of incurable infections and diseases, craft a support plan for a family who is experiencing these challenges" or "Write an editorial article that offers a defense for supplying weapons to another country." In this case, our observations may be the most useful way of determining proficiency. Summative assessment has a hard edge when we feel compelled to always give a written test, but our learners' understanding is not fully captured when assessed this way.

A key to softening the edges of summative assessment is to demonstrate not only instructional agility but also *assessment agility.* This means we can adapt our assessment processes to meet both our own and our students' needs in the moment, if needed. Sometimes even the most careful planning does not anticipate the actual context of an assessment experience. We have to be willing and able to adjust our assessment processes (timing, method, context), if need demands it. When our classroom experiences reflect a wide variety of growth and learning opportunities, students will naturally be ready for summative assessment at different times. When we are ready in these instances, we build our own confidence and skill as educators and ensure our assessment practices align with our own needs and values. Our pre-assessments and formative assessments will signal when students are approaching readiness. We should have a strong sense of how students will synthesize and apply understanding when the time comes. This means we may need to be ready to offer these opportunities in ways and at times we didn't necessarily expect. This is critical for softening the edge for students and honoring their intellectual needs. Continuing to practice skills that are already fully developed is frustrating for learners and a waste of valuable instructional time. This is another reason why considering how summative assessment could occur before beginning instruction is so important: we ready ourselves for any eventuality.

As we decide our method for assessing student learning, we also want to be sure we are matching our assessment to our learners. Emotional and social safety are paramount for students to truly show what they know. Choosing our method is as much about ensuring a supportive environment as it is about a connection to the learning goal. A strong assessment method does both.

Ensure Reliability

Once we have chosen possible assessment methods, we need to ensure we have a degree of reliability in the pattern of assessment evidence. Nicole Dimich Vagle (2015) states, "Reliability and validity depend on teachers being intentional about the type and frequency of student work used to make instructional decisions and report progress" (p. 36). This requires us to have versions of the same proficiency measures across assessment formats. For example, if we assess students using a large-scale project, we can add a quiz to make sure they haven't given us a false positive of their understanding, or we can invite them to write a journal entry that asks for synthesis of thinking after they have given an oral presentation on the same learning goal. These are ways to make sure our validation is reliable.

One of the ways we can soften the edge for ourselves is to ensure that we are comparing assessment information using like data. We can accomplish this with greater efficiency when assessing more than one goal at a time if, instead of organizing a test by the kinds of questions we are asking (short answer, matching, long answer), we organize our assessment events by learning goal. We may even opt to explicitly state the learning goal we are assessing at the beginning of a set of questions or prompts. In this way, we can ensure we have the opportunity to validate proficiency of each learning goal. This validity increases when we assess with our colleagues. However, it is difficult to do this efficiently when questions are scattered throughout an assessment. In these instances, we may find ourselves held hostage by scores and helpless to organize interventions efficiently.

Organizing our assessments by learning goal opens up options for both ourselves and our students. For example, when a student does poorly on a demonstration of a single learning goal but does well on others, we may decide to reassess only in the area needed. This prevents us from reassessing students on goals on which they have already demonstrated proficiency. We can also begin to notice areas where students need to spend additional time exploring the learning goal, and we can flexibly group students according to their needs. Structuring our assessments by learning goal helps us respond to student needs in a much more timely and targeted fashion.

This approach also invites us to engage students in reflection and self-assessment. Whether the assessment is summative or formative, progress becomes very clear when the organization of the assessment by learning goal leads students to see their growth. They can better monitor their own progress and celebrate their learning when they know what each assessment moment is capturing. In this way, we can help our learners see that learning is continual; that each learning goal builds on the one before it, either through the content or the processes they use to master the content. So even when an assessment event is summative in nature, students can access their strengths and challenges and set goals that will apply to their next learning goal. The stories are theirs, and their understanding of how they are developing is essential.

To further this end, we may consider directly embedding a rubric at the beginning of each assessment experience (placing it at the front of each section devoted to a learning goal) or allowing students to access it (posting it before a performance, for example), so more specific indicators of proficiency can guide the learners' demonstration of proficiency. Utilizing a rubric to capture the key criteria within a learning goal allows us to apply it to any variety of summative assessment formats because it is the key understanding (identified as the proficiency stage on the learning continuum) that is being assessed, not a particular task.

When a rich performance task asks students to do several things to fully demonstrate learning, it is difficult to separate the assessment into learning goals. This is another reason it is important to address all goals on learning continuums. The various degrees of proficiency for multiple goals can be shared with students ahead of time. Because students will have practiced the goal's individual targets, they will already be familiar with the criteria and both assessing and reflecting on the goals separately will be possible, even with a complex task.

When the summative results are shared with students under these circumstances, it is important to share the degree of proficiency for each goal separately and cite examples of this demonstrated degree. This way, reflection and discussion based on clarity for both our learners and ourselves will follow.

Ensure Clarity When Sharing Results With Students

As part of our overall strategy for designing strong summative assessment processes, we should also decide, ahead of time, how we will share summative results with students in order to ensure clarity for our learners. This is where softening the edge and attending to everyone's needs may feel a little challenging, depending on the structures and processes already established in our specific learning contexts.

The myriad of ways assessment results are communicated and interpreted in education is staggering. In some districts or schools (depending on how decisions are made), summative verification is communicated using percentages, while in other contexts, letter grades are the norm. Some districts are gradeless and learning information is shared solely through feedback, and yet, in others, information is communicated using alpha codes or key descriptors. Given the degree of autonomy schools or systems have in communicating summative results, and our desire to utilize assessment to share learning with our students (while supporting their intellectual, emotional, physical, and social needs), it is essential to establish clarity with our learners from the outset.

Whatever the context, teachers can soften the edge of summative assessment by being clear about which methods they will use to communicate degrees of learning and how they will make their decisions transparent to the learners in the classroom. There should never be any mystery about the meaning of a summative assessment decision. If students are going to walk alongside us as they live their learning stories, they have to understand the language and processes we use in relation to summative assessment. We cannot explore learning stories using different processes and assessment terms, or the plot will get lost in the details. We can also soften this edge by being unfailingly consistent in how we report summative information to learners. When a shared language and processes are developed and supported over time, the message becomes more important than the symbol we choose. Learning steps to the forefront and placing a value on the learning recedes.

If we are going to use the learning continuum with students, the way we share information with them must reflect and align with the language and processes inherent in the continuum. When we talk about building readiness, exploring a learning goal, and demonstrating proficiency, and then we report a number or letter value at the end of a summative assessment, we must ensure students understand how those two things connect. When students are engaged in enriched understanding, they must be able to see how this impacts their efforts on a summative assessment. Clarity is essential if we are going to create a climate of trust and transparency that supports the whole person.

Understanding Redemonstration

The term *redemonstration* is perhaps better clarified by referring to it as *continual learning. Redemonstration* is the act of providing additional artifacts of learning to correctly infer degrees of understanding and skill. If that isn't happening, then redemonstration is not working for either the teachers or the students. Continually revisiting whether a practice is supporting growth of the whole student is helpful when navigating the practicalities of everyday life in classrooms.

Great diversity exists in learning environments from kindergarten through twelfth grade. However, the terms *redemonstration* or *reassessment* are used most often in middle and high schools. In primary grades, teachers use these terms less because there is not always a summative event that defines the demonstration. In these classrooms, students may simply demonstrate learning when they are ready in a myriad of ways (during a game, while exploring a puzzle, during a discussion), and this learning is usually preceded by feedback and structured conversations. Summative assessment is monitored through these conversations and observations in what are often *emergent learning experiences*. Many early learning classrooms are play based and exploratory in nature, with students taking the lead for the content and contexts and the educators facilitating deeper thinking through questions and purposeful conversation. Assessment information is collected in the moment and can vary from student to student. For many primary grades teachers, the only time they really think about summative assessment is when the report-card deadline arrives (or when they are engaging in formalized testing).

However, in middle and high schools, this learning and assessment cycle is a little different. There are often specific summative events that measure specific and targeted information administered to the whole class at the same time, and redemonstration can follow these events. Some questions we may ask ourselves when considering redemonstration include the following.

- "How will I know when a student has truly learned more?"
- "Does offering the opportunity to redemonstrate mean I must create multiple summative assessments, or is it simply a matter of fixing errors on the initial assessment?"
- "How do I connect reassessment to growth for learners so they don't just assume they will have a chance to redo their work forever? Or should they be offered the chance to redo their work forever?"
- "How do I manage this when most students are ready to move on? Do I hold everyone back for one person?"
- "Do I commit all my noon periods to reassessment?"
- "How do I honor the need for reassessment opportunities alongside my own need for sanity?"

These questions are completely valid and speak to the complexity of our learning spaces and the needs of the people within them. Multiple answers are possible, depending on a teacher's context. To help us navigate the waters of redemonstration and address both teacher and learner needs, consider these three circumstances that may warrant a redemonstration of learning.

1. **Conflicting evidence:** We have conflicting evidence of the degree of learning a student has shown. Our summative and formative data are not telling us a clear story; we need more information.
2. **Invalid assessment:** We feel the assessment tool, environment, or external circumstances affecting the learner may have hindered a valid assessment the first time around.
3. **Student growth:** The student has grown since the last assessment, and we want to acknowledge and capture this growth.

Let's examine each of these three circumstances and consider how to approach each in ways that support both our learners and ourselves.

Conflicting Evidence

Making decisions about proficiency when there are varied results can seem like a hard edge for educators. Perhaps a student is able to answer a question that explores enriched understanding but has difficulty with the proficiency prompts. In this case, did the student reach the learning goal? Or maybe one day the student was able to solve a problem connected to the learning goal, while the next day, the student experienced a challenge with a similar performance task. What tripped up the student the second time? Was it a lack of understanding or something different?

Stops and starts are a normal part of the learning process. Certainly the challenge for teachers is to determine when a proficiency demonstration reflects strong understanding. Added to this is the complexity of the human condition. Our learners have bad days. They find a particular way the prompt is phrased unfamiliar. They don't connect practice to performance in ways we expect. These are all normal parts of being a learner in incredibly complex learning environments.

On top of this, as educators, we have stops and starts too. Sometimes our questions are not as strong as we think or they contain bias, unclear phrasing, or assumptions. Other times, our professional judgment is affected because we are tired, preoccupied, or overwhelmed. This is also normal. This is why giving both ourselves and our students the time and space to understand proficiency is an important way to create a soft edge. It is also why it is vital to really understand our learning goals, so when we experience hesitation while verifying learning, we can revisit and re-explore when needed.

Redemonstration may occur when the summative assessment event shows results vastly different from previous formative results and observations or previous summative events. In these instances, assessment data are considered holistically (summative and formative delineation is not as important as looking at all the assessment data available in order to make a decision about redemonstration). The teacher has conflicting assessment data and may need to seek out further evidence of learning. It is helpful to remember that a teacher has a responsibility to both support learning and collect evidence of this learning as it progresses over time. While formative assessments don't "count" (in terms of a summative grade calculation), they help both teachers and students understand the trajectory of learning over time. This is all part of making strong redemonstration decisions. At the end of the day, the teacher is responsible for making a summative professional judgment about how students are doing on each learning goal. All assessment data available to us help us understand the degree to which a learner has developed proficiency. The whole assessment picture is important in helping us decide whether we can be sure our most recent summative assessment process reliably communicated an accurate representation of understanding or whether we need to seek more evidence in order to be secure in our summative decision.

We need to feel comfortable asking students again to show us what they have learned. This may mean rewriting an exam or revisiting a performance task. If we aren't sure, we have to ask. It may be as simple as a conversation or a request to expand further on the student's answer. Our job when summatively assessing is to really figure out what learning a student has acquired and whether he or she can act on this learning using the actions articulated in the learning goals. As we become more experienced with reassessment, we will become more familiar with the learning goal parts that give students extra challenge. We may offer refined instruction as a result of our own experience with learners, or we may develop alternate tools to verify growth. This will take time and experience, but it is a soft edge to grant ourselves and our students permission to explore how best to grow and capture that growth. This is the art of teaching.

Invalid Assessment

There are times when our best intentions at creating a summative assessment to capture learning fall short for a variety of reasons. Sometimes those reasons are within our control and sometimes they are not. Whatever the case, we must be open to redemonstration of learning.

There are also times when our assessment tool fails to capture the understanding identified in the learning goal. We may find we are assessing the individual targets without inviting synthesis and application. Or perhaps we have asked questions that are too difficult or developmentally inappropriate for both our learners and the goals. These difficulties may only reveal themselves when we are in the midst of validating proficiency. In these moments, we may have to accept that we didn't ask the right questions or invite aligned thinking. We may have to reassess.

Even when our summative assessment is strong, the assessment environment may inhibit accurate verification. Perhaps unanticipated circumstances presented distracting noise or uncomfortable temperatures, or maybe there was a lack of needed supports. For example, when we allow a summative assessment to be administered by a guest teacher, this may prevent students from asking clarifying questions and teachers from monitoring students as they are assessed and detecting inadvertent challenges. Even environmental factors such as a lack of resources (especially if summative assessments are being completed outside the classroom) or the inability to access needed strategies may prevent a true picture of student learning. Any external factor that inhibits students in their ability to demonstrate their learning may require a reassessment.

Finally, there are times when students' life circumstances make showing their learning too difficult. Perhaps a conflict outside the classroom is preoccupying. Maybe a student did not eat or sleep prior to being assessed and these factors are just too difficult to overcome. Students have lives that extend well beyond the reaches of our classrooms and honoring the whole person means acknowledging this fact and allowing redemonstration to occur at a time that makes sense for our learners.

In instances when students are not ready to summatively demonstrate (and we will know this from our formative assessments), we may choose to wait until they are ready or take the summative snapshot but allow redemonstration after further engagement in the learning cycle. We should encourage this practice and use formative evidence, observations, and, when appropriate, feedback from both students and parents to support our decisions regarding when to permit redemonstration.

Student Growth

The final occasion that may necessitate reassessment occurs when our learners have clearly grown their understanding in relation to a learning goal. Many of our learning goals are broad and recursive, meaning there is a high likelihood that students will be offered additional opportunities to practice skills and develop understanding, even after a learning goal has been summatively assessed. Essential questions will likely reach past a single learning goal. As Rick Wormeli (2011) says, "True competence that stands the test of time comes with reiterative learning. We carry forward concepts and skills we encounter repeatedly, and we get better at retrieving them the more we experience them" (p. 24). In these cases, we want to check proficiency again so we can alter our professional judgment when necessary.

Redemonstration may occur immediately following a summative assessment or in the midst of new units or new learning goals. In fact, students can show what they know at any time, in any number of ways. The learning goals are often intended to develop through practice over the course of a school year. While we may move on to new contexts, we will often revisit certain skills and concepts over and over. This does not mean, however, that students should be permitted to ask to be reassessed at any time. It does not mean they just have to fix a few errors to get a better grade. Reassessment is about demonstrating new understanding. It requires professional responsibility by educators to make accurate judgments. We need to engage students in reassessment discussions to develop a shared understanding about the responsibilities everyone holds in our classrooms and the role assessment plays in supporting growth.

This recursive perspective invites us to reimagine the practice of final exams. Instead of viewing them as the moment when we figure out what a student knows, we could look at them as a final opportunity to redemonstrate learning. Presumably, students have practiced and reflected, been formatively assessed, and been offered feedback. They will likely even have been given the opportunity to show what they know prior to any final assessment. This means we will already have data to support inferences about the degree of proficiency a student has attained. In this way, we are free to tailor an exam to meet a student's need and our own need to form a professional judgment. Perhaps an exam aligned with the learning goals could be offered in portions. Students would only take those portions where they have not yet reached proficiency. Maybe all students take the final, but some engage in prompts that invite enriched thinking and connection across multiple learning goals. We could even eliminate an exam if we have already verified learning in other ways. Our choices are based on a knowledge of our learners and their learning goals.

Students may also be invited to have a voice in these decisions. As they become more skilled at reflecting and setting personal goals, they will have a sense of where learning needs to be developed. They may choose to address particular prompts on a final exam because they are ready and committed to offering new evidence of learning. Shared decision making leads to greater student investment.

When we are clear about the degree of understanding students have attained after they demonstrate learning in a safe environment using a valid and appropriate summative assessment, then we will feel comfortable making professional judgments about proficiency.

Facilitating Student and Adult Buy-In

Concerns and questions about reassessment can often surface with adults as well as students. Myron Dueck (2014) notes, "Retesting may require a community to embrace a cultural paradigm shift. If one of the central purposes of the school system has been to sort and rank students, retesting will be seen as challenge" (p. 112). Many parents and even educators may be unfamiliar with the concept of redemonstration (and how it is similar to and different from just offering students a retest), and there may be concerns about a lack of fairness or equity. It is possible that colleagues or parents may question our decision to invite redemonstrations of learning in certain circumstances in our classes, and so we might need to be prepared to explain our philosophical beliefs about learning and the whole student and how these beliefs will manifest in our reassessment and redemonstration practices. We can share our belief that the learning goals are non-negotiable, while the time and means are flexible. We may want to be prepared to defend differentiation and that supporting all learners means different things for each person.

A different kind of concern may arise with regard to students. While we may agree that some students need more time and opportunity than others to adequately demonstrate learning, the difficulty occurs when students perceive no need to put forth an effort or adequately complete the work the first time because they can always redemonstrate at will. In some cases, the results of this interpretation can culminate with teachers running themselves ragged assessing and reassessing the same work until the students grow tired of the exercise, developing a hard edge for teachers and students alike.

One of the most effective ways to create the conditions for strong reassessment through professional judgment is to engage our learners in an assessment context that is personally relevant. As Dimensions Educational Research Foundation, Nancy Rosenow, Christine Kiewro, and Tina Reeble (2011) assert, "Inspiring children to see the excitement and purpose of true learning so they will want to develop skills and interests is really the goal of every dedicated teacher" (p. 6). If the reasons for learning and then showing learning are connected to something learners care about—something that holds intrinsic accountability—then students will naturally want to do well from the very beginning. For example, if they know that at the end of a unit they will have to write and mail a letter to a musician they respect, they will have a vested interest in ensuring the letter is coherent, persuasive (if needed), and engaging. We would work on it through inquiry and continual feedback until it is ready. This more closely resembles the learning cycle paradigm in primary grades. If things didn't go well for a student, we could try another letter, but the chances of this happening are lower than if the only reason for writing the letter was because the teacher said so and it was for a grade.

This may seem like an oversimplification of a very complex issue, but it bears consideration when we come up against a hard edge of assessment. Engagement is strongly connected to assessment. Not getting the best effort from our students and feeling like we are working harder than our learners are symptoms of a system not grounded in authentic learning. Summative assessment has morphed into a transaction rather than a rich experience. We will find it harder and harder to make strong professional judgments because our summative assessment practices are not grounded in relevant experiences for our learners and we may not feel sure we have gathered the very best learning evidence from our students.

Certainly, everything we do in schools cannot always be connected to an authentic purpose and real-life audience for every student. Sometimes the best purpose for students is the work is fun or it will maintain good relationships with their teacher. That's okay. However, we could think about meaningful contexts a little more when we are considering ways to soften the edges of summative assessment by ensuring both ourselves and our learners are finding relevance in the work. The purpose for learning has to extend beyond *because I said so* or *because it is in the textbook*. When these reasons are the only purpose for engaging in learning, our students' summative assessment results hinge on compliance and, for some students, that hinge is very loose. The purpose must connect to the student. When that happens, the hard edge of summative assessment can soften and students will engage in the process because it matters to them.

Final Thoughts

Summative assessment is the way we verify learning and determine proficiency. It is an essential part of the learning cycle. To develop summative assessments that are reliable, accurate, and transparent, we need to feel comfortable considering the whole needs of our students alongside the intention of the learning goals. Summative assessment is about developing confidence in our ability to professionally judge the degree to which every student has developed the understandings and skills articulated in learning goals. It is also about supporting our learners as they embark on this process. We measure the specific skills and understandings reflected in the goals and eliminate factors that may invite inaccurate conclusions. Above all, our summative assessment practice must:

> Demonstrate a positive belief about children. This implies more than just saying, "I have a positive belief about children." It involves maintaining positive high expectations for

> their academic progress as well as their social-behavioral development, encouraging them to be the best they can be, and providing them opportunities to be successful beyond performance on tests. (Kochhar-Bryant, 2010, p. 93)

Summative assessment practices with a soft edge celebrate students' learning as a result of exploration and practice in supportive, reflective, and engaging learning environments created and facilitated by expert educators.

Questions for Reflection

The following questions for reflection have been divided into three sections: (1) architecture, (2) student response, and (3) personal response. The architecture questions invite consideration of how we design our assessment processes to ensure our assessment choices reflect learning accurately and reliably. The student response questions prompt us to consider assessment choices from the perspective of the learner. The personal response section asks us to reflect on our own beliefs about assessment and consider these beliefs in relation to decisions we may make. Each question is intended to act as a catalyst for deeper thinking and may lead to new questions. Taking time to reflect on one or two at a time, through journaling, conversation, or as part of a group discussion, can help determine aspects of assessment that may have a hard edge and those that we have successfully softened. See the reproducible "Recognizing Hard Edges in Summative Assessment" (page 157) for an additional resource to help identify summative assessment practices and circumstances that can create hard edges, and see the reproducible "Softening the Edges of Summative Assessment" (page 162) for specific and practical recommendations of ways to ensure soft edges with summative assessment.

Architecture

- How do you know when it is time for a summative assessment? Do you ever summatively assess students at different times? How do you respond when a student has demonstrated proficiency earlier than others?
- How much time do you have to consider the kinds of learning evidence you may see for learning goals? Do you need more time?
- How often are you able to work with colleagues to discuss and plan summative assessment?
- How confident are you that your summative assessment measures learning goals in their entirety?

- How do you make decisions about the form a summative assessment will take?
- How often do you summatively assess a learning goal? Is it enough? Too much? How do you know?
- How often are students permitted to redemonstrate a learning goal? Is this process difficult or easy for them? For you? Do you have a defined process for engaging in this practice?
- Do you ever include criteria not in the learning goal in a summative score? Why or why not?
- How often do you administer bonus points? Under what conditions?
- Do you administer zeroes? Under what circumstances? Does your school or district have a policy? How do you think about it?
- To what degree are your summative assessments organized by learning goal?

Student Response

- How prepared are your students for summative assessment?
- How do they respond when receiving summative assessment results? What does this indicate?
- What kind of language do students use when discussing summative assessment? What does this language say about their beliefs? What does it indicate about edges?
- To what degree are students clear about the meaning of symbols or information they receive in relation to their summative assessments (letter grades, percentages, ratios, check marks, and so on)? How do you know?
- How much time do students have to practice and refine before a summative assessment? Are there ever any surprises?
- Are any of your students visibly stressed by a summative assessment? Why? How could you soften this edge?

Personal Response

- To what degree do you think students are being challenged by your summative assessment practices? Is the challenge appropriate? Do you think your summative assessment is making things too easy? Too difficult?

- How confident are you in your summative decisions? Do you have a strong sense of the degree of proficiency your students possess on the learning goals? How do you know?
- How much time do you spend calculating a grade? How much number crunching do you do following a summative assessment?
- How do you feel when assessing and delivering summative results? What does this indicate?
- How often do you apply professional judgment to assessing? When does it occur? Do you ever change your mind?
- How often do you reflect on your summative assessment tools? Is it enough?
- How much time do you spend on summative assessment compared to formative? Do you feel burdened by grading?
- Have you ever allowed a student another chance at a summative assessment because you knew it was fair or equitable? What were your reasons?

Recognizing Hard Edges in Summative Assessment

How do we recognize when our summative assessment practices have hard edges and lack alignment with our beliefs and values and the needs of the whole person? The following sections describe some indicators to watch for.

Forgetting About the Learning Goal

When we lose sight of the learning goal and, more specifically, the action within the learning goal, we may find ourselves asking students to spend inordinate amounts of time on memorization that doesn't serve a higher purpose. Certainly knowing facts and details can support an analysis or lead to strong solutions, but when memorization is done for the sole purpose of regurgitation for points, the edges of both assessment and learning have become very hard, and intellectual potential is undermined.

Splitting Hairs

When we begin to depend on technicalities to articulate the difference between percentage points or summative grades, our need for professional confidence is diminished and a hard edge forms. When we find ourselves saying things like, "You lost half a percentage because of this missed comma" or "I docked two points for forgetting to name all six examples of an invertebrate," we have shifted from thinking and talking about learning to thinking and talking about how a grade was calculated. This is a slippery slope into game playing, compliance, and disengagement.

Focusing on Quantifying Learning Instead of Developing Learning

There are times when we get so caught up in trying to assign the right mark to student work that we forget our real goal is to make sure our grades reflect strong, proficient learning. When we find ourselves worrying that our grades are not reflecting a bell curve or an even distribution (some 90s, some 80s, some 70s, and so on), we may have stumbled on a hard edge of assessment. In these cases, if we spent as much time thinking about how to guarantee successful summative demonstrations as we did figuring out how to measure and quantify learning, we would have classrooms of students who experience proficiency, and measuring *degrees of ineptitude* would become far less important to us than working to eradicate ineptitude.

Making Assessment a Guessing Game

If a summative assessment is truly a verification of proficiency related to learning goals, then all key aspects of the learning goal should be assessed. If our assessment practices have been building readiness skills and understanding through formative assessment and feedback, and they have been focused on a shared understanding of a learning goal, then no aspect of a summative assessment should be a surprise. If it is important enough to learn, it is important enough to measure. Even more accurately, if it was important enough to measure, it was certainly important enough to learn. The two are reflections of each other. No games. No surprises.

Measuring Criteria Not in the Learning Goal

When we measure criteria outside learning goals (such as things like behavior, completeness, and neatness), we are creating confusion and encouraging compliance from students. Our assessment communicates what is important, and when we measure external factors, we are miscommunicating what is important. For example, points for a title page or coloring neatly rarely reflect an entire learning goal. By marking them, we are stating that they are the most important things to learn. To remedy this and still encourage students to take pride in their efforts, it may be helpful to consider these types of nonacademic descriptors as non-negotiable. In this way, we work alongside students to make sure these items are completed if they are important. When a student hands in an essay without a title page when we have requested one, we simply hand it back and ask for it to be completed. Docking points communicates that we are willing to accept less than the best from our students. Assigning points for outside criteria assigns them an importance that is misplaced. This creates a hard edge and is counterintuitive.

Administering Summative Assessment Empty of Meaningful Context

Summative assessment without a meaningful context is empty assessment. It completely neglects the whole student and the need to make sense of the world by applying skills and understanding in a context that matters. It diminishes the importance of learning and the experiences that have led to this learning. It also diminishes the importance of the learning goals by reducing them to simple test items that depend on recall.

Allowing Students to Opt Out of Assessment

Giving zeroes for missed work allows students to opt out. This action communicates several things to students about our beliefs and motivations. First, it shows we have little faith in a student's ability to learn and demonstrate that learning. Second, it shows that we cannot create contexts in which the student wants to succeed; in essence, we give up. Third, it shows that the student's only responsibility is to declare the intention to learn. The learning itself is not the student's responsibility because when he or she chooses to disengage, we permit it by assigning a zero. Myron Dueck (2014) explains the futility of this approach: "Academic threats have lost their potency for students who are already disillusioned with their school experience and thus inclined to think, 'If I'm already failing, why should I care about another zero?'" (p. 14). Richard DuFour (2015) explains a solution to this challenge: "I contend that the best way to teach students responsibility is to insist that students do what responsible people do. Responsible people do the work. Responsible people seek assistance when they are struggling to succeed" (p. 184).

Applying Blanket Scores to Multiple Learning Goals

The edge of assessment is hard when scores are meaningless to teachers, students, and families. When we do not organize summative assessment by learning goal and, instead, calculate an overall score and enter it into each goal, we have undone our work to accomplish learning goal–based assessment. This results in a misrepresentation of proficiency or lack of proficiency. We have to be prepared to break down the proficiency measures by goal, so goal setting and feedback are targeted and meaningful. A single score communicates nothing and does not, in any way, support growth, accuracy, or reliability.

Encouraging Hoop Jumping

We must avoid the narrative that says the most important thing in school is to fulfill the teacher's expectations on any given day. We want students to express their thinking, make choices, and build independence and confidence. We want the learning goals to guide our work, not the particular brand of summative assessment each teacher chooses. When our language ("Get this done" or "Just hand it in") and our actions (allowing students to give less than their best or assigning random work) support hoop jumping, this is all we will get from our learners, who are capable of and need so much more.

Making Summative Assessment Stressful, Difficult, and Unenjoyable

Summative assessment does not have to be what happens *after* all the fun. Assessment, when contextualized with an authentic audience and purpose, can be highly engaging, inviting students to truly invest in their own demonstration of learning. As Cassandra Erkens (2009a) says, "When our assessments are engaging, we almost can't *stop* learning from happening!" (p. 23). Summative assessment should be a celebration of hard work, not a punishment.

Giving Bonus Points

We may think we are doing students a favor by offering bonus points for effort and compliance, but we are most definitely not. This practice demonstrates little faith in students' ability to achieve proficiency on their own and reduces clarity in the communication of learning to students and families. We may find ourselves wondering if students achieved proficiency by demonstrating learning related to the learning goals, or if they have fallen short but achieved a higher score because they complied with unrelated requests (such as handing an assignment in early, including pictures, memorizing labels, or lining up quietly). We want clarity and accuracy in our assessment practices, and bonus points do not support these aims.

Administering a Summative Assessment Without Practice

We have to work very hard to avoid getting caught in the assign-assess paradigm (wherein we simply assign tasks and then grade them, making no time for formative assessment, feedback, or practice). If everything students do is calculated into a grade, students stop taking risks. If learners are assessed before having the chance to build readiness and explore the learning goal, the edges have become unbearably hard. The learning cycle must include practice, formative assessment, feedback, and self-assessment prior to summative assessment. To determine how learning may unfold, preassessments are first needed to help teachers determine the amount of practice and instruction necessary. Then, formative assessments are essential to build a culture of risk taking, problem solving, creativity, and engagement. As David Culberhouse (2014) says, "The problem with being answer-focused is that we begin to ask fewer and fewer questions, as we already have the answers. We become less and less inquisitive, less and less creative, and less and less innovative." Simply assigning and assessing is no fun for anyone.

References

Culberhouse, D. (2014, May 14). *The creative leader: Part 2* [Blog post]. Accessed at https://dculberh.wordpress.com/2014/05/14/the-creative-leader-part-2 on December 1, 2015.

Dueck, M. (2014). *Grading smarter, not harder: Assessment strategies that motivate kids and help them learn.* Alexandria, VA: Association for Supervision and Curriculum Development.

DuFour, R. (2015). *In praise of American educators: And how they can become even better.* Bloomington, IN: Solution Tree Press.

Erkens, C. (2009a). Developing our assessment literacy. In T. R. Guskey (Ed.), *The teacher as assessment leader* (pp. 11–30). Bloomington, IN: Solution Tree Press.

Softening the Edges of Summative Assessment

Strong summative assessment must first allow prior appropriate opportunities to practice, rehearse, research, seek feedback on, and engage in self-assessment. This does not mean there shouldn't eventually be a time when we verify understanding and independent proficiency. However prior to the summative assessment, students need to actually be allowed to *learn.* They also need to be allowed time to recognize and verify their own learning. This leads to truly empowered learners who are no longer dependent on a teacher to define their growth. To support strong learning and build confidence and hope, here are ways to soften the edges of summative assessment.

Convey Joy and Optimism When Discussing Learning and Assessment

We must talk about learning as being fun and accessible. We should not have to scare students into learning. We need to avoid talking about *big tests* and *huge assignments*. This makes learning sound scary. Some students experience tremendous anxiety when we talk about things in this way. Articles in the news speak to this stress and the ramifications for our learners (Dwyer, 2014; Strauss, 2013). They lose their confidence which, as Tom Schimmer (2014) notes, is essential for success: "There is nothing more important to a student than confidence—with it, students can learn anything; without it, they'll learn nothing" (p. 16).

Learning is fun and school is interesting. If it isn't, then we need to try a different approach. Fear and learning do not go hand in hand.

Spend Time Exploring and Developing an Assessment Philosophy

When our actions and choices are grounded in our values and beliefs, assessment edges soften. To discover our beliefs and understand how to live them authentically through our assessment practices, we may need to read books, talk with colleagues, and attend professional learning sessions about assessment. We may have to step back often and ask ourselves whether the choices we are making serve ourselves and students in the long term. We should hold high standards for ourselves and our students by consistently affirming that our practices are reflecting a belief in ourselves and our learners (and haven't slipped into a grade-generation mentality). Sharing our philosophy with our students ensures accountability to our beliefs.

Observe and Assess Continually as Part of Instruction

When we watch and listen to students as they learn, we can make decisions that soften the edges of summative assessment for both ourselves and our students. For example, when we increase the amount of observation during practice and formative learning time, we can document emerging proficiency and decrease the number of learning goals to assess summatively at the end of the unit. This, in turn, honors the students' learning as it manifests and reduces the time we spend marking unnecessary summative assessments when we have reliably verified that students have reached proficiency earlier on. We could ask ourselves how often a student needs to demonstrate learning before we are confident in our own inference about their proficiency. Our answer may allow us to feel comfortable determining when a student is proficient, even when it occurs before we intended to measure it. Furthermore, when we verify learning earlier in the learning cycle, we can engage students in developing enriched understanding and give them time to practice and explore extended learning.

Understand the Difference Between Work and Learning

While work and learning are connected, they are not synonymous. Fixating on the work instead of the learning intended to emerge from the work can often limit flexibility in our summative assessment approaches. This is why understanding our learning continuum is so important. If we can remain focused on proficiency indicators and the various targets that precede proficiency, we can avoid the hard edge of frustration when students do not complete the work. We can begin to ask ourselves what the right work is. We can imagine opportunities to approach learning in multiple ways. We can distill the most important pieces and make sure the experiences associated with those pieces are engaging and well supported. We want more for our students than working *just to work*.

Put Summative Assessment in Its Place

There is a clear place for summative assessment in the learning cycle. It is important to verify learning and share this information with students and families to celebrate, enlist supports, or determine future actions. However, summative assessment is not the reason for schools or for learning. It should not be viewed as the end of learning, as the final word on the value of learning, or as the communicator of potential and ability. Summative assessment verifies learning at a moment in time and allows educators to determine the degree to which learners have achieved proficiency related to learning goals. Summative assessment has reached its potential when it blends seamlessly with everyday learning. Carol Ann Tomlinson (2005b) says of summative assessment:

> [It provides] opportunities throughout a unit for both student and teacher to understand a given learner's progression at a particular moment in the flow of the unit. [Summative assessments] call on students to express their understanding of the genius of the topic, using essential skills and habits. They are a natural part of instruction, not an intrusion or interruption in it. (p. 162)

We can put summative assessment in its place when we view it as a natural phase of learning for one or more learning goals, leading directly into the next learning goal and the experiences and explorations that follow.

Make Sure Students Are Ready

The softest edge of summative assessment for both teachers and students occurs when every student is prepared to demonstrate proficiency when the time comes. There is nothing like confidence in knowing we can do something well, and in being the teacher who helped that happen for the learners in our classrooms. Myron Dueck (2014) recalls a time when he did not engage in this practice: "I believe that my former strategy of surprising my students on test day frustrated the most capable learners and discouraged the most vulnerable" (p. 71). Engaging in transparent practices, just as we engage our students in assessment, communicates a belief that the learning stories are theirs and that they are our partners in the development of learning. This kind of equality is key for nurturing independent, engaged learners who are willing to take risks and explore learning goals with confidence and competence.

Separate Behavior and Achievement Data

Assessing behavior is important and suitable in many contexts (measuring skills like collaboration, organization, persistence, or handing in assignments on time, for example), but when behavior is addressed through achievement data, it muddies communication around summative assessment and overall academic proficiency. For example, when we reduce grades if assignments are handed in late or when we increase grades if learners are quiet and cooperative, the summative assessment result can miscommunicate proficiency or lack thereof. Instead, we should assess learning goals separately from behavioral goals. Practically speaking, this means refraining from using academic assessment to punish students for behavior such as failing to complete work, handing in assignments late, or refusal to comply with classroom rules. Certainly consequences are appropriate for these challenges, but they must fall outside academic assessment. By revisiting our work with the learning continuum and determining the building blocks for exploring our learning goals, we can focus our summative assessment on the academic proficiency indicators.

Be Prepared for Students to Occasionally Redemonstrate Across Reporting Periods

Learning can be revisited at any point, and redemonstration may not completely align with reporting. For example, we may choose to add a question onto the end of a unit exam assessing the previous unit's learning goals. Not all learners would necessarily attempt the question, but if they did redemonstrate proficiency, their new assessment result would replace their older one, and their grade in a previous reporting period may change. In these cases, despite a lack of proficiency in the original term's grade, the students can be reassured that learning is continual and that a learning goal can be revisited in the next reporting period. This softens the edge for students and for teachers, too, because reassessment can be held off during the week prior to report cards to support balance and sanity.

Avoid Group Grades

Collaboration and group problem solving are powerful instructional approaches. When our learning environments capitalize on the ideas of many, creativity and capacity building become part of the everyday experiences of our learners, and this supports the development of the whole student. However, instruction and learning are separate from summative assessment, and determining individual learner proficiency by assessing group efforts can be misleading. Our professional responsibility to infer the degree to which each student can demonstrate learning goals means we need to be crystal clear about who knows and can do what. Strong group collaboration creates a synergy that is undeniably advantageous to advancing understanding and productivity but, at some point we want to determine how each member of the group is advancing his or her learning. Ken O'Connor (2007) summarizes:

> Group scores may not accurately reflect the achievement of each student and therefore would be unfair for some members of the group. This problem can be addressed by recognizing that cooperative learning is essentially a learning activity, *not* an assessment tool. (pp. 48–49)

Our instructional planning can tap the potential of collaboration, while our assessment architecture can be designed to assess individual degrees of proficiency. We can have both.

Allow Summative to Become Formative When New Evidence Replaces Old

Getting hung up on separating summative events from formative events can be counterproductive in many contexts. When the learning experiences emerge out of student interests, questions, and experiences, and observation is a prominent source of assessment information, we are always on the lookout for demonstrations of proficiency. We can be comfortable with the idea that learning today may be *replaced* by learning tomorrow. In these cases, the only time assessment is summative is when we report progress to stakeholders. Otherwise, learning is always ongoing. New evidence replaces old in a highly organic fashion that honors the whole student. This continuous model of learning opens up the learning space and softens the edges for us and our students. The monitoring and capturing process becomes far more natural and less regimented.

Foster Emotional Safety

We have to be especially cautious with the language we use about summative assessment. Summative assessment has the potential to foster or destroy hope. We must be insistent on "regarding the child first and foremost as adequate and complete, without references to purposes and achievements, or social attachments for that matter, by which she has to justify her worth" (Lamb, 2001, p. 214). We have to remember that students come first in our classrooms. Their emotional safety and feelings of worth surpass the results of any assessment event.

Mix It Up

We need to feel encouraged to administer alternate versions of a summative assessment when allowing for redemonstration. Summative assessment verifies learning, and there are multiple forms of learning. We want to be completely sure learning has grown, so asking students to apply their learning in new contexts is reasonable and even desirable.

Bring the Learners Into the Conversation

Softening the edges of our summative assessment practices by truly examining our own and our students' needs (intellectual, emotional, social, and physical) can be challenging. There are things that need to be sorted out. There are beliefs that need to be challenged. There are habits that need to be adjusted. None of this is easy for teachers or for students. Years of exposure to traditional grading practices make a change to assessment that supports exploration, deep learning, and responsibility difficult to understand, especially for high school students. We have to be willing to share our beliefs and reasons for trying new approaches with our learners. We need to allow them to ask questions and seek reassurance that this new assessment approach will not result in lower grades, aimless work, and a reduction in emotional, social, physical, or intellectual safety. It can be surprising how deeply embedded assessment understanding is in our students. Many have come to believe that a score reflects their ability, their potential, and their value as students. We have to teach our learners that their value rests in who they are and how they engage in the things that are important to them.

References

Dueck, M. (2014). *Grading smarter, not harder: Assessment strategies that motivate kids and help them learn.* Alexandria, VA: Association for Supervision and Curriculum Development.

Dwyer, L. (2014, October 3). When anxiety hits at school. *The Atlantic.* Accessed at www.theatlantic.com/health/archive/2014/10/when-anxiety-hits-at-school/380622/ on November 16, 2016.

Lamb, W. W. H. (2001). The "whole child" in education. *Journal of Philosophy of Education, 35*(2), 203–217.

O'Connor, K. (2007). *A repair kit for grading: 15 fixes for broken grades.* Portland, OR: Educational Testing Service.

Schimmer, T. (2014). *Ten things that matter from assessment to grading.* Boston: Pearson.

Strauss, V. (2013, February 10). Test anxiety: Why it is increasing and 3 ways to curb it. *Washington Post.* Accessed at www.washingtonpost.com/news/answer-sheet/wp/2013/02/10/test-anxiety-why-it-is-increasing-and-3-ways-to-curb-it on November 16, 2016.

Tomlinson, C. A. (2005b). Quality curriculum and instruction for highly able students. *Theory Into Practice, 44*(2), 160–166.

CHAPTER

7

Systems of Reporting

My youngest daughter had an eighth-grade teacher who used social media to share the learning stories in her classroom. Intrigued at the teacher's invitation to be part of this experiment, I positioned myself to receive notifications from her when she shared these stories, and I waited for the first communication. It arrived in the second week of school in the form of images of learners, including my daughter, engaged in a science experiment. Their faces were a mix of interest and excitement as they conducted their lab, and I was surprised at how much joy it brought me in my busy adult day to witness this learning artifact. I found it compellingly reassuring, and the posts that followed as the year progressed continued to bring me these same feelings. I felt like I was opening a window into my daughter's day of learning. When the first reporting period arrived and I opened my daughter's report card, I realized I now had a context for the symbols I saw—they actually meant something. The story of my daughter's and her classmates' learning had been made visible to me, and I felt a role by witnessing and supporting her learning story. Our conversations about school expanded because of this single experiment by her teacher, and for that I am grateful.

While I was fortunate enough to receive this additional insight into my daughter's learning, it is entirely possible that some schools depend almost exclusively on report cards and subsequent parent-teacher conferences to capture and report the progress of student learning. While this is often the reality, it is not necessarily sufficient for creating a soft edge in our assessment and reporting practices. These two methods of communication alone do not always fulfill parents' needs to clearly understand their children's learning stories. Supplementary forms of communication can serve to provide a context for the grade on the report card and ensure that parents feel secure in the relationship between home and school. In order for this security and clarity to occur, it is worthwhile to pay attention to the reporting process, which is fundamentally connected to assessment. Tomlinson (2005a) shares, "Experts in the area of grading suggest that society develop 'reporting systems' rather than only 'report cards' as means of conveying multiple messages about a student's learning" (p. 268). Student learning is complex and multifaceted, and assessing and reporting this learning requires a system that attends to the varied needs and expectations of students and their families.

The relationship between the education system and students' families is pivotal to the success of the whole student. Reporting is often the primary way schools engage parents in the educational progress of their children. In order to enhance the traditional view of reporting, it is important to understand that a reporting system extends beyond the issue of report cards and standardized exam results. Instead, reporting systems communicate achievement, progress, engagement, and behavior within learning contexts; reporting systems communicate the learning stories of students.

In this chapter, we will explore reporting both in terms of how to share students' grades and how to communicate their learning stories in a broader sense. We will also explore how to communicate and even co-construct shifts in how assessment is undertaken in our classrooms by designing effective reporting systems. Developing a shared language around assessment and reporting is critical to increasing family investment in our schools and the work we do to support learning for the whole student.

Understanding Reporting

Establishing and maintaining a supportive relationship is important work, and the layers of complexity associated with this work make it worthy of focused attention. Any adult who has been through the education system has a belief about where school fits in the scheme of things, and this placement varies from person to person. Negotiating a purposeful relationship with students' families can be challenging, given the variety of needs of educators, learners, and families. Some parents want to be deeply involved in their children's education and want to be notified of progress in detail and often. Others are happy to leave the work of schools up to the schools and only want to be notified when there is a problem.

It is next to impossible to capture a consistent sentiment regarding how much families and schools should be connecting. In turn, teachers have varying philosophies about the role parents should have in the lives of their children while at school. It is difficult to find a balance, soften the edges of our assessment and reporting, and meet the needs of everyone. However, there is no denying that in the growth and development of the whole student, both the school and home environment of the child are integral. In fact, Kochhar-Bryant (2010) notes, "Educational research has provided evidence that the participation of parents and other family members is the most crucial factor in a child's potential benefit from education and related services" (p. 32). When the school and home work together, the student is able to experience education in the most positive way possible. A well-considered and executed reporting system enriches the dynamic between the educational context and the family context by enhancing communication, increasing celebration, and creating an open forum for questions and conversations.

While parents may prefer different levels of connection to and information about what their students are doing in the classroom, one thing they have in common is they want to know that we notice their children. They want to be reassured that we will take care of them—nurture their whole beings and develop their potential. Ultimately, reporting is a conversation between people who care about students. It opens a conduit of communication with families, serving as a catalyst for conversation. When we design our reporting systems, we might consider the following questions: How do we demonstrate our ability to see each student? How can we celebrate individual growth and interests? How do we communicate our desire to develop our learners and share this development with our family partners? How do we share the joy we take in spending time with their precious children? These questions frame our reporting decisions. Our actions speak louder than our words, so we have to be vigilant in our communication with families.

There is a greater story to tell than can be told in even the best report card. No report card can communicate a robust story of learning. It's frustrating to have to distill an entire term or semester of exploring, thinking, practicing, and demonstrating learning into a single code. When we consider the complexity of the stories being lived in classrooms, this frustration is to be expected. Instead of trying to work and rework these codes, let's step back from these practices and return to our intent. Engaging families in our schools and developing a shared understanding both of what we are trying to accomplish and how our learners are engaging in our classroom environments require us to be purposeful in our reporting decisions. We have the ability to portray much more complex learning stories by utilizing multiple ways of sharing and celebrating. By embracing some of these options, we more accurately reflect the experiences of students in our classrooms.

Designing Effective Reporting Systems

When we consider how we will engage in reporting practices that communicate student learning and invite families to become invested in the work of schools, it is helpful to think of reporting as a *system* beyond a single event. Reporting is an integral part of the learning cycle and is embedded in the processes of instruction and assessment. When it is done with integrity and transparency, reporting becomes essential for creating and reflecting learning experiences that are responsive to students' needs. Instead of being considered the end of the learning cycle, reporting can serve as a springboard to a new cycle of learning and sharing. As learners take increasing responsibility for their own growth, the reporting process can even become indiscernible from learning itself. It becomes part of the celebrating, sharing, and reflecting that students do every day.

For a reporting system that is valuable, accurate, and engaging, we should consider the following questions.

- How will we assess academic growth in relation to curricular outcomes?
- How will we assess and report behavioral growth that supports learning?
- How will we utilize assessment results to formulate a professional judgment about learning?
- How will we report the results of our professional judgment?
- How will we share evidence of learning? How will we encourage student reflection on this evidence? How will we celebrate growth with families?
- How will we engage in conferences and meetings that promote student engagement and communicate hope?
- How will we ensure we have created a shared language and common understanding of our academic and behavioral learning goals and the assessment practices we use to capture these goals?

With our answers to these key questions guiding the creation of a reporting system, there are several components to keep in mind that will help support our development of effective reporting systems, including ensuring alignment, supporting and reporting behavioral growth, making a strong professional judgment, determining how to report results, and sharing learning stories. Each component is intended to add a layer of clarity and engagement to our reporting systems, while at the same time inviting personalization and flexibility, depending on your context. When reporting systems work well, they flow naturally out of learning experiences and reflect the assessment processes we have spent time exploring in this book.

Ensure Alignment

The foundation of our reporting system needs to reflect alignment between our assessment work and our learning goals. For this reason, it is important to report academic growth in relation to the learning goals. This does not necessarily mean we need to include every single learning goal in our report cards; there are many ways we can share this level of detail. However, when we report academic growth, it must be based on the professional judgments we have formed from engaging in and assessing the learning goals each day.

This complete alignment, from planning to learning to assessment and reporting, greatly increases the clarity and accuracy of our reporting system. To accomplish this, we always return to our continuums and our own deep understanding of what the goals are asking students to learn and demonstrate. Strong reporting practices are an indicator of a strong understanding of both our learners and the goals we are working together to achieve. When we use the learning continuum as the basis of planned learning experiences, self-assessment, goal setting, and feedback, we demonstrate transparency and clarity for all invested parties. This is how a shared language is developed over time and the edges are softened.

One benefit of this alignment is that it supports shared responsibility for learning. As we use consistent language built around a common understanding of the learning goals in our classrooms, students become our partners in creating a shared language with their families. Over time, students begin to discuss learning in terms of the continuum. They bring home samples of their work with this language. They celebrate their successes in relation to the learning goals. In this way, their families come to understand the relationship among their children, the knowledge and skills they are developing, and the assessment practices of the teacher and students together. This co-construction of understanding embeds reporting within the learning cycle rather than placing it at the end, apart from the learning.

Support and Report Behavioral Growth

As we focus on the education of the whole student, we cannot ignore the importance of teaching and reporting the development of behaviors and competencies that support lifelong learning. The ability to work collaboratively to solve problems, take risks, develop autonomy and responsibility, and demonstrate empathy and compassion are all important human qualities. Our focus on the learning goals does not supplant the importance of these behavioral qualities—an important part of a reporting system to communicate growth in these areas. As with academic goals, behavioral goals must be taught, practiced, and assessed regularly. Educators know how vital these behaviors are not only to learning but to students' experiences in a shared classroom space, and they are deserving of focused attention. As John Hattie (2015) asserts:

> We have many achievement measures; we would do well to augment this arsenal with more measures of learning, such as the extent to which students can engage in collaborative problem-solving, deliberate practice, interleaved and distributed

> practice, elaboration strategies, planning and monitoring, effort management and self-talk, rehearsal and organisation, evaluation and elaboration and the various motivational strategies—the 'how to' aspects of learning. (p. 13)

Behavioral strategies and processes are how learning gets done and are worthy of assessment and reporting.

Assessing behavioral growth separately from academic growth requires the development of a process to monitor learning in these areas. We can develop rubrics and observe students for indications of behavioral learning. When gaps exist, explicit reteaching can address student needs. Practice may be necessary, and self-assessment and feedback can exist in the same way it does for academic learning goals. Essential questions may guide this exploration. Table 7.1 shows a sample of criteria to assess that indicate behavioral growth, and the accompanying essential questions for students to guide learning in this key area of development. These criteria and questions could be shared with families to build an understanding of how learning can be supported both inside and outside school.

Table 7.1: Behavioral Assessment Criteria and Essential Questions

Criteria	Essential Questions
Attitude contributes to learning	• Why does everyone's opinion matter? How can I be a good listener? When is it good to share and when is it good to listen? • Why is it important to respect others' things? How do I want others to treat my things? • How can I be a good classmate or friend? • Why does what I am learning matter to me? How can I show that I am ready to learn? • Why should I try new things? How can I do that and still do well? • Why are mistakes good? How can I show I have learned from mistakes? • What do I wonder? How can I ask good questions? Why are questions important?

Criteria	Essential Questions
Follows directions and classroom routines	• What are my responsibilities in class? How do I know what to do each day? • What things happen every day in class? • When is it important for me to make decisions? How do I make good decisions? How do I know when my decisions are good? • How can I become involved in my own learning? • How can I keep track of directions and instructions? What strategies can help me with this? • How does my teacher explain things? How can I get ready to listen? • How can I move from one activity or environment to the next smoothly and productively? How do I know when to change directions?
Completes coursework on time	• How do I know when something has to be done? How can I keep track of this? • Why should I always be careful with my work? How can I learn what this means in every learning experience? How do I know when I am not being careful? • How can I show I am proud of what I know and can do? • How is learning going to happen today? How can I make sure I am doing what I need to? What do I do when I think we are moving too fast or too slow? • How will I know when I am done with something and ready to move on to something new?
Organizes work and workspace	• What parts of the classroom do I need to take care of? How do I know if I am taking care of things? What does that mean in each class? • What does it mean to be organized? How does it look and sound? • How can I make sure I leave a space as clean as when I came to it? • How can I share my thinking in a clear way? Who can I ask to check that my thoughts are clear? What does the teacher expect from me?

continued →

Criteria	Essential Questions
Works effectively in groups	• How does working well in a group sound and look? How does it feel when I am working well with others? • How can I check to make sure everyone is having a say? How can I make sure my opinion is heard? • What do I need to do when I am working in a challenging group? • What is expected of me in this group? What is expected of everyone? • How can I make everyone feel good about their efforts? • How do strong groups work together? • What do I do when I disagree with someone in my group? What do I do when others are disagreeing? What skills help me with conflict and problem solving? • What is my role today? How do I know when to listen and when to speak? • How can my group stay focused on our work? What strategies can help us if we get off track?

Source: © 2014 North East School Division, Saskatchewan. Used with permission.

It is critical for collaborative teams of educators to consider behavioral expectations in the same way they consider the criteria for academic learning. Allowing our gut feelings or current frustrations about a specific behavior event prior to a reporting period influence our behavioral reporting is unfair and a hard edge for both teachers and students. We must be prepared to assess behavior regularly and base our reporting processes on a strong understanding of a learner's behavior over time. Behavior is, quite simply, another type of learning goal.

Make a Strong Professional Judgment

Whether we are reporting on academic or behavioral goals, we depend on our ability to collect the right information to make a strong professional judgment. Developing a consistent approach to making decisions about the degree to which a student has achieved proficiency can only happen when we are clear about what we are assessing, why we are assessing it, when it is time to reassess, and how we will know whether a student has met the learning goal. We have to feel confident in our understanding and be prepared to utilize collected information to determine whether the most recent data represent actual proficiency or the most consistent data give us the clearest picture. As stated previously, depending on an electronic gradebook to tell us how students are doing reduces our ability to use our reporting and hardens an edge for everyone interested in knowing how students are doing and in meeting their needs. We have to be prepared to utilize assessment results to formulate a professional judgment about student learning.

When we make summative judgments, verify proficiency related to learning goals, and report this information to students and families, we must utilize our professional knowledge of both our learners and the learning goals to construct an idea of how much learning and growth have occurred and where we need to focus next. When multiple measures of a single learning goal have occurred, it is often appropriate to replace old evidence with new and report the most recent information. It would be very comfortable to assert this rule and never look back, or program the gradebook to default to the most recent data and feel confident in the resulting report. However, we know the complexity of human beings and our learning environments often prevent us from depending on a single rule all the time. We have to bring a knowledge of our learners to decisions we make around reporting—decisions that reflect confidence in our knowledge of student learning.

Our understanding of our goals and learners is especially important when we look in our gradebook and see a wide variety of summative results for a single learning goal. Perhaps one day the student was only able to work within the building readiness stage, but the next day the student demonstrated proficiency. We may ask ourselves, "Were all my assessment events good assessment events?" "Did they measure the learning goal in its entirety each time?" If we believe an assessment has fallen short, we may consider using that evidence as formative evidence only and seek more information in a different way. If each assessment was strong, we may begin to ask ourselves, "Did the learners struggle with a particular piece the first time, and do we know this learning gap was addressed the second time?" If so, then the most recent evidence is the most reliable. Alternately, we may choose to examine the most consistent result: "Did the student do well the majority of the time and a single outlier at the end is offering a different result?" In this case, we may choose to defer to the most consistent result or we may choose to reassess to be sure. In any case, we are taking our professional responsibility seriously and seeking more information when needed before reporting our decisions to families.

The responsibility to make a professional judgment does not diminish when we are obligated to report assessment data in percentages, letter grades, or some other coding variation. It may certainly feel more complex, but the same underlying philosophy applies. Inherent in making a professional judgment about degrees of learning and then reporting this result is ensuring a shared understanding of what the report is communicating on behalf of the teacher to anyone who will be receiving the information. Any system can support or erode clarity and harden or soften an edge.

Determine How to Report Results

How we report our assessment results can sometimes be what causes us the most angst as whole educators. This decision may be ours or it may be determined for us. In a perfect world, we would completely align our reporting practices with our assessment of the learning goals using the levels of our continuum. However, in many cases, this is not possible. When we are asked to report grades using a system different from the one we have been using for our formative assessment and in our conversations about learning, creating a shared understanding is more challenging. This is why a *system* of reporting is so important.

To begin to ensure transparency and clarity in our reporting system, we need to be clear about the meaning of any number, alpha code, or other system of collecting data and reporting. In traditional systems, we may find ourselves simply adding everything together and dividing by the total. In this case, the percentage represents old evidence mixed with new—strength mixed with challenge. Perhaps we try to be a little more refined and group the numbers into categories (assignments, tests, and so on) and weight them before adding and dividing. However, in doing so, we place the focus on the type of assignment as opposed to the learning goals. When a parent asks for clarification about a teacher's mark when using this approach, the teacher may say, "Well, your child received the mark she did because I took 25 and added it to 14, 36, and 21. That gave me 96 out of a possible 120. I divided the 96 by 120, multiplied by 100 and her mark was 80 percent. That was on her assignments, which I weighted at 75 percent. This gave her a 60 out of 75. On her final exam, she got 80 percent, which was 20 out of 25. Add those two together and your daughter received 80 percent."

When we find ourselves saying things like this, we may be struggling with clarity and transparency, and we have certainly lost sight of our learning goals. Notice that not once in this explanation did the teacher discuss learning. He did not refer to the learning goals. Not once did he share how the student demonstrated learning, the feedback the student received, the goals the student set, or the learning experiences the student engaged in. The teacher just explained how he calculated the mark.

In order to engage parents in conversations about learning, we have to focus on the learning itself. In the above example, the teacher might have said, "Your child was able to show a strong understanding of these three targets, but the last two will need some additional attention and practice. My plan is to engage your child in small-group targeted instruction with some of her peers for a few minutes each day next week and then give her some practice questions. I will reassess and make sure she is learning what she needs to. If things don't go well, I will be sure to let you know, but I have confidence in her." A learning goal–based approach allows the focus to remain firmly on student growth and allows teachers to consider which evidence is most accurate and to narrow our focus and re-engage learning when needed. It offers a transparency that cannot be achieved with magic math.

If using a blended system of rubrics and percentages or letter grades, we need a coding table or other agreed-upon method of converting one system to the next. Judith Arter and Jay McTighe (2001) refer to this kind of conversion as applying a *logic rule*. They urge, "Don't use strict percentages when translating rubric scores to letter grades" (p. 79). Instead, they say, "Develop a logic rule for converting the descriptions associated with each score point to a grade that reflects a performance standard" (p. 81). For example, a system may decide that a student can receive a letter grade of an A when no more than 10 percent of the assessment results are less than proficient (in other words, exploring or building readiness) and 40 percent of the assessment results demonstrate enriched understanding. Having a consistent, collectively agreed-on approach for working in a blended system helps students understand how their attempts at learning impact their grades. Considering the connections between formative assessment, summative assessment, and reporting can ensure that reporting emerges from learning and assessment, and not the other way around.

To ensure the greatest accuracy possible in a percentage system (where accuracy is most challenging), converting rubric scores to percentage points should occur at the last possible moment, just prior to reporting. This way, the conversations around learning in relation to the learning goals are consistent and clear. Making a professional judgment about degrees of proficiency is much easier when we are considering four levels of proficiency as opposed to one hundred (Guskey, 2015; Schimmer, 2016). The conversion to a percentage can occur once we have made professional decisions about the degree to which each student has demonstrated proficiency for each learning goal.

Regardless of the conversion method used, there are three things to keep in mind when using a blended system.

1. On individual assessments, we must avoid simply treating our continuum as four equal parts of a whole, assigning a 25 percent, 50 percent, 75 percent, or 100 percent score to each box. This is a misleading representation of the intention of and learning represented by the learning continuum. When discussing learning in relation to the continuum, any number at all can be problematic because it miscommunicates the intention of the continuum to support growth (and not assign value).
2. We should organize our gradebook according to learning goals. This facilitates professional judgments and instructional and assessment decisions that support the whole student. Using this method, we can

consider most recent evidence as well as the most consistent. We can focus on learning outcomes and document behavior separately.

3. When making professional judgments during reporting time, when letter grades or percentages may be required, we need to feel able to take time to consider the best ways to nurture future learning while still being as accurate as possible with percentage scores or letter grades. For example, moving from 88 percent to 100 percent or from an A to an A+ should not be insurmountable. We have to remember that these students have achieved proficiency on multiple assessment opportunities. Moving forward should result in high grades without question.

In addition to how we will report learning, we must consider how much information to share with families. The question we have to ask ourselves is, "How and when can we best engage families to invest in their children's education while ensuring this investment is informed, relevant, and co-constructed?" It is challenging to find the sweet spot between too much and not enough information. A single numerical score completely eliminates the learning story and stalls further discussions about goal setting, interventions, and specific celebrations. However, printing a multipage report card to document proficiency (with accompanying anecdotal comments) in relation to every single learning goal can be completely overwhelming for parents.

To reach the right balance, consider alternative reporting methods that include multiple layers of information that parents can access depending on what they want to know. Some school districts opt to approach academic reporting in more than one way to try to meet the needs of diverse family contexts. First, they issue a report card that synthesizes the learning goals into broader themes, strands, or contexts (for example, writing in ELA or number sense in mathematics). These areas represent multiple learning goals. In this case, a teacher's gradebook is organized by the learning goals, and information is collected by goal. However, the gradebook also shows how these results are rolled up into the themes, strands, or contexts within each subject. This way, the report card is on one double-sided piece of paper. Teachers apply professional judgment to their results for each learning goal, and then the goal results are collected into summary scores. We can then add a second layer of reporting by sharing the gradebook with parents. This way, if families wish to have more specific information, they can log into the online gradebook and access additional assessment data. However, there are valid concerns associated with this approach. How do we ensure our gradebook clearly communicates learning and still honors the flexible nature of data collection over time? Perhaps asking parents is the most effective way to determine how much is right.

It is important to acknowledge that teachers do not often have the autonomy to decide what report cards look like or which codes and symbols will be used to represent learning; these kinds of decisions are often made at the school or district level. However, we can advocate for shifts in thinking whenever we have the chance. We can also implement valid and reliable assessment practices in our classroom contexts so that no matter what our report cards look like, they actually reflect degrees of proficiency. Schimmer (2016) asserts, "We must change how we think about grading—our mindset—before we can make any physical changes to our grade reporting structures and routines" (p. 3). Our daily assessment practices are within our control and we have the option to refine our assessment practices and enhance our reporting tools with a system that more fully communicates the story of learning.

Share Learning Stories

Once we have decided how to report academic and behavioral growth, we need to consider how to share the learning story in other ways. Consider the code or score that we place on a report card as a single, small piece of the overall reporting architecture. By sharing learning in multiple contexts, we embed reporting in the learning cycle, expand how we engage both students and their families, and invite reflection. Portfolios, conferences, parent evenings, communication tools, and social media are all ways to expand how we invite families to invest in the work in our classrooms. We can encourage student reflection on formative and summative assessment as well as the final reporting and engage them in thinking about their processes as they look at multiple products. We can celebrate growth by sharing learning experiences over and above the report card. This is the power of a strong and aligned reporting system.

Portfolios

Portfolios (including digital portfolios) are a compilation of artifacts of student learning that may be used to document growth, invite reflection, share information, and assess learning. Portfolios can be part of a reporting system when learning artifacts are shared with parents and family members. When conversations and reflection result, they can enhance parental understanding of a student's learning story as well as build new learning within the learning story itself.

While working with a group of teachers on encouraging student reflection through digital portfolios, a colleague once said, "It is no longer about saving [the work we do]; it is about sharing." How profound. This idea reflects how many students function in the world today. Learning can reach beyond the walls of schools and be shared with wider audiences. Digital portfolios (or other methods of gathering learning samples in one place) can serve the dual purpose of acting as a catalyst for reflection and engaging a broader audience. As Dimensions Educational Research Foundation et al. (2011) assert, "Learning is powerfully supported by having shared experiences with others . . . truly deep learning happens when children are highly motivated to gain information and then communicate their understanding back to others" (p. 6). Harnessing this power and using it as part of a reporting system can enhance communication with families and, ultimately, investment in students' learning journeys.

A portfolio is not simply synonymous with a scrapbook. Portfolios move learners beyond collecting their work in one place to engaging them in thinking and metacognition in more profound ways. Sharing becomes part of how we invite students to tell their individual learning stories, while developing them at the same time. Portfolios also invite us to have much-needed discussions with students about why we share, who we share with, when to share, and how to protect ourselves when we engage a larger audience. Portfolios (digital or not) offer ways to assess and report that are more inclusive of the process rather than being product focused. They allow us to look not just at the product but at how we construct a product through a complex process. Sometimes, portfolios allow us to see a much wider picture than one assessment event can. This means we can offer feedback in a more timely fashion and engage in conversations with students anytime and from anywhere to really see where they are stuck and when they are ready to fly. We can encourage students to connect us to their thinking. In this way, a tool we may choose to use to enhance our reporting system can also become a tool to enhance learning.

The beautiful thing about the use of portfolios is we can also engage parents in offering feedback, celebrating growth, and encouraging reflection. Families become important characters in students' learning stories. This is very powerful in supporting and developing the whole student and softening the edges of our assessment practices. It supports a connection between home and school that can only occur when all parties are invested and informed.

Conferences

Portfolios shared over the course of a year can greatly enhance the formalized conferencing processes many schools use to engage families. Many schools depend on some variation of a meeting or conference to discuss student learning face to face. Sometimes this meeting is between the parent or guardian and the teacher and sometimes students lead the process. How we choose to engage is as varied as the people involved, but if we are going to nurture the whole student, we must be prepared to facilitate conferences and meetings that promote student engagement and communicate hope.

The advantage of student-led conferences is they provide us with a way of "encouraging pupils to come to their own reflective decisions about the matters at stake" (McLaughlin, 1996, p. 15). Inviting students into the conferencing process gives them a sense of ownership over their own learning and decisions for enriching and enhancing future learning opportunities. Letting students tell their own stories celebrates competence and confidence.

The best way to ensure a successful student-led conference is to give students time to prepare. Engage them in metacognition and reflection prior to the meeting. Allow them to process their growth and make decisions about their future prior to talking with the teacher and their families. Student-led conferences are not about justifying grading decisions or setting a random goal (for example, keep my locker cleaner or make my handwriting neater). Goals set before and during a conference should connect to the learning continuums and the specific growth strategies and processes. Consider the following exemplars.

- One of the criteria in narrative writing is to reveal the characters' motives through emotional responses to events. Next time I write a narrative essay, before writing, I will spend more time considering the emotional impact of events on the characters.
- The criteria for proficiency in this ratios learning goal is to be able to solve multistep problems using ratios. When I encounter a multistep problem, I will be sure to take time to carefully analyze the prompt before beginning so I am clear about what is being asked.

In these examples, the goals are grounded in specific growth criteria and developed through self-assessment and feedback. In an effective student-led conference, students define and create their learning stories and set their own goals.

In circumstances where students are not directly part of the conference, it is important to bring the learner perspective into the discussion. Student work can serve as the foundation for in-depth discussions about how learning is progressing and where additional supports and interventions may be needed. Any goals that students have taken the time to articulate can be shared. This invites a focus that rests on the future as opposed to the past and ensures positive and proactive discussions, which creates a soft edge for everyone.

Parent Evenings

We may decide to offer additional formal methods of parental engagement, such as parent evenings, in order to develop a shared language and understanding and share students' learning stories. During these events, both teachers and students explain how shifting assessment practices can be very powerful. Students are often the biggest advocates of a learning goal–based approach and will understand and invest deeply in the process when they personally feel the benefits. Honoring the voices of teachers, students, and families builds a shared investment in establishing a culture of rich learning through common understanding and consistent support.

Communication Tools

The communication tools that many of us currently utilize as a matter of daily business can be viewed as part of a reporting system. Letters, phone calls, newsletters, and emails can often support parents' understanding of both the types of learning opportunities students are having and the successes and challenges they are experiencing. Emails and phone calls have the added benefit of two-way communication, where ideas can be exchanged back and forth, building up relationships and supporting a shared understanding. As with any aspect of a reporting system, we are seeking to enhance understanding of the learning stories of our students, with a focus on future growth and an optimistic perspective.

Social Media

Social media is a great way for students and teachers to share the story of learning and enhance our reporting systems. Twitter, Facebook, and online blogs are just some of the ways we can work with our students to communicate how they are learning and to celebrate growth and reflection. On their own, social media posts do not provide enough information for parents about the individual growth of their children, but together with other methods of sharing, they can paint a powerful picture of the joy and complexity of learning in our classrooms.

Develop Clarity

Because of the degree of planning, instruction, and assessment we engage in every day, we need to be relentless in developing clarity in our reporting processes. We can help students see the connections between what they are doing and what they are learning, and we can share these connections with families through conversations, work we send home, conferences, and any other means we use to engage in learning discussions. As students get older, we can be upfront about how reported grades are determined. We have to be vigilant in our decision to remove unclear assessment practices from our repertoire. The true measure of clarity occurs when students can articulate exactly what they are learning and where they are focusing attention *before* the report card is issued. There should never be any secrets or confusion. When students understand how their learning is captured, their families will come to understand it too. Whatever decisions we make regarding assessment and reporting, we must make sure everyone understands.

This transparency is especially important when we are in the middle of shifting assessment philosophies and processes. There are times when we make decisions about our practices that seem dramatic (if they happen mid-year, for example), and we must be clear about this journey with students and families. This means we have to be comfortable with the philosophical beliefs that drive our decisions. Explaining to students and parents our beliefs about assessment in relation to learning is an important step. When we communicate these beliefs and explain the assessment practices we will use to reflect these beliefs, families will develop the understanding that our assessment practices will neither diminish the expectations we have for our learners nor the degree of responsibility students hold for their own learning. When we change things like our redemonstration processes for example, we should expect to receive some questions about fairness. We must explain how our practices align with a belief in our learners' strengths and abilities. We want parents to understand that we will not compare students to each other. Rather, student learning is measured in relation to learning goals. This will be a new approach for many adults—different from what they experienced in school. We want them to understand how this approach tells more, not less.

If we are unsure of the reasons for changes we are making because they have been mandated by others, and we haven't had time to wrestle with the underlying philosophies, we must give ourselves time to explore what the changes mean. This may mean that to soften the edges of our assessment and reporting processes, we need to read current literature, watch webinars, and engage in deep conversations with colleagues. It is essential to engage in this process with people who possess diverse perspectives. Doubts and questions from our colleagues often mirror those of parents, and working through some of the challenges in environments of trust prepares us to welcome questions from students and families when the time comes.

Final Thoughts

Ensuring our students feel fully seen and heard as whole people is one of the most powerful ways to nurture their humanity. Reporting is a critical way to share with families the degree to which we have seen and heard their children. Through an effective reporting system, we can work alongside students to share the best parts of their learning and their plans for the future.

A strong reporting system flows out of effective planning built on a strong understanding of learning goals. Assessment criteria and architecture are clarified in advance of instruction, and learning experiences emerge in response to preassessment, formative assessment, and self-assessment information. When all these pieces are in place, reporting becomes a continuation of a learning story that has been long in the making. The learning goals and the students drive instruction and reporting, not the other way around. Learner needs are at the forefront, and the edges of our assessment practices are softened.

When we take time to ensure our reporting system flows out of strong assessment, the message we send to students and their families is that the students and their learning are what matter most. As educators, we have to be clear in our own hearts about the things we do before we can ever hope to clarify understanding with our partners. We must be willing to make time to explore our assessment and reporting practices in a personally meaningful way, so when we make changes, it is because we decided to do so, in ways that made sense to us. We also need to allow ourselves to feel what we feel as we refine our assessment processes. This work requires perseverance and fortitude in addition to an ability to forgive ourselves for past decisions and actions. When we develop renewed confidence, we are positioned to invite students into the conversation, allowing them the space to decide ways to share their own progress and celebrate their own successes. Ultimately, the learning stories belong to the students, and reporting is the part when families are invited to support and celebrate. Teachers no longer have all the responsibility for sharing learning stories. This is a soft edge for reporting.

Questions for Reflection

The following questions for reflection have been divided into three sections: (1) architecture, (2) student response, and (3) personal response. The architecture questions invite consideration of how we design our assessment processes to ensure our assessment choices reflect learning accurately and reliably. The student response questions prompt us to consider assessment choices from the perspective of the learner. The personal response section asks us to reflect on our own beliefs about assessment and consider these beliefs in relation to decisions we may make. Each question is intended to act as a catalyst for deeper thinking and may lead to new questions. Taking time to reflect on one or two at a time, through journaling, conversation, or as part of a group discussion, can help determine aspects of assessment that may have a hard edge and those that we have successfully softened. See the reproducible "Recognizing Hard Edges in Reporting" (page 189) for an additional resource to help identify reporting practices and circumstances that can create hard edges, and see the reproducible "Softening the Edges of Reporting" (page 193) for specific and practical recommendations of ways to ensure soft edges with reporting.

Architecture

- How do you report academic information to families? Do they receive too much information? Not enough? Why? How do you know?

- How will you report behavior and other critical competencies that exist outside the learning goals?
- To what degree are you able to build a relationship with families? How often do you connect? In which ways?
- Have you asked for feedback about your reporting system? Who would you ask? Why?
- What are all the ways you celebrate learning with families? Is it enough? Too much? How do you know?
- How often do you apply professional judgment before reporting? Do you feel adequately equipped to do so? Do you feel able to communicate rationale if needed?
- How do you engage students in longitudinal reflection about their growth and development? Do you use portfolios or some other method of collecting artifacts? Why or why not?
- How do you communicate concerns with families? Is it a good approach? Why or why not?
- To what degree do families understand the assessment language on any items you share with them? How often do you explain things? Co-construct them?

Student Response

- Are students clear about how learning is reported? How do you know?
- To what degree do students know what will be reported prior to the report cards going out?
- Have families or students ever been surprised by reported results? Why did this happen?
- To what degree is each student hopeful following a reporting period? How do you create and sustain hope? How does this lead to a softened edge?
- To what degree are learners involved in conferences and meetings? Is this an appropriate amount? Why or why not?
- Do you have strong relationships with your students? Do they perceive the same thing? How do you know?
- To what degree are self-assessment and goal setting connected to reporting?

Personal Response

- Are you satisfied with your reporting system? Do you feel like you have enough opportunities to share successes and challenges with families?
- How comfortable are you with communicating with families? Which aspects are less stressful and which are most stressful? Why? What does this indicate about edges?
- How do you approach written comments? Do you find your approach personal enough? Do your comments reflect individual students? What purpose do comments serve?

Recognizing Hard Edges in Reporting

How do we recognize when our reporting practices have hard edges and lack alignment with our own beliefs and values and the needs of the whole person? The following sections describe some indicators to watch for.

Reporting Behavior as Part of an Academic Score

We need to find ways to consider behaviors and report concerns and celebrations to parents without losing clarity about our reporting of academic learning. We should do both separately, as opposed to combining them into a single score. If we are assessing behavior, we must utilize tools that document learning over time, just as we do with academic learning. We need to be prepared to teach, intervene, reteach, and respond to concerns. Our reporting of behavior has a hard edge when we make reporting decisions minutes before our reporting deadlines or based on our feelings about students in the moment, as opposed to using data and opportunity for learning and growth. It is unfair to ourselves and our learners to make these kinds of professional judgments without deep consideration of what we expect and how we collect data to support our decisions.

Giving Marks That Lack Clarity

If we are spending inordinate amounts of time trying to manipulate a gradebook, calculate a mark, or justify the result we finally share, then we are sacrificing time we could be spending on formative assessment and feedback. When we calculate grades through a series of complicated mathematical maneuvers, there is a strong chance our reporting system is less about a conversation and more of a mystery to the people who matter the most: the students and their families. Students make decisions about us based on the decisions we make about them. Mysteries erode trust and indicate a hard edge.

Talking Only About Grades and Points

If our language around assessment and reporting continually falls back to grades and points ("This is for a grade" and "This will be on your report card"), we are severely limiting authentic engagement and student investment opportunities. Myron Dueck (2014) asserts, "Schools have trained students to be grade-focused rather than learning-focused" (p. 101). Furthermore, when we fail to illustrate the progression of learning through the variety of assessments (formative, preassessment, summative) we are implementing, then we are missing out on a conversation that is so important. The things we should be reporting to families are the stories of amazing things that happen inside our schools every day. We have a lot to be proud of and so do our students.

Failing to Ensure Reporting Emerges From the Learning Goals

When our reporting is disconnected from the learning goals, it prevents rich discussions about self-assessment, feedback, and goal setting. When this happens, we can become disconnected from the learning cycle and instead focus on generic goals and figuring out ways to talk about challenges while avoiding conflict with families. This is a tremendously hard edge for teachers and promotes complete student disengagement in the process. When our reporting processes align completely with what we do every day in our classrooms, amazing clarity and growth can occur.

Allowing a Computer Program to Define and Communicate Learning

A computer program, no matter how strong, is not a teacher. Letting a machine make an important decision about student learning is the equivalent of giving away our professional expertise. It is our responsibility to report the degree to which we infer student learning, and ignoring this responsibility is ignoring the power we have in our classrooms. Our professional judgment, not the computer's algorithm, matters more.

Communicating Challenges Too Late or Not at All

Whether it is because we have failed to assess learning in a timely fashion or simply want to avoid uncomfortable conversations, it is ultimately ill-advised to fail to communicate students' learning challenges to them and their families. Both parties are critical to student success, and our strategies to support learning must be timely and used alongside students and their families. Experiencing difficulty is part of rich learning, and embracing these challenges and moving forward from them are the gifts of our education system.

Focusing Too Much on the Challenges

Nobody wants to be confronted with a long list of failures. Facing a laundry list of problems can be overwhelming to both students and their families. This is why considering the root causes of challenges, whether behavioral or academic, is so important. In this way, we can address the *first next thing* instead of everything all at once. For example, instead of informing parents that their child can't read at grade level, it may be more helpful to share that we are working together on self-monitoring strategies to identify when comprehension breaks down. Furthermore, growth must start from a position of strength. Honoring a learner's strengths sets up everyone for optimism.

Assuming We Know What Parents Want

When we catch ourselves saying things like, "Parents don't care about . . ." or "Parents don't need to know . . ." we may be lingering in the realm of assumptions. Developing an authentic relationship with families is no less important than our relationship with their children. Reporting decisions, whether they occur inside our classrooms or on a larger scale, should be done in consultation with families. We may ask parents, "How do you want to hear about your child's learning?" "How much is too much and how much is too little?" "How do you prefer to be contacted?" "What do you want to know?" We can ask questions like these in parent surveys, during a parental engagement evening, or through phone calls. By engaging in rich discussions with our parent partners, we craft a shared purpose and process for surrounding learners with support and encouragement.

Leaving Students Out of the Conversation

Adults make most of the decisions in our education system. We decide what students will learn, when they learn it, and under what time constraints. We notify students when it is time to stop thinking about one subject and move on to another. We tell students who they are thinking for and how much their thinking is worth. It is essential to shift some of these decisions to the learners so they develop the independence, autonomy, and efficacy so essential for the development of their whole selves. Furthermore, students can serve as the strongest advocates for assessment change and are often the best equipped to explain shifts in assessment practices to their families. When we fail to include them in the assessment conversation, we fail to leverage incredible potential.

Not Allowing Students to Prepare for Student-Led Conferences (or Not Being Clear About the Purpose)

Student-led conferences sometimes falter because their purpose is not clear to everyone involved. Once we understand that we are engaging in a rich discussion about learning progress and the processes that support it, we can begin to make decisions about how to prepare students for the discussion. Like anyone without adequate time to reflect, learners cannot be expected to lead a discussion about themselves. This is a difficult process for some students and, in supporting the whole student, we must purposefully prepare them. Simply eliminating students from the conferences may seem like an easy solution, but we can lose a rich partnership in the process.

Putting Impersonal Comments on the Report Card

The narratives we use to explain what we see and hear in our classrooms can support students' shifting views of who they are as learners. Comments on a report card can seem inconvenient, but the choices we make in sharing what we know about students can impact their perception of our level of commitment to their growth. When we are able to write our own comments, we might consider avoiding comments like "Thanks for being in my class" or "We will be learning fractions in the next unit," and instead write, "Joey's contributions to class discussions show a strong understanding of the content we have been exploring" or "Maria has set a personal goal to use models when exploring math questions. I am excited to see if this approach works well to build her understanding." In cases where we must choose from a bank of comments and have no option to personalize, we might consider *noticing* our learners by adding components to our reporting system (such as portfolios, blogs, or email) in addition to report cards. Using our students' names and personalizing our comments are part of a larger reporting system that aims to *notice* students and honor who they are.

References

Dueck, M. (2014). *Grading smarter, not harder: Assessment strategies that motivate kids and help them learn.* Alexandria, VA: Association for Supervision and Curriculum Development.

Softening the Edges of Reporting

How can we soften the edges of reporting to families? Here are a few things to consider.

Work on the Relationship

A report card and subsequent conference can seem very impersonal when they are with people we don't know very well. That being said, some of us teach hundreds of students a year, and developing a relationship with each student and family can seem next to impossible. Developing relationships amid the demands of a busy classroom and teaching schedule can seem daunting. This is where formal processes (conferences, writing workshops, reflection circles, and portfolios that have interaction built in, and so on) that support self-assessment, reflection, and peer engagement are so important. In addition, having a reporting system that invites students to communicate their own learning stories through portfolios and work samples supports the development of these essential relationships. Classrooms that utilize social media platforms and digital portfolios find connecting with families easier and more manageable. As an educator, holding all the responsibility for developing a school-family relationship is exhausting and unnecessary. Sharing this responsibility with students and parents makes our work an exercise in partnership. Consistent practices create clarity and community with much less effort than systems that confuse and mask the work we do together. Furthermore, when an entire school works together to facilitate learning goal–based experiences and authentic and aligned assessment practices, we increase clarity exponentially and build true school-home partnerships (DuFour, DuFour, Eaker, Many, & Mattos, 2016).

Embed Reporting Throughout the Learning Cycle

Learning does not end with reporting. Constructing ways to embed reporting in the learning cycle supports the understanding that reporting reflects learning at a particular time and place; as conditions and contexts change, learning continues to develop and allows us to illustrate growth. Supporting intellectual activity and future opportunities requires a continual, constructive conversation about the learning goals and how they address broader skills and competencies. Because the goals rest within a larger context of lifelong learning for students, the need for dialogue, reflection, and goal setting cannot be ignored.

Use Portfolios as a Catalyst for Reflection

Portfolios can serve the dual purposes of documenting learning and analyzing growth. This positions them to be useful to students, teachers, and families. Jeffry Overlie (2009) explains, "Teachers need to set aside time for students to do a periodic portfolio review and reflect on specific probing questions pertaining to their understanding" (p. 190). This review moves a portfolio from a collection of *stuff kids have done* to a springboard for future learning experiences.

We must ensure portfolios serve a meaningful purpose for students and teachers. We can invite students to choose an item of pride—an item that challenges them and that demonstrates growth. Portfolios indicate a hard edge to assessment when we spend hours posting and organizing student work to share. This hard edge can become softened when we invite students into the process, sharing the ownership for portfolio creation. We can also invite our learners to curate their portfolios based on what we intend to do with them (select examples of strong learning if we are celebrating, or select a sample that is not complete if we are encouraging reflection and revision, for example). This way, we are spending our time wisely and meaningfully. Regardless of the learner's age, he or she should be invited to use the process as part of learning. Portfolios are more than a collection of artifacts. When used to their full potential, portfolios invite deep reflection that is difficult to do with day-to-day work.

Stay Curious

We would be hard pressed to find the perfect assessment and reporting system for every teacher and student in every context. Our environments change, our students have unique needs, and our own knowledge and skill develop over time. One of the most important ways to soften the edge of reporting is to allow ourselves the time and space to try new things and adjust them when they don't work. When a practice doesn't quite align with our beliefs, we need to feel comfortable to explore it further, discuss it with our colleagues, and sort out how to make it better. Accepting a grading program without understanding how it generates a grade, or sharing learning only at reporting periods because it is what everyone else does, can be uncomfortable when these practices don't align with our beliefs about assessment and the whole student. Teacher professionalism depends on our ability to make these kinds of decisions for ourselves and our students. We have to exercise the right to stay curious, ask questions, and seek more information.

References

DuFour, R., DuFour, R., Eaker, R., Many, T. W., & Mattos, M. (2016). *Learning by doing: A handbook for Professional Learning Communities at Work* (3rd ed.). Bloomington, IN: Solution Tree Press.

Overlie, J. (2009). Creating confident, capable learners. In T. R. Guskey (Ed.), *The teacher as assessment leader* (pp. 181–201). Bloomington, IN: Solution Tree Press.

Conclusion

I remember a time early in my career when a father visited my sixth-grade classroom and told me of the stress his daughter was feeling about an upcoming science exam. He said he understood why I had been asserting the importance of the exam, but some of the statements I had made in an effort to motivate students to study were actually causing stress for his daughter. She did not need reminders to review because she already had been doing so for weeks. My statements to the whole class (but actually directed at one or two students) were resulting in distress for this student and creating a very hard edge in my assessment practices.

I was floored at my ignorance. I had been oblivious to how my own actions were affecting her mental well-being. That conversation changed the way I asked students to complete the work. It alerted me to my need to empathize with my students, consider all their needs, and redirect behavior and learning on an individual basis as opposed to the whole class. Most of all, it reminded me of the humanity of my students and the impact I had on their overall well-being.

Learning is a relationship between the learner and his or her world. Like all relationships, it is complex, challenging, joyful, fulfilling, draining, affirming, and essential. When we approach learning in our schools and classrooms, we must be aware of the role we play in nurturing this relationship and the complex nature of the learning we are inviting our students to engage in. Previous experiences, prior knowledge, and life circumstances impact a learner's willingness to take risks, explore new territory, experience challenges, and celebrate growth. Through the choices we make every day in our classrooms, we have the ability to shift this impact in new and positive directions and soften the edges for both ourselves and our learners. How we choose to position students in relation to their own learning further impacts how their relationships with themselves will develop over time. If we are going to invite a student to demonstrate strong learning, we must be willing to attend to the needs of the whole student with agility, empathy, and compassion. This is the soft edge of education.

Assessment is a window into our students' hearts and minds. It is a way for us to hear their voices, determine their engagement, gauge their passion, and validate their growth. Without strong assessment architecture, we cannot capture this essential information and leverage it into possibilities for our learners. When done well, assessment can lift students to places where they did not imagine they could travel. It can diminish their self-doubt and encourage engagement. All assessment types serve a critical purpose in helping us impact and support our students' learning stories.

Just like us, students' lives are about continual change and movement; there isn't an end to learning once a learner graduates. Education is a negotiation, a conversation, a catalyst, an invitation. We have to trust students' abilities to learn, and we have to trust our ability to facilitate that learning using assessment in ways that support the whole student. We have to give ourselves space to try new things, explore new ways of assessing, and observe the impacts on our students. We deserve the space to learn alongside our students, and our students deserve the best we can give. As Penny Kittle (2008) explains:

> My students and I are the most powerful forces in my classroom, not the tests. I'm learning every day, every class, with every student. They still drive my teaching, planning, and thinking. . . . I'm still the one who knows my students best. (p. 4)

We have both the gift and the responsibility to keep the edges of assessment soft for both ourselves and our students. It is not easy, but the rewards are astounding.

APPENDIX

Sample Learning Continuums

The following samples illustrate how each stage of the learning continuum fits together to develop student proficiency and enrich learning goals in a variety of subjects and grade levels.

Table A.1: Sample Learning Continuum for English Language Arts in Grade 6

Standard				
Analyze how a particular sentence, paragraph, chapter, or section fits into the overall structure of a text and contributes to the development of the ideas (RI.6.5; NGA & CCSSO, 2010a).				
	Building Readiness	**Exploring the Learning Goal**	**Clarifying Proficiency**	**Enriching Understanding**
Skills and Knowledge	• Understand the use of vocabulary (within a sentence, paragraph, chapter, section) and the text structure (main idea, supporting details or ideas, message, author, and meaning). • Know how to analyze, support an analysis, and track idea development throughout a text. • Identify strategies for improving comprehension. • Recognize text forms and structures.	• Recognize and identify key text structures (sentence, paragraph, chapter, section, stanza, and so on). • Engage in and comprehend the main idea and supporting details of literary texts. • Analyze relationships between various elements and ideas in literary texts. • Compare parts of a text to the whole text and analyze the relationship in terms of both structure and meaning.	• Recognize text structures by name and attribute. • Engage in texts for meaning. • Analyze the relationship between text structure and the development of ideas to communicate meaning. • Support analysis with details and examples from texts. • Engage in analysis independently.	• Assess how sentences, paragraphs, chapters, or sections impact the message within a text; determine which parts have the greatest impact on ideas in various texts. • Craft alternative portions of a text to alter the development of ideas. • Analyze increasingly difficult texts with unique text structures and explain how the parts impact the whole. • Compare texts with similar messages and examine their structures to determine the impact of structure on message.

	Building Readiness	Exploring the Learning Goal	Clarifying Proficiency	Enriching Understanding
Questions	• What is the vocabulary I need to know? How can I develop my understanding? • What is an analysis? How do I best support my ideas? • How can I be sure I understand what I am reading? How will I know when I don't understand? • What is a text form? What is a text structure? How do they help the author develop the message?	• What are some of the key structures in literary texts? • What is the message in this text? • What are the supporting details that help us understand the author's message? • How do authors structure their texts? Why do they make the decisions they do? How do their decisions affect us as readers? • How does part of a text connect to the whole? How would the meaning change if that part were missing or structured differently?	• How does the structure of a text contribute to its overall meaning? • Why do authors make the structural choices they do? • How do an author's choices impact a reader's understanding of the author's message?	• Which parts of a text have the greatest impact on the development of ideas? • What happens to the message when the structures are changed? How can you show this? • How do some authors utilize unique structures to develop their ideas? Why do they do this? • How do texts with the same message use structures differently? What is the impact? Does it change the way the ideas are developed?

Table A.2: Sample Learning Continuum for Writing in Grade 1

Standard				
Write and share stories and short informational texts about familiar events and experiences in a minimum of five sentences (CC1.4; Saskatchewan Ministry of Education, 2010).				
	Building Readiness	**Exploring the Learning Goal**	**Clarifying Proficiency**	**Enriching Understanding**
Skills and Knowledge	• Determine what makes a sentence a sentence. • Recognize the difference between informative texts and stories. • Explore how sentences connect to one another in a larger text. • Explore how to use details to make the writing stronger. • Learn about capital letters and end punctuation.	• Recognize and craft complete sentences, using correct conventions. • Decide on a topic based on personal knowledge. • Choose details that inform. • Order sentences so they make sense. • Understand how thoughts make up sentences and sentences make up compositions.	• Write at least five complete sentences. • Create a clear and informative message based on personal knowledge. • Support ideas with relevant details. • Sequence ideas logically. • Use appropriate language conventions.	• Compose increasingly longer and more complex informational texts. • Craft informational texts about something less familiar. • Use descriptive language (adjectives and adverbs). • Use varied punctuation for purpose.

	Building Readiness	Exploring the Learning Goal	Clarifying Proficiency	Enriching Understanding
Questions	• How do I know when one sentence ends and the next begins? • Where do I go for ideas for my writing? • How is a sentence different from a word or a paragraph? • What are details? • How do I explain something to someone else?	• Which punctuation marks should I use and why? • Where do I go to get information if I need it? • What am I trying to tell and what details do I need to explain? • What order works best for my writing?	• How do sentences fit together when I am explaining something? • Where do I get my ideas? • How can I use details to make my information more interesting? • How do I order my sentences? • How do I use punctuation and capital letters to help readers understand my writing?	• How can I make my writing more interesting? • How can I explain more things to my readers? • How can I add words that make my writing more interesting to read? • What are some punctuation marks I can use besides a period?

Source: Adapted from Saskatchewan Ministry of Education, 2010.

Table A.3: Sample Learning Continuum for Senior Environmental Science—Human Populations

Standard				
Investigate technologies and processes used for mitigating and managing resource use, waste generation and pollution associated with a growing human population (ES20-HP1; Saskatchewan Ministry of Education, 2016).				
	Building Readiness	**Exploring the Learning Goal**	**Clarifying Proficiency**	**Enriching Understanding**
Skills and Knowledge	• Define sustainability. • Explore population growth, including data and impacts. • Explore the connection between environmental factors and human population growth. • Investigate concerns that currently exist in relation to population growth. • Explore how resources are used and waste is managed around the world.	• Investigate the factors that support human populations. • Investigate factors that cause resource use and waste generation. • Investigate decisions humans make in relation to resource use and waste management. • Identify ways humans are solving problems associated with popula-tion growth, waste man-agement, and resource use.	• Describe environmental factors and medical advancements that support human populations. • Analyze and assess ways human actions impact (pluses and minuses) the environ-ment, includ-ing waste management. • Describe technologies and processes that assist in environ-mental and population sustainability. • Propose solutions to human population concerns.	• Propose more in-depth solutions to concerns relating to populations and sustain-ability, and assess the challenges associated with these solutions. • Explore more complex contexts relating to human populations and decisions. • Explore the tension between economic goals and sustainability. • Explore additional technologies and processes in this area.

	Building Readiness	Exploring the Learning Goal	Clarifying Proficiency	Enriching Understanding
Questions	• What do we mean by sustainability? • How are human populations changing and why is this happening? • What are some environmental factors that affect human populations? • Why are humans so concerned about human population growth? • How do we use resources and how is this different from elsewhere? What does this mean for humans?	• What factors support human populations? What factors are a concern to human populations? • How do humans make decisions that negatively and positively affect themselves? • What kinds of things are people working on to solve some of the problems associated with population growth, waste management, and resource use?	• Which environmental factors and medical advancements support human populations? • How do human actions impact the environment, both positively and negatively? • How do technologies and processes promote environmental sustainability? • How do humans resolve some of the challenges associated with population growth?	• How can we solve the problems associated with population growth, resource use, and waste management? • How do economic goals and sustainability relate? How is this relationship positive and how is it challenging? • What are some lesser-known technologies and methods currently being used or explored to mitigate or manage challenges?

Source: Adapted from Saskatchewan Ministry of Education, 2016.

References and Resources

Ai-Girl, T. (2004). *Exploring children's perceptions of learning.* Singapore: Marshall Cavendish Academic.

Ainsworth, L. (2003). *"Unwrapping" the standards: A simple process to make standards manageable.* Denver, CO: Advanced Learning Press.

All Things Assessment. (2016a). *Assessment architecture.* Accessed at http://allthingsassessment.info/assessment-architecture on November 10, 2016.

All Things Assessment. (2016b). *Instructional agility.* Accessed at http://allthingsassessment.info/instructional-agility on November 10, 2016.

Anderson, L. W., & Krathwohl, D. R. (Eds.). (2001). *A taxonomy for learning, teaching and assessing: A revision of Bloom's taxonomy of educational objectives.* New York: Longman.

Andrade, H., & Du, Y. (2007). Student responses to criteria-referenced self-assessment. *Assessment and Evaluation in Higher Education, 32*(2), 159–181.

Arter, J., & McTighe, J. (2001). *Scoring rubrics in the classroom: Using performance criteria for assessing and improving student performance.* Thousand Oaks, CA: Corwin Press.

Bateson, M. C. (1994). *Peripheral visions: Learning along the way.* New York: HarperCollins.

Bennett, S., & Kalish, N. (2006). *The case against homework: How homework is hurting our children and what we can do about it.* New York: Three Rivers Press.

Bernard, C. (1999). *Experimental medicine.* Herndon, VA: Transaction.

Biggs, J. B. (1987). *Student approaches to learning and studying* [Monograph]. Hawthorn, Australia: Australian Council for Educational Research.

Black, P., & Wiliam, D. (1998). Assessment and classroom learning. *Assessment in Education: Principles, Policy and Practice, 5*(1), 7–74.

Bloom, B. S. (Ed.). (1956). *Taxonomy of educational objectives: The classification of educational goals.* New York: Longman, Green.

Bowie, L. (2014). Teacher evaluation system is latest education battleground. *Baltimore Sun*. Accessed at www.baltimoresun.com/news/maryland/sun-investigates/bs-md-teacher-evaluations-20140628-story.html on November 17, 2016.

Braque, G. (1952). *Le jour et la nuit: Cahiers de Georges Braque*. Paris: Gallimard.

Burns, A. (1992). Teacher beliefs and their influence on classroom practice. *Prospect, 7*(3), 56–66.

Camera, L. (2016). High school seniors aren't college-ready. *U.S. News and World Report*. Accessed at www.usnews.com/news/articles/2016-04-27/high-school-seniors-arent-college-ready-naep-data-show on November 17, 2016.

Chappuis, J., Stiggins, R. J., Chappuis, S., & Arter, J. A. (2012). *Classroom assessment for student learning: Doing it right—Using it well* (2nd ed.). Boston: Pearson.

Clandinin, D. J., & Connelly, F. M. (1995). *Teachers' professional knowledge landscapes.* New York: Teachers College Press.

Clandinin, D. J., & Connelly, F. M. (2000). *Narrative inquiry: Experience and story in qualitative research.* San Francisco: Jossey-Bass.

Coles, R. (1989). *The call of stories: Teaching and the moral imagination.* Boston: Houghton Mifflin.

Commission on the Whole Child. (2007). *The learning compact redefined: A call to action—A report of the Commission on the Whole Child.* Alexandria, VA: Association for Supervision and Curriculum Development. Accessed at www.ascd.org/ASCD/pdf/Whole%20Child/WCC%20Learning%20Compact.pdf on August 28, 2015.

Covey, S. R. (1989). *The seven habits of highly effective people: Restoring the character ethic.* New York: Simon & Schuster.

Culberhouse, D. (2014, May 14). *The creative leader: Part 2* [Blog post]. Accessed at https://dculberh.wordpress.com/2014/05/14/the-creative-leader-part-2 on December 1, 2015.

Davies, A. (2011). *Making classroom assessment work* (3rd ed.). Bloomington, IN: Solution Tree Press.

Dimensions Educational Research Foundation, Rosenow, N., Kiewra, C., & Reeble, T. (2011). *Growing with nature: Supporting whole-child learning in outdoor classrooms.* Lincoln, NE: Dimensions Educational Research Foundation.

Dueck, M. (2014). *Grading smarter, not harder: Assessment strategies that motivate kids and help them learn.* Alexandria, VA: Association for Supervision and Curriculum Development.

DuFour, R. (2015). *In praise of American educators: And how they can become even better.* Bloomington, IN: Solution Tree Press.

DuFour, R., DuFour, R., Eaker, R., Many, T. W., & Mattos, M. (2016). *Learning by doing: A handbook for Professional Learning Communities at Work* (3rd ed.). Bloomington, IN: Solution Tree Press.

DuFour, R., & Eaker, R. (1998). *Professional Learning Communities at Work: Best practices for enhancing student achievement.* Bloomington, IN: Solution Tree Press.

Dwyer, L. (2014, October 3). When anxiety hits at school. *The Atlantic.* Accessed at www.theatlantic.com/health/archive/2014/10/when-anxiety-hits-at-school/380622/ on November 16, 2016.

Elliott, S. N., Kratochwill, T. R., Cook, J. L., & Travers, J. F. (1996). *Educational psychology: Effective teaching, effective learning* (2nd ed.). Madison, WI: Brown & Benchmark.

Erkens, C. (2009a). Developing our assessment literacy. In T. R. Guskey (Ed.), *The teacher as assessment leader* (pp. 11–30). Bloomington, IN: Solution Tree Press.

Erkens, C. (2009b). Paving the way for an assessment-rich culture. In T. R. Guskey (Ed.), *The principal as assessment leader* (pp. 9–28). Bloomington, IN: Solution Tree Press.

Erkens, C. (2015, July 23). *Collaborative common assessments: Getting to instructional agility* [Blog post]. Accessed at http://allthingsassessment.info/2015/07/23/collaborative-common-assessments-getting-to-instructional-agility on July 7, 2016.

Goodwin, M. (2009). Matchmaker, matchmaker, write me a test. In T. R. Guskey (Ed.), *The teacher as assessment leader* (pp. 89–109). Bloomington, IN: Solution Tree Press.

Guskey, T. R. (Ed.). (2009). *The principal as assessment leader.* Bloomington, IN: Solution Tree Press.

Guskey, T. R. (2015). *On your mark: Challenging the conventions of grading and reporting.* Bloomington, IN: Solution Tree Press.

Hall, P., & Simeral, A. (2015). *Teach, reflect, learn: Building your capacity for success in the classroom.* Alexandria, VA: Association for Supervision and Curriculum Development.

Hattie, J. (1992). Measuring the effects of schooling. *Australian Journal of Education, 36*(1), 5–13.

Hattie, J. (2009). *Visible learning: A synthesis of over 800 meta-analyses relating to achievement.* New York: Routledge.

Hattie, J. (2015). *What works best in education: The politics of collaborative expertise.* London: Pearson.

Heflebower, T. (2009a). Proficiency: More than a grade. In T. R. Guskey (Ed.), *The teacher as assessment leader* (pp. 111–133). Bloomington, IN: Solution Tree Press.

Heflebower, T. (2009b). A seven-module plan to build teacher knowledge of balanced assessment. In T. R. Guskey (Ed.), *The principal as assessment leader* (pp. 93–117). Bloomington, IN: Solution Tree Press.

Hume, K. (2008). *Start where they are: Differentiating for success with the young adolescent.* Toronto: Pearson Education Canada.

Jussim, L., & Eccles, J. (1992). Teacher expectations II: Construction and reflection of student achievement. *Journal of Personality and Social Psychology, 63*(6), 947–961.

Kittle, P. (2008). *Write beside them: Risk, voice, and clarity in high school writing.* Portsmouth, NH: Heinemann.

Kochhar-Bryant, C. A. (2010). *Effective collaboration for educating the whole child.* Thousand Oaks, CA: Corwin Press.

Kohn, A. (2006). *The homework myth: Why our kids get too much of a bad thing.* Philadelphia: Da Capo Press.

Kramer, S. V. (2009). Engaging the Nintendo generation. In T. R. Guskey (Ed.), *The teacher as assessment leader* (pp. 227–247). Bloomington, IN: Solution Tree Press.

Kryza, K., Duncan, A., & Stephens, S. J. (2009). *Inspiring elementary learners: Nurturing the whole child in a differentiated classroom.* Thousand Oaks, CA: Corwin Press.

Lamb, W. W. H. (2001). The "whole child" in education. *Journal of Philosophy of Education, 35*(2), 203–217.

Marzano, R. J., & Pickering, D. J. (2007). The case for and against homework. *Educational Leadership, 64*(6), 74–79.

McLaughlin, T. H. (1996). Education of the whole child? In R. Best (Ed.), *Education, spirituality, and the whole child* (pp. 9–19). London: Cassell.

McTighe, J., & Wiggins, G. (2013). *Essential questions: Opening doors to student understanding.* Alexandria, VA: Association for Supervision and Curriculum Development.

Mehrens, W. A., & Lehmann, I. J. (1987). Using teacher-made measurement devices. *NASSP Bulletin, 71*(496), 36–44.

Merton, R. K. (1948). The self-fulfilling prophecy. *Antioch Review, 8*(2), 193–210.

Metacognition. (2016). In Merriam-Webster.com. Accessed at www.merriam-webster.com/dictionary/metacognition on September 8, 2016.

Moss, C., Brookhart, S., & Long, B. (2011). Knowing your learning target. *Educational Leadership, 68*(6), 66–69.

National Governors Association Center for Best Practices & Council of Chief State School Officers. (2010a). *Common Core State Standards for English language arts and literacy in history/social studies, science, and technical subjects.* Washington, DC: Authors. Accessed at www.corestandards.org/assets/CCSSI_ELA%20Standards.pdf on September 14, 2016.

National Governors Association Center for Best Practices & Council of Chief State School Officers. (2010b). *Common Core State Standards for mathematics.* Washington, DC: Authors. Accessed at www.corestandards.org/assets/CCSSI_Math%20Standards.pdf on September 14, 2016.

Nehring, J. (2015, August 25). We must teach for "range" and "depth." *Education Week.* Accessed at www.edweek.org/ew/articles/2015/08/26/we-must-teach-for-range-and-depth.html on July 7, 2016.

O'Connor, K. (2007). *A repair kit for grading: 15 fixes for broken grades.* Portland, OR: Educational Testing Service.

Overlie, J. (2009). Creating confident, capable learners. In T. R. Guskey (Ed.), *The teacher as assessment leader* (pp. 181–201). Bloomington, IN: Solution Tree Press.

Palmer, P. J. (1998). *The courage to teach: Exploring the inner landscape of a teacher's life.* San Francisco: Jossey-Bass.

Palomares, S., & Schilling, D. (2008). *Educating the whole child: Social development and self-awareness activities for the early years.* Austin, TX: Pro-Ed.

Patel, N. V. (2003). A holistic approach to learning and teaching interaction: Factors in the development of critical learners. *International Journal of Educational Management, 17*(6/7), 272–284.

Reeves, D., & Reeves, B. (2016). *The myth of the muse: Supporting virtues that inspire creativity.* Bloomington, IN: Solution Tree Press.

Ritchhart, R., Church, M., & Morrison, K. (2011). *Making thinking visible: How to promote engagement, understanding, and independence for all learners.* San Francisco: Jossey-Bass.

Robinson, K. (2015). *Creative schools: The grassroots revolution that's transforming education.* New York: Viking.

Rodgers, C. R. (2002). Voices inside schools: Seeing student learning—Teacher change and the role of reflection. *Harvard Educational Review, 72*(2), 230–253.

Rodgers, C. R. (2006). Attending to student voice: The impact of descriptive feedback on learning and teaching. *Curriculum Inquiry, 36*(2), 209–237.

Rog, L. J. (2014). *Struggling readers: Why Band-Aids don't stick and worksheets don't work.* Markham, Ontario, Canada: Pembroke.

Rotherham, A. (2015). Stop the testing circus. *U.S. News and World Report.* Accessed at www.usnews.com/news/the-report/articles/2015/05/21/stop-the-standardized-testing-circus on November 17, 2016.

Saskatchewan Ministry of Education. (2010). *English language arts 1.* Accessed at www.edonline.sk.ca/bbcswebdav/library/curricula/English/English_Language_Arts/English_Language_Arts_1_2010.pdf on November 9, 2016.

Saskatchewan Ministry of Education. (2016). *Environmental science 20.* Accessed at www.edonline.sk.ca/bbcswebdav/library/curricula/English/Science/Environmental_Science_20_2016.pdf on November 9, 2016.

Schimmer, T. (2014). *Ten things that matter from assessment to grading.* Boston: Pearson.

Schimmer, T. (2016). *Grading from the inside out: Bringing accuracy to student assessment through a standards-based mindset.* Bloomington, IN: Solution Tree Press.

Schmoker, M. (2004). Start here for improving teaching and learning. *School Administrator, 61*(10), 48–49.

Schnellert, L., Datoo, M., Ediger, K., & Panas, J. (2009). *Pulling together: Integrating inquiry, assessment, and instruction in today's English classroom.* Markham, Ontario, Canada: Pembroke.

Stiggins, R. J., Arter, J. A., Chappuis, J., & Chappuis, S. (2004). *Classroom assessment for student learning: Doing it right—Using it well.* Portland, OR: Assessment Training Institute.

Strauss, V. (2013, February 10). Test anxiety: Why it is increasing and 3 ways to curb it. *Washington Post.* Accessed at www.washingtonpost.com/news/answer-sheet/wp/2013/02/10/test-anxiety-why-it-is-increasing-and-3-ways-to-curb-it on November 16, 2016.

Taylor, L. (2015). Teachers' unions fight standardized testing, and find diverse allies. *New York Times*. Accessed at www.nytimes.com/2015/04/21/education/teachers-unions-reasserting-themselves-with-push-against-standardized-testing.html on November 17, 2016.

Thalheimer, W. (2008). *Providing learners with feedback—Part 2: Peer reviewed research compiled for training, education, and e-learning*. Accessed at http://willthalheimer.typepad.com/files/providing_learners_with_feedback_part2_may2008.pdf on November 4, 2016.

Thompson, M., & Wiliam, D. (2007, April). *Tight but loose: A conceptual framework for scaling up school reforms*. Paper presented at the annual meeting of the American Educational Research Association, Chicago, IL.

Tomlinson, C. A. (2005a). Grading and differentiation: Paradox or good practice? *Theory Into Practice*, *44*(3), 262–269.

Tomlinson, C. A. (2005b). Quality curriculum and instruction for highly able students. *Theory Into Practice*, *44*(2), 160–166.

Tomlinson, C. A., Brimijoin, K., & Narvaez, L. (2008). *The differentiated school: Making revolutionary changes in teaching and learning*. Alexandria, VA: Association for Supervision and Curriculum Development.

Tomlinson, C. A., & Imbeau, M. B. (2010). *Leading and managing a differentiated classroom*. Alexandria, VA: Association for Supervision and Curriculum Development.

Tomlinson, C. A., & McTighe, J. (2006). *Integrating differentiated instruction and understanding by design: Connecting content and kids*. Alexandria, VA: Association for Supervision and Curriculum Development.

Vagle, N. D. (2009). Inspiring and requiring action. In T. R. Guskey (Ed.), *The teacher as assessment leader* (pp. 203–225). Bloomington, IN: Solution Tree Press.

Vagle, N. D. (2015). *Design in five: Essential phases to create engaging assessment practice*. Bloomington, IN: Solution Tree Press.

Vygotsky, L. (1978). *Mind in society: The development of higher psychological processes*. Cambridge, MA: Harvard University Press.

Webb, N. L. (2002). *Depth-of-knowledge levels for four content areas.* Accessed at http://schools.nyc.gov/NR/rdonlyres/2711181C-2108-40C4-A7F8-76F243C9B910/0/DOKFourContentAreas.pdf on September 6, 2016.

Wiggins, G., & McTighe, J. (2005). *Understanding by design* (Expanded 2nd ed.). Alexandria, VA: Association for Supervision and Curriculum Development.

Wiliam, D., Lee, C., Harrison, C., & Black, P. (2004). Teachers developing assessment for learning: Impact on student achievement. *Assessment in Education: Principles, Policy and Practice, 11*(1), 49–65.

Wormeli, R. (2011). Redos and retakes done right. *Educational Leadership, 69*(3), 22–26.

Index

J

K

L

M

N

O

P

Q

R

S

T

U

V

W

Z

Essential Assessment
Cassandra Erkens, Tom Schimmer, and Nicole Dimich Vagle
Discover how to use the power of assessment to instill hope, efficacy, and achievement in your students. Explore six essential tenets of assessment that will help deepen your understanding of assessment to not only meet standards but also enhance students' academic success.
BKF752

Mindful Assessment
Lee Watanabe Crockett and Andrew Churches
It is time to rethink the relationship between teaching and learning and assess the crucial skills students need to succeed in the 21st century. Educators must focus assessment on mindfulness and feedback, framing assessment around six fluencies students need to cultivate.
BKF717

FAST Grading
Douglas Reeves
Embrace effective grading procedures that have the power to reduce failure rates and encourage learning. Discover practical strategies teachers and administrators can use to ensure their grading practices center on four essential criteria: fairness, accuracy, specificity, and timeliness.
BKF647

Proficiency-Based Assessment
Troy Gobble, Mark Onuscheck, Anthony R. Reibel, and Eric Twadell
With this resource, teachers will discover how to close the gaps between assessment, curriculum, and instruction by replacing outmoded assessment methods with proficiency-based assessments. Learn the essentials of proficiency-based assessment, and explore evidence-based strategies for successful implementation.
BKF631

Visit SolutionTree.com or call 800.733.6786 to order.